Dialogues of

ALFRED NORTH WHITEHEAD

Alfred North Whitehead

" . . . his face, serene, luminous, often smiling, always benign . . ."

Dialogues of
ALFRED NORTH WHITEHEAD

as recorded by
LUCIEN PRICE

Max Reinhardt : London

First published 1954

Set in Baskerville
MADE AND PRINTED IN GREAT BRITAIN BY
WILLIAM CLOWES AND SONS LTD.,
LONDON AND BECCLES

" . . . from this source we have derived philosophy, than which no greater good ever was or ever will be given by the gods to mortal man."

Plato: TIMAEUS

" . . . and this place is sacred, to all seeming—
thick set with laurel, olive, vine; and in its heart
a feathered choir of nightingales makes music.
So sit thee here on this unhewn stone . . ."

Sophocles: OEDIPUS AT COLONUS

CONTENTS

[vii]

INTRODUCTION

BY

Sir David Ross

Boswell set an example for all time of the possibility of recording for posterity the very words of a venerated master; he has had few successful followers, but Mr. Price must be numbered among these.

To be worthy of mention in the same breath as Boswell's *Johnson*, a book must fulfil two conditions. In the first place, the man depicted must be worthy of depiction. Whitehead *was* worthy of it. He had a wide and well-stored mind, deeply interested not only in the fields of mathematics, physical science, and philosophy, to which his books are devoted, but, as the following pages testify, also in history, in politics, and in literature. He was trained in an old and old-fashioned school; and his magazine article on Sherborne is one of the best of all defences of the English public-school system. He never lost his love of the classics, and his devotion to Plato grew as his life advanced, and never failed. But in the years spent in Cambridge, England, his mind settled down to its main interests, in mathematics, in logic, and in physical science. This was a time when new ideas were stirring, both in logic and in physical science, and both at Cambridge and in the years (1910–24) which he spent in London Whitehead played a large part in the development and statement of these ideas. When he was sixty-three, an age at which most people begin to think of retirement, there came the dramatic invitation to begin a new life in America. He accepted the invitation with enthusiasm. There have been other British subjects—Lord Bryce and Lord Lothian are examples—who have been singularly at home in the American scene, but no one has ever been more so than Whitehead. He wrote copiously—too copiously, perhaps, for his reputation, for it is often difficult to follow the precise sequence and content of his ideas—but always suggestively. His home became a centre of simple but charming hospitality (in which his wife played almost as great a part as himself), both to colleagues and to students. I suppose that it would be true to say of him that he never made an enemy nor lost a friend.

The second requirement for a successor (I will not go so far as to say a rival) to Boswell's *Johnson* is the finding of a fit person to tell the story. This requirement Mr. Price satisfies to the full. It is clear from the book that, like Boswell, he elicited many of the best remarks made by his hero. His training as a journalist-reporter, and his habit of writing down his notes at the earliest possible moment, enabled him to give an exact and lively account of Whitehead's conversation. Those who wish to find an appreciation of Whitehead's scientific and philosophical thought will look elsewhere—to Lord Russell's account (in *Mind* for 1948) of Whitehead's share in the writing of *Principia Mathematica*, to Professor Quine's article in *The Library of Living Philosophers*, to Professor Emmet's account of Whitehead in *The Proceedings of the British Academy for 1947*, and to Professor Broad's discriminating essay in *Mind* for 1948. But of Whitehead as a man, a man of wide interests, a man whose conversation was always wise and sometimes witty, Mr. Price's account is a masterly one.

PROLOGUE

THE century between 1850 and 1950 is peopled with careers which no writer of fiction could have invented. Such extravagant vicissitudes are generally associated with men of action, but they can equally befall men of thought, and the revolution in thought during the past century has, if anything, been the more violent. What novelist could have imagined a career so intricated with an epoch so explosive as Whitehead's? Anthony Trollope? Trollope could have managed the start of it, for the story begins in an English parsonage, but as soon as it leaves the neighbourhood of Canterbury Cathedral and Archbishop Tait, who used to drive over for Sunday dinner to the vicarage of St. Peter's, Trollope's imagination would not have been up to it and neither would his intellect. It is almost as if Whitehead himself was aware of this, for has he not said:

> *Literature must in some sense be believable, whereas experiences of human beings in fact develop beyond all powers of conjecture. Thus Social Literature is conventional, while History exceeds all limitations of common sense.*

★   ★   ★

Whitehead's is a three-volume life. Volume I, Cambridge University; Volume II, London; Volume III, Cambridge, Massachusetts. He also said that he had a sense of having lived three lives in three successive epochs; the first, from 1861 to 1914; the second, during the war of 1914–1918; and the third, after that first world war.

This "Tale of Three Cities" begins quietly. He is son and grandson of schoolmasters, then his father becomes a parson. As parson he is an *Old* Testament man, and his prophetic

[1]

thunders reverberate under the barrel vault of a Norman church. The whole scene is picturesque—Ramsgate, fronting the Narrow Seas between England and the Continent, those narrow seas which "are the parents of all free governments in the world—Holland, England, the United States. The Pilgrim Fathers were their offspring." Not far away are the grim walls of Richborough Castle, built by the Romans; a mile inland from Ebbes Fleet beach, where the Saxons had landed, is the spot where Augustine preached his first sermon; and only sixteen miles away is Canterbury Cathedral, where ninety years ago, as still today, a little boy could look on the very spot where Thomas à Becket was murdered, and see the armour worn by the Black Prince. History for this lad was not something learned out of a book; he rubbed elbows with it every day and took it in at eyes and nostrils.

Although Whitehead always regarded himself as the East Anglian that he so typically looked and was—fair, ruddy, blue-eyed—there was one of those slight mixtures in the stock which, as he had observed time and again in history, provide a variant. One of his grandmothers was Welsh, her maiden name had been Williams, and he was so different from his brothers that it was attributed to the Celtic strain.

He was born on February 15, 1861. A frail child, he was taught at home by his father and spent much of his time out of doors with an old gardener to whom he retained a lifelong gratitude for having first let him see the light that can shine in obscurity. Winters he would visit his grandmother in London. She was the widow of a military tailor and lived in a town house, 81 Piccadilly, from whose windows overlooking the Green Park he used to see Queen Victoria, then a middle-aged widow and not too well liked, go by in her carriage. His grandmother was a wealthy woman, but, said he, "She made the mistake of having thirteen children," which somewhat reduced their several inheritances. She also must have been a redoubtable character, for the linch-pin who held the family together was the housekeeper, Jane Whychelow, and she it was who read aloud the novels of Dickens to the little boy as he sat on a hassock hugging his knees beside her grate fire.

His schooling is not less picturesque. He was sent to Sherborne as an adolescent lacking four months of his fifteenth birthday. In 1941 that school celebrated its twelve-hundredth anniversary. It dates from Saint Aldhelm and claims Alfred the Great as a pupil. The monastery buildings are still used and its abbey is one of the most magnificent in existence, with tombs of Saxon princes extant. During his last two years here young Whitehead's private study was a room reputed to have been the abbot's cell and he worked under the sound of the abbey bells—"the living voices of past centuries"—brought from the Field of the Cloth of Gold by Henry VIII and given by him to the abbey.

The curriculum, he remarked in after years, struck him as having been about right for that period and place. "We read Latin and Greek as the historical records of governing peoples who had lived close to the sea and exerted maritime power. They were not foreign languages; they were just Latin and Greek; nothing of importance in the way of ideas could be presented in any other way. Thus we read the New Testament in Greek. At school—except in chapel, which did not count— I never heard of anyone reading it in English. It would suggest an uncultivated religious state of mind. We were religious, but with that moderation natural to people who take their religion in Greek." English grammar he never studied; that was learned out of the grammars of Greek and Latin.

These boys were not overworked. There was time for athletic sports and private reading, which with him meant poetry, in especial Wordsworth and Shelley, but also much history. He was a good athlete and finally a prefect. As Head of the School, he was called upon to cane a boy who had stolen money. "Either he had to be caned before the school or expelled. I don't say that I did right, but I caned him."

Whitehead's classical training stuck; it was cultivated by him for the rest of his days, and as the twentieth century went on and so many men of science were found to be lamentably lopsided, this benign balance in him between science and humanism became one of his unique distinctions. It was a common saying that "Whitehead has both."

*   *   *

At the age of nineteen, when he went up to Cambridge University, he was already a good mathematician. The method of instruction at Cambridge in those days was largely Platonic, free discussion among friends, and he has said that he learned as much from conversation as from books. Once when asked how he was able to write *Science and the Modern World*, one chapter each week during the academic year while carrying his regular teaching schedule at Harvard, he replied, "Everything in the book had been talked over for the previous forty years."

He becomes a fellow of Trinity in 1885, at the ripe age of twenty-four—Trinity College, Cambridge, one of the most splendid educational foundations on earth. And now comes the great experience in which he found that rare jewel, true humility.

For the previous two centuries it had been comfortably supposed that Sir Isaac Newton had discovered the laws of the physical universe for ever. Then befell the thing. Let me try to quote Whitehead's own words as nearly as I can remember:

"We supposed that nearly everything of importance about physics was known. Yes, there were a few obscure spots, strange anomalies having to do with the phenomena of radiation which physicists expected to be cleared up by 1900. They were. But in so being, the whole science blew up, and the Newtonian physics, which had been supposed to be fixed as the Everlasting Seat, were gone. Oh, they were and still are useful as a way of looking at things, but regarded as a final description of reality, no longer valid. Certitude was gone."

It still is. But how many others have learned? This collapse of certitude where certitude was supposed to be least assailable affected his thinking for the rest of his days. Gone was the Everlasting Seat, yet he noticed how repeatedly even men of science themselves who knew this story would come forward with discoveries in the tone of, "Now at last we have certitude!"

In due season he formulated his reply:

> *The Universe is vast. Nothing is more curious than the self-satisfied dogmatism with which mankind at each period of its history cherishes the delusion of the finality of its existing modes of knowledge. Sceptics and believers are all alike. At this moment scientists and sceptics are the leading dogmatists. Advance in detail is admitted; fundamental novelty is barred. This dogmatic common sense is the death of philosophic adventure. The Universe is vast.*

We thus arrive at what he termed "the fallacy of dogmatic finality." It is one of the least popular of his doctrines. When tried out in conversation or in the public prints, its heresy is sensed with astonishing celerity, for people who do not know what it is that they don't like, do know that they don't like it ... bristle and growl at the sensed presence of spooks.

*   *   *

Next scene, Dickens's "Bleak House." By no means imaginary, it is a flint-stone mansion which stands on the seaward-thrusting headland at Broadstairs; it *is* bleak, and its walls shake to the thundering shock of surges in winter storms. Here Alfred Whitehead encountered Evelyn Wade, daughter of an Irish military family. Reared in Brittany, she had been schooled in a convent and had come in girlhood to live in England. They were married in December 1890 and lived in Cambridge for the next twenty years. Eight of these, from 1898 to 1906, were in the Mill House at Grantchester, a seventeenth-century farmhouse with thatched roof, seated at its ease in a lovely garden. Near it is a pool mentioned in Chaucer.

Here was no cleavage between town and gown. Their participation in the life of the village was lively; they took a flier in setting an example of teetotalism, for at that time the village was rather drunken, and they accepted quite a measure of responsibility for the needy and for their own servants, which savoured of a lingering eighteenth-century squiredom even stretching on back towards feudalism. This experience let Whitehead into an understanding of English character and folkways which he was able to relate to his wider philosophical generalizations and which helped to humanize his abstract thinking. He was also in the thick of liberal politics. "It was exciting work. . . . Rotten eggs and oranges were effective party weapons and I have often been covered with them. But they were indications of vigour, rather than of bad feeling."

"At what period of your life," he was once asked, "did you begin to feel that you had a grasp of your subject?"

He replied, somewhat brusquely for him, "Never."

It then appeared that for sixteen years at Cambridge he had had a constant tussle with insomnia, and each September after a summer's sojourn in the English countryside, in Kent, or in some little village by the sea, he would wonder whether he could ever again sustain a year's teaching. The insomnia never affected his work, however, and in London it diminished and finally ceased. At the same time, during eight of these years in Cambridge, he was reading theology. This was all extracurricular, but so thorough that he amassed a sizable theological library. At the expiry of these eight years he dismissed the subject and sold the books. A Cambridge bookdealer was willing to give quite a handsome figure for the collection. It then appeared that the pay must be taken in books at his shop. So he went on an orgy of book-buying until he had overdrawn his account.

* * *

In mid-career and with three children, he and his wife deliberately pulled up stakes and moved to London. This was a venture of faith without definite prospects. "I took a bottle-washing job," said he, "at London University." This lasted three years, then a professorship was made for him, and a dozen years later he was president of its senate.

This experience of the problems of London, extending for fourteen years (1910 to 1924), transformed my views as to the problems of higher education in a modern industrial civilization. It was then the fashion—not yet extinct—to take a narrow view of the function of universities. There were the Oxford and Cambridge type, and the German type. . . . The seething mass of artisans seeking intellectual enlightenment, of young people from every social grade craving for adequate knowledge, the variety of problems thus introduced—all this was a new factor in civilization. But the learned world is immersed in the past.

The nineteenth century ended on August 4, 1914. The Whiteheads' two sons, North and Eric, were in the first world war and the younger, Eric, an aviator, was killed. Their daughter, Jessie, entered the Foreign Office. Only as one came to know them gradually year after year did one even remotely understand how Eric's loss was felt. Finally they could talk of him eagerly and with laughter, but Whitehead once said that the most vivid wordings of grief or attempts at consolation by those masters of speech, the English poets, to him "only trivialized the actual emotions." It was the end of Volume II.

*   *   *

His invitation to Harvard came in 1924, a complete surprise. The letter was handed him by his wife on an afternoon which was dismal without and within. He read it as they sat by their fire, then handed it to her. She read it, and asked, "What do you think of it?" To her astonishment he said, "I would rather do that than anything in the world."

The manner of their having come is not yet generally known. Mr. Lowell, of course, as president issued the invitation, but the idea had originated with Lawrence Henderson and the funds for Whitehead's professorship were furnished by the Henry Osborn Taylors. This was not known to the Whiteheads themselves until many years afterward.

Now comes Volume III. In 1924, at the age of sixty-three, Alfred North Whitehead in a new land begins a new life and by far the most brilliant and productive part of his career. How quietly, how gently this great light rose over Harvard. The sky begins to shine with the white radiance of eternity. Once more the department of philosophy is spoken of as it had been two decades earlier in the *floruit* of William James, Josiah Royce, George Santayana, and Hugo Münsterberg. Then began appearing one major work after another: *Science and the Modern World* in 1925, *Process and Reality* in 1929, his most difficult but the one which he said he had "most wanted to write," *Adventures of Ideas* in 1933, in which admittedly there is more of Whitehead the man than in any other, and, in 1938, *Modes of Thought* . . . the list of published works is of course much longer.

At Harvard it was expected that he would write but not do much teaching. He did both. His lectures came thrice weekly, and instead of allowing his students a twenty-minute conference, he gave them a whole afternoon or a whole evening. "From that inspiration a man comes back with a changed tone." And the traffic was two-way, for Whitehead felt that he needed contact with young minds to keep his own springs flowing. "It is all nonsense," he said, "to suppose that the old cannot learn from the young."

More than professorial, this association was also personal. For at least thirteen years beginning midway in the 1920's and lasting into the 1930's, one heard of "evenings at the Whiteheads'," one night a week of open house to students, although anyone was welcome. These entertainments were of the simplest: conversation, hot chocolate to drink, and cakes to nibble. The students helped make and serve the chocolate, the conversation was their own, skilfully encouraged by host and hostess. In fine, the evenings were theirs, not the Whiteheads'; they began coming timidly in pairs for mutual protection, then by the half-dozen. They were asked to bring their girls, and brought them. Finally they came by the score, from sixty on up to ninety-eight of an evening. So here was a salon in the eighteenth-century French meaning of that term, brought off in an academic town with young men and women on cookies and hot chocolate. But there was also decanted that heady vintage which exhilarates but does not inebriate, conversation with the Whiteheads, and that means both Whiteheads, for he himself once said, "By myself I am only one more professor, but with Evelyn I am first-rate."

*   *   *

One May morning in 1932 my telephone rang. Mrs. Thaddeus DeFriez, whose husband, a young victim of the wartime pestilence in an army camp in 1918, had been managing editor of the *Boston Globe*, spoke:

"I am having the Whiteheads to dinner tomorrow. Could you come?"

"Sorry, but I am all packed and ready to leave for the Berkshires."

"They are frail, and getting on in years. You had better change your mind." (I changed my mind.)

The acquaintanceship with Whitehead developed slowly. For its first half-dozen years, 1932 to 1938, I was merely one of scores, even hundreds, who came and went in that dwelling. He once said that conversation should begin on a quiet note: "People should be allowed to talk commonplaces until they have got the temperature of the room. Climate is a good topic. The weather will do." Some deliberation of that sort is mirrored in the opening pages of these dialogues; the reader, too, is growing acquainted with Whitehead gradually.

But after about two years his personality exerted a peculiar force. He and his ideas seemed to permeate everything. By an odd quirk of imagination he became identified with one of the noble passages in music, those pages in the finale of Brahms's Fourth Symphony, that great *passacaglia*, where the theme is sounded by horns in goldenly glowing sustained notes above sonorous arpeggii in the darker registers of the string choir, violoncelli and violas (the measures from 113 to 129). Apparently there was no other connection except that of grandeur.

Then *he* disappeared. Oh yes, there remained his voice, clear, resonant, kindly, deliberate and perfectly articulated, British in tone and accent; there was his face, serene, luminous, often smiling, the complexion pink and white, the eyes brilliant blue, clear and candid as a child's yet with the depth of the sage, often laughing or twinkling with humour. And there was his figure, slender, frail, and bent with its lifetime of a scholar's toil. Always benign, there was not a grain of ill will anywhere in him; for all his formidable armament, never a wounding word. But his physical presence had become, as it were, only a transmitter, so intense was preoccupation with his ideas. He, the thinker, seemed to have vanished in the vastness of his own thought. Had this happened only once . . . but it happened so often, happened invariably. And something else happened too: time after time, going over to Cambridge after a day's work and feeling too fatigued to sustain a consecutive conversation, I would come away at midnight after four or five hours' lively interchange with him, exhilarated as with a raging flame of life. Did he emanate an electricity of the spirit?

It used to puzzle me that other guests could take that flood of powerful and original ideas, to all appearances, so coolly. Was he, then, merely one of many, and was nothing unusual going on? Could they pick up such conversation in a hundred other places? For my part, neither in America nor in Europe had I heard its like, and scarcely expect to hear its like again. If it was in books, what were the titles of the books? It was not in books, not even, as he later said, in his own books.

But, "What is so very wonderful here?" someone asks after having read these dialogues. I suggest that Whitehead's thinking makes its effect slowly. It is like a maxim of conduct, of no value unless put into practice; or like music, silent unless performed; or like seeds, sterile unless planted and cultivated. People say of Whitehead's books, "I read him, am stirred and interested, but afterwards I can't remember what he said." The same is true of Beethoven's *Diabelli Variations* and the *Republic* of Plato.

*   *   *

Be warned. Some of the matter in these dialogues is acutely controversial. There are books in which there is something to please everyone, and let us hope this will not prove entirely displeasing, yet I think it may be said with becoming modesty that in the following pages will be found something to annoy everybody, including myself. A frontiersman does not enjoy at one and the same time the zest of adventure and the placid comfort of a settled community. If some do not care for Whitehead's critiques of Christian theology or his dissent from Hebraic thought, no more do I care for some of his judgments about music and poetry, which happen to be *my* religion; for it makes a difference whose religion is gored. But for his part, he moved at a serene altitude above controversy:

Mine be some figured flame that blends, transcends them all.

He was not there to dogmatize—dogmatic finality he held in abhorrence—and I was not there to dispute Whitehead (which in any case I was totally incompetent to do). My function was to help keep the conversation moving and the ideas flowing. Never a dispute, "the worst of dispute is that it spoils a good discussion." In consequence, if some of the ideas which ensue are found offensive, I can only say with Todger Fairmile in *Major Barbara* (as reported by Bill Walker):

> " *'E looks up at the sky and sez, 'O that I should be fahned worthy to be spit upon for the gorspel's sake!' 'e sez.*"

And besides, to record the conversation of an eminent man is likely to be a thankless task. Even those who have done it best have earned, the one two hundred years, the other one hundred years of such epithets as flunkey, valet, toady, ass. Add to this that nowadays everybody is supposed to be as good as everybody else—if not better—and hence a becoming deference argues deficiency in self-respect. From any such presumed equality I emphatically dissent. Your informant was *not* as good as Whitehead, and the intellectual disparity was quite as pronounced.

My posture was that of a sixteen-year-old English lad, deckhand on the Leyland Line freighter *Devonian*, which used before the war of 1914–1918 to dock at East Boston near St. Mary's House for Sailors. A Londoner by birth, his name was Charles Bailey (pronounced Choles Beyley), and so well bred was he that when on closer acquaintance it was permissible to ask, the question was put:

"Charles, you tell me your parents are poor and that you grew up on the docks of East London. Then how did this happen?"

And Charles, with becoming modesty, replied:

"I was taught to mind me manners in the presence of me betters."

Those golden words are still as shining as the day they were issued from the mint. When we come now to the Dialogues—

"Choles, let me mind me manners in the presence of me betters."

*   *   *

Dialogues is merely a convenient title, though the obvious one. Any notion of its challenging the Platonic precedent would be absurd. The two are, on the contrary, antithetical; Plato's dialogues are contrived to sound like spontaneous conversation, Whitehead's actually are spontaneous conversation, even to the several speakers often obeying the Socratic injunction to "follow the argument where it leads." Even here some of Whitehead's remarks must be read in the strict historical context of the exact date on which they were uttered, and this is one of the points he explicitly made, that what interests a later age in such conversations is how people felt and what they thought about events while they were still going on and before any final judgment was possible. This is something which seldom gets told, for the human race, being denied foresight, dearly loves prophetic hindsight; and more than one highly qualified historical scholar, reading some of these pages in typescript, promptly fell into that trap, protesting:

"He really should have known better than that!"

"But did you, in 1934, or in 1944?"

This element is, however, not large because for the more part Whitehead did not talk of ephemera. His interest in daily events ignited his mind and he always thought freshly as the event turned up, but the true wave length of his thinking was one which opened centuries.

It will be noticed that certain themes run through these dialogues from beginning to end. They are easily identifiable. Repetitions these returns of theme are not; at each recurrence the idea is seen in some novel aspect. It would have been easy enough to combine these recurrences into a single comprehensive statement of the idea; to have done so would have been inexcusably to falsify the document. Instead, the themes are allowed to return, each time in a different key and varied as to rhythm, harmony, tempo, figuration. This quasi-musical form, though quite unpremeditated, is even more pronounced. (There would be a preliminary beating-up of the game, any game, then the hunt was up and off it would go.) Themes and counter-themes would be stated, as in a sonata movement, then a moment would come when Whitehead's mind would take over, as in free fantasia or as a cadenza for the solo instrument. In this the whole movement would come to a climax, after which the accompanying instrument, or instruments, would strike in again to a gradual subsidence and a quiet close.

A visual metaphor was supplied by Mrs. Whitehead: "His thinking is a prism. It must be seen not from one side alone but from all sides, then from underneath and overhead. So seen, as one moves around it, the prism is full of changing lights and colours. To have seen it from one side only is not to have seen it." One-sided seeing is what Whitehead called "half-truth"— "There are no whole truths; all truths are half-truths. It is trying to treat them as whole truths that plays the devil." (The arithmetical quips to which this lends itself were all made long ago.)

The notion that such return of themes is mere vain repetition is thus excluded. My function was not to cut, hack, and mutilate, but to record what was said.

Very well then, what was said? How authentic is this text? In the practice of writing down dialogue from memory as nearly verbatim as one can, the first thirty years are the hardest. My practice began as a schoolboy on January 1, 1901; it continued as a shorthand reporter of lectures, then as a newspaper reporter (who soon discovers that if he produces pencil and paper within view of a person unaccustomed to being interviewed, the unfortunate creature promptly congeals); and after that, years of saving the discourse of all sorts and conditions of men, eminent and obscure. Then by 1932, when this association with Whitehead began, the recording of conversation had become merely some more of the same thing, though it might be well to add that memory is likely to be more exact forty-eight hours later than it is after twenty-four hours—as though the longer interval gave the matter time to strike bottom and rise again to the level of consciousness. This is like the experience of a listener at a concert; immediately afterward, the themes may be hard to recall; the next day or the next after that they return of themselves. But Whitehead, foreseeing that the accuracy of these records (which I do not guarantee to be one hundred per cent) might be questioned, said on one of the last evenings when we were together:

"You had better insert a remark to say that these have been read by us and that they correspond to what was said. Otherwise, people might not believe it. I wouldn't have believed it myself. . . ."

Then just how accurate do I myself think they are? In the run of general conversation where it is merely an affair of picking up cues and following the train of thought, albeit with an ear for characteristic idiom, they are often verbatim; when it comes to Whitehead's longer speeches, his use of language had such flavour of mathematical precision, his command of English was so masterly, and the thinking itself was so compact that moments would come when I listened with secret consternation: "How can I retain all that? How can I hope to get it written with anything like the distinction he is giving it in oral delivery?" The answer is that often I do not. My appeal is to the sign that was posted up in the dance hall of a western mining camp:

Don't shoot the pianist. He is doing his best.

*   *   *

So it went for nine years, 1932 to 1941, and the book was half written before anybody, including the writer, knew it was to be a book. The Whiteheads did not know I was recording their conversation and there was no reason why they should. "Thrift, Horatio." The conversationally baked meats did furnish forth the journalistic tables. When they did, a copy of the editorial was duly sent him (his name was never mentioned in print), this partly in order to play fair and partly to learn whether the matter had been accurately retained and properly understood.

Then came the second war. Their son and his wife were in London under the bombing, and their grandson also in England was, as Mrs. Whitehead said, "for it." As a diversion these dialogues up to the autumn of 1941 were typed and sent them. Nothing was said about publication until the December of that year. The philosopher's view of their possible value will be found in the conversation of that date. Did the knowledge that they were to be saved impair spontaneity? It was never given a thought. There was too much else that was more interesting.

After his retirement, in 1937, the number of their guests had to be restricted. A good many callers still came, some from far corners of the earth, but advancing years and deafness made entertainment on the previous scale impracticable. And yet, although the larger gatherings may have elicited more aspects of his thought and revealed more sides of his personality, as time went on and the dialogues were among four or even three, he seemed to delve deeper into the ideas which were peculiarly his own. As touching subject matter, he had never liked to be quizzed about his published works. There they were, in print, to be read. He had done his best to make them intelligible. Let us go on to something new.

He was now in his eighties. There was not the least evidence that his intellectual powers were waning. In fact, the current was being stepped up. During those final years at their apartment in the Hotel Ambassador, when our sessions might begin as early as seven-thirty in the evening and last until after midnight, he would finish fresher than he began. The name of the hotel often made me think of Henry James's novel *The Ambassadors*, for ambassador in the highest sense Whitehead surely was.

The retention of his power he owed to moderation in all

things. His abstemiousness was marked. He ate sparingly. Table wine was admissible. No smoking. He seemed never to have craved stimulants. The sight of this ruddy octogenarian, clear-eyed, clear-skinned, without a mark of the customary male indulgences, was, as time went on, not the least of his impressiveness. Another and greater impression was the spectacle of his living, in a four-room apartment, a larger life, more free, more spacious of spirit and intellect than most others could have lived in affluence. One grows accustomed in filial piety to indulging the aged in crotchets and caprices. In him there was nothing to excuse. His calm, his magnanimity, the vastness of his concepts reduced the trivialities of daily living to their true dimensions, yet at the same time abstract principles were raised into issues which must be stood up for stoutly. He was not above the battle, but the battle was on higher ground. This gave him a peculiar quality. He had met and solved more problems than most of us are aware of as existing at all. One felt that here was a man who was not afraid—not afraid of those common enemies of mankind: illness, poverty, old age, misfortune, death; and then he was not afraid of the vast enigmas of human destiny or the immensities of the universe. In those awesome spaces he was at home and at his ease. This is what it means to be a philosopher, to have made friends with the enemy and to have domesticated the infinite in one's own soul. People sensed in him the habit of victory, and all those victories, long since forgotten by him, were there beside him invisibly working and fighting, and lo! his mountain was full of chariots and horsemen.

He once said that the Bible, instead of ending with the Revelation of Saint John, should have closed with the Funeral Speech of Pericles. Two sentences from that speech belong, the one at the beginning of these dialogues, the other at the end of his life:

We have no black looks or angry words for our neighbour if he enjoys himself in his own way.

And:

> *The whole earth is the sepulchre of famous men; and their story is not graven only on stone over their native earth, but lives on far away, without visible symbol, woven into the stuff of other men's lives.*

For a figure worthy of the Periclean Age had walked into our epoch.

The Dialogues

I

SEVENTEENTH anniversary of the United States's entrance into the first world war. The declaration of war came on a Good Friday, a historic irony which no one seemed to notice at the time. This had occupied us at editorial conference and was still in my thoughts as I went out to Canton to dine with the Whiteheads. Their youngest son, Eric, an aviator, had been killed in the war.

By telephone I had understood that dinner was to be at six. Having hustled out to Mattapan Square by train, and by taxi up to their house on Canton Avenue overlooking the Blue Hills, I was informed that dinner was not until seven. They relieved my embarrassment tactfully. A young Dr. Nichols, physician at some big hospital in London, who with his wife had landed in this country for the first time only the day before, met me—relatives of the Whiteheads, I gathered. Presently a message came.

"Won't you go into the study and chat with Mr. Whitehead till dinner-time?"

He was seated at his writing table beside two windows, his head ruddy and luminous from late-afternoon sunshine which poured over him. Rising, he said:

"How fortunate that you did come early! My afternoon was broken up and I was just loitering till dinner-time."

We chose two armchairs by the fire. He talked about newspapers.

"American newspapers give a totally wrong impression by their headlines. When one comes to read their small print, he finds that they are written by very sensible people, and in their space allotments they are much more fair to political opponents than English ones. English papers are better written as a whole, but when the writing in American papers does rise, I think it rises higher."

"That coincides with some experience of mine. Last summer I was writing an article on the exhibition of Wagner's manuscript scores at Bayreuth for the London *Times*. It was not as well written as it would have been for the *Boston Globe*. The *Times* wants all the colour washed out of the style."

It appeared that he, too, was aware that the day was an anniversary, and spoke of how far wide of reality are the books by professors about the World War:

"They conscientiously examine state papers, but what have state papers to do with it? The condition of fear that reigned from 1900 to 1914 was unspoken, almost subconscious. People forbore to mention it, hoping thereby not to detonate the explosive, but the dread was always there. Only for a few years after 1870, when it was evident that France would not attack, was there a sense of security in England. The real history does not get written, because it is not in people's brains but in their nerves and vitals."

"Suppose our American culture were wiped out: whom have we produced so far who would stand as a lasting contribution to the world?"

"Walt Whitman."

"Not Emerson?"

"I read Emerson a good deal when I was younger, but if my good neighbours, the Forbeses, will pardon me for saying so," (they are grandsons of Emerson) "he was not so original. But Whitman brought something into poetry which was never there before. Much of what he says is so new that he even had to invent a form for saying it. Whitman seems to me to have been one of the few very great poets that have ever lived. He can stand easily beside the really great European poets. . . . If

English civilization had perished prior to the year 1500, the loss would not have been great. Chaucer is not of the stature of Dante or Homer, and though we have some fine cathedrals, English Gothic is not really as good as French Gothic; but if you destroyed the English civilization from 1500 to 1900, you would make the world much poorer, for it did add something important to the development of the human spirit."

"At Winchester College last summer I noticed something which struck me as a bit of measurement," I said. "Reginald Coupland had taken Sam Morison and me down from Oxford to show us where he went to school, and, in passing those cubicles of the top-form boys I noticed on their study tables texts of Aeschylus, Thucydides, and others of the Great Age, not 'study' texts, edited for schoolboys, but the Teubner *Opera*, the regular brass-knuckled article. 'Are these boys studying the fifth-century dramatists and historians already?' I asked Coupland. He said, 'No. They're reading them on their own.' In Harvard, you were doing well if you read those authors in the original by your sophomore or your junior year. I was flabbergasted."

"You must remember," Whitehead cautioned, "that at Winchester the boys are a selected group, with a very special kind of training to which they are well adapted. In that groove they acquire astonishing proficiency, but they would be quite ignorant out of it. They would know a great deal about Roman customs in the period of the Punic Wars, but very little, perhaps nothing, about urgent problems of their own land and time. They do well at the universities and make names in the professions and as colonial administrators and civil servants. The creative arts? I do not think you will find many of them excelling there. They write well, but not very imaginatively. American students are less well-informed but more eager to learn; English boys are less eager but more informed. The American boy knows less about what interests him more, the English boy knows more about what seems to interest him less." He said this with a laughing twinkle in his bright blue eyes.

"Yes," I conceded, "but all over Europe the cultural soil is so much deeper."

"You place too much stress on soil. It isn't soil. You are the same people as Europeans. You have access to the whole of European history. Americans are too diffident."

"It strikes me that our writers don't *know* enough."

"It is true that most great writers did know quite a lot. But it is possible to know too much. What is wanted is an immense *feeling* for things. And the danger in old civilizations is that the teaching may be *too* good. It damps students down. They know too much about what has been done, they write well, but without freshness. It is so fatally easy for a good period in art to die down into scholasticism and pedantry, for the life to go out of it. Oxford has taught the classics for centuries, and for centuries Cambridge virtually refused to teach literature and taught mathematics, and yet twice as many poets came out of Cambridge as out of Oxford."

"At least, no one can complain that our epoch doesn't provide plenty of excitement to write about. The trouble with history is that there is too much of it."

"If you want a striking parallel of our time," said Whitehead, "read Neale's life of Queen Elizabeth.[1] Point for point it is like ours: uncertainty, no one could have the least idea of what would happen, and Elizabeth's chances of assassination were excellent; and then there was Mary Stuart, for if she survived Elizabeth, either she would become queen and the work of the Reformation be undone, or else there would be the worst of civil wars. And yet that age put forth its astounding achievement."

"Are ages of upheaval favourable to creation?"

"I fancy they are, if not too prolonged and too violent. In the Elizabethan there would have been quiet weeks when nothing

---

[1] *Queen Elizabeth*, John Ernest Neale, Astor Professor of English History, University of London. Jonathan Cape, 1934.

much was happening and a poet could be at his play-writing. And then there is the incentive of any one great figure doing good work. It sets off a lot of others."

"How about the possibility of one or two great artists exhausting an epoch or an art-form? The Renaissance takes a drop after Michelangelo, and grand opera since Wagner has been a 'Tristan, Junior.' "

"That does happen. Such figures come at the end of an epoch. The danger is when the great themes have been superlatively well done, and the later workers come to secondary themes or refinements or niceties, and art or thought gets drawn off into shallows. That is fatally easy. I mean such themes as a mother's love for her child, something so universal that to express it sounds trite, and yet the medieval sculptors and Renaissance painters could express it with unbelievable beauty: but it is no good trying to imitate them. I have the feeling that the very greatest art gets created only in periods and about subjects as to which there is the very greatest enthusiasm and unanimity and popularity. It speaks to the common people, and when art begins to break up into coteries I do not think it is of much significance. When these coteries begin saying, 'This is too fine for the vulgar to understand,' I doubt if it is very good or great art.

"Our own time is a period of break-up and perhaps our thinkers haven't yet got their bearings in the new era. That may be what is putting them off. The assumptions of the nineteenth century are shaken, and one of the symptoms of it is satirical biography. Lytton Strachey, whom I knew and enjoyed, writes with amazing gusto and familiarity of the Victorians, but when a party of contemporaries says, 'Let us sit down and have a quiet laugh over those stuffy creatures, Dr. Thomas Arnold and Queen Victoria,' he may be very amusing, and may be getting at their weak spots, but he isn't writing about what gave them their moral energy or what carried their century along. And your second crop of such scoffing is likely to be a sorry one.

[23]

I think your generation caught the break-up harder than the one now growing up. They never knew a different world, but yours did. Take such a fifteen-minute conversation as we are having now: we are talking earnestly. Their attitude is, 'What is there to choose between one fifteen minutes and another, so long as it is enjoyable? Why should there be any difference? What is the purpose? What is the value? What is the goal?' "

"But you and I do *not* believe that this fifteen minutes is no more important than any other fifteen minutes," I said with some emphasis.

"That is because we belong to a generation which did feel that certain experiences were more valuable than others, and did have a sense of whither it was bound."

The question arose whether science, or a scientific age, was hostile to poetry. He said:

"I think if some of the great poets had lived in our time they might have been not poets but scientists. Shelley, for example; I think it quite possible that he could have been a chemist or physicist. Take Professor Ames of Dartmouth, a man whose discoveries in the field of psychology and optics have made him eminent in Europe and America. If you were to talk with him you would at once discover that you were speaking with a poet and a mystic."

(It struck me that just that thing does happen in the play *Wings Over Europe* by Robert Nichols and Maurice Browne. The scientist is a young Shelleyan poet-idealist.)

Here Mr. George Agassiz was shown in, and while he and Professor Whitehead discussed briefly some affairs of Harvard University, of which Mr. Agassiz is an overseer, there was time to take in the room. It is a large chamber with a peaked roof carried on open beams, and there is a brick fireplace wide enough for three-foot logs. This study is walled with books. The upholstery for the hearth settee and armchairs is a pale green, cool and restful, but the log fire was a grateful warmth against the lingering chill of April. The writing table and secretary are well daylighted, but his working place is evidently the deep armchair beside a south-west window, with a writing board to be held across his lap.

From that window one looks over a wide vista of rolling hills, meadows, and woodland. It was now past sunset, and under a clear sky of early spring, the interfolding hill contours against the horizon were twilight purple.

*   *   *

Mrs. Whitehead was in the living-room on her chaise longue. A good deal had happened. Their daughter, Jessie, while skiing on Mt. Washington had broken her neck. For weeks her life had hung as by a thread. When this siege was over, Mrs. Whitehead had had a heart attack. She was pale, but still had her sparkle. Tall, slender, white-haired, and gowned in black, she looked much more the *grande dame* than the invalid, though her dinner was brought on a tray. We others went out to the table, but the door was open so that she could join the conversation, which she did at intervals.

Before dinner was announced she was reading aloud with great gusto some of the opening parts of *John Brown's Body*, which they had all read and liked. Mrs. Nichols came in and was introduced, a handsome young Englishwoman of the black-haired, blue-eyed type, frank and friendly.

At the table, since the three English people continued the theme of American literature as it seemed to me out of courtesy, a shift was negotiated by someone's saying that Dickens's *Bleak House* is one of the few novels which (like the long catalogues of occupations in Whitman's poems) does give some sense of the immense range and variety of social life.

"Yes, all but at the top," said Dr. Nichols.

"Dickens was good at the bottom and middle," said Mr. Agassiz, "but poor at the top; Thackeray was good at the top but poor below the middle."

"In my time at Cambridge (I went up in '83) no one

read Dickens," said Whitehead. "He was considered beneath notice."

"Because poorly written?" asked Mrs. Nichols.

"Largely, I think."

"Of course, Thackeray can write."

"But," she was reminded, "you remember Chesterton's remark about him: that he thought a good many things were going to last which *weren't* going to last. 'He didn't know enough ignorant people to have heard the news.' "

"Dickens," said Whitehead, "didn't begin to be generally read by the university people and the cultivated classes, I think, until along in the 1890's."

"What carried him then? Did the socialists help him?"

"No, not a bit, I should think."

"I was thinking of the Fabians. Their tracts began in 1884."

"No. He came in on his own, along with poor-law relief and housing reform."

The talk veered to slum clearance, the victory at the polls of the Socialists for control of the London County Council, and its frightening the government to put out a huge slum-clearance scheme "which," said the professor, "they had been dangling but didn't really mean to do anything about"; comparison of London and New York slums, London having at least the advantages of more durable buildings and little or no fire risk. They spoke of how strange it seemed to see wooden houses but thought they fitted into our landscape more naturally, and Professor Whitehead added, "One of the first distinctive notes in the American city I noticed is the prominence of the fire brigades."

"Before we leave the novelists, what has happened to George Eliot?" I asked.

"She *has* tumbled off, hasn't she?" said the professor. "I wonder why. *Middlemarch* is a great book."

Mrs. Whitehead spoke from the living-room:

"Have you tried reading her lately?"

"Yes," said I.

"So have I. As I remembered it, she was rather gorgeous, and so she is still in spots, but didn't you find long intervals very prosy and ponderous?"

"What an awkward question! Yes, I did. But there was a time in my twenties when I swore by her, and now one sword at least her right shall guard."

"It was the same with me," said Mrs. Whitehead, "and I had to stop enthusiastically urging my friends to read her."

"That's dangerous," said Whitehead. "For years I have been extolling the Old Testament prophets. True, I hadn't read them recently, but as I remembered, they were quite sublime. Then I tried reading Isaiah. I couldn't go him."

"What was wrong? Did the JEPD,[1] the way the different versions of the Old Testament are cut and pasted, put you off?"

"No. It was the ranting, and wandering from the point. I found that when talking of the Old Testament prophets I should have to change my line."

"Do you remember what Strachey says about prophets?"

"No."

"It is in his essay on Carlyle. He says Carlyle had a low opinion of artists and would have preferred to be remembered as a prophet. Now to be a prophet one must have three qualifications, a loud voice, a bold face, and a bad temper. (Strachey got that joke from Aristophanes, but it's none the worse for that.) But, asks Strachey, who, in any case, remembers prophets? Isaiah and Jeremiah, perhaps, but then they have had the extraordinary good fortune to be translated into English by a committee of Elizabethan bishops!"

"Tell them about Strachey's remark at our house on Jane Austen," said Mrs. Whitehead.

---

[1] JEPD: Jahvist, Elohist, Priestly, and Deuteronomist elements in the Old Testament. "That is to say, in an average chapter of Genesis we may read a verse written in the ninth century, followed by one written in the fifth, a gap of four hundred years. And sometimes the gap will occur in the middle of a verse."—*The Rise of the Greek Epic*, Gilbert Murray. Oxford University Press, 3rd ed., 1924, page 109.

"It was when we were living in Cambridge, along toward the end of our time there and Strachey was down staying with us. He said he had been reading Jane Austen. 'You?' said I. 'What is there in Jane Austen for you?'—'Passion!' says Strachey."

"All the same," said Mr. Agassiz, more as one thinking aloud, "satire is the soured milk of human kindness."

"How singularly humourless the Bible is," remarked the doctor. "I wonder why."

"You would be gloomy, too," said Whitehead gravely, "if you had Jehovah hanging over you."

"But what a contrast with the Greeks and their laughter," said Mr. Agassiz.

"Where does it come in?" asked Mrs. Nichols.

"Aristophanes."

"Yes," said Whitehead, "but I think humour is a bit later than the stage to which the prophets belong. I think humour is a later thing, and Aristóphanes is a bit special. Is there any, or much, humour in Homer?"

"Besides," said the doctor, "the Jewish scriptures were religious literature."

"Yes," said Whitehead, "and when writing is new, men don't set down what they regard as trivialities, and mischances they do regard as trivial even now in primitive tribes. Some of our fellows who were out in Africa with the Negroes during the war tell of how the Negroes went down to a stream for something and came back roaring with laughter. What was the joke? Why, a crocodile had suddenly popped out of the water and snatched one of their fellows off. One of *their* fellows, mind you; not a white."

This came as we were rising from the table. A spring shower was falling. It could be heard making a musical patter overhead, for the living-room roof, like that of the study, is carried on oak beams stained black, with white plaster in the intervals. Glass doors in three pairs open to a terrace that fronts westward, giving view across lawn and garden to the Blue Hills from which Massachusetts takes its Indian name. The room is large and cheerful with its huge fireplace, some quite choice mahogany chairs and lounges upholstered in a French-gray satin, a suggestion of the Empire style, and flowers on side tables and mantelshelf, tulips, jonquils, narcissuses, and lilies of the valley.

"When you were speaking at table of Lytton Strachey," said Mrs. Whitehead, whom the return to the living-room had brought back into the conversation, "I wanted to quote those verses by Miss Wordsworth of Lady Margaret Hall:

> *If all the good people were clever*
> *And those that are clever were good,*
> *This world would be nicer than ever*
> *We dreamed that it possibly could.*
>
> *But it seems as though seldom if ever*
> *Do the two hit it off as they should,*
> *The good are so harsh to the clever,*
> *The clever so rude to the good.*

"Then should clever portrait painters," asked Mrs. Nichols, "flatter good but stupid and perhaps homely sitters?"

"When John Sargent's portraits of some wealthy but disagreeable sitters were being exhibited in New York," observed Mr. Agassiz, "a Harvard professor murmured at my ear, 'Imitations of Immorality.'"

"Sitters, too, have their rights," said Mrs. Whitehead, and told of their recent adventures with a portrait painter. "He first did one of me. Eleven mortal mornings I sat, until he asked if I wished to see how he was getting on. Of course I knew that such first views aren't altogether happy, so I did not expect too much. He asked what I thought of it. I said, 'Well, of course, one never knows how one looks.' He worked some more. He all but counted the hairs of my head. When it was finished he showed it to his wife. She said, 'It is frightful! Why it isn't even a likeness. What are you planning to do with it?' 'I am going to have it framed and give it to Mr. Whitehead, keepsake style.' 'You are not,' said she, 'you are going to tear it up.' Whatever became of it I never did learn but some time afterwards he confided to me, 'You see, I wasn't really interested in the subject: what interested me was the medium!' "

"And what about the one he painted of me?" asked Mr. Whitehead.

"It looks," said Mrs. Nichols, "as if you were about six years old."

"Yes," said Mrs. Whitehead, "and he still had that same look twenty years later when I married him and for a good many years after that." She smiled with reminiscent, and slightly grim, relish. "I learned to know what it meant and to keep quiet!"

"When he was painting it," said the philosopher blandly, "I chatted along to him, but he kept stopping to scribble notes on paper till I wanted to ask, 'I say, are you an artist or an amanuensis?' And then he wanted to involve me in a controversy of his. You see he went abroad and brought home an Italian tomb, quite a beautiful one, I thought, and he had it put up in the middle of the museum, but then he went away again for a year and when he came back it was gone, quite disappeared. He finally found it down in the basement. But he couldn't get it up again. He tried to get me in on his side. He said, 'If only you will come in with me I think your influence will be tremendous, sufficient to get it restored to its rightful place of dignity.' 'But what good would I be?' I asked. 'I know nothing about art. All I know is that your tomb is quite beautiful.' 'That's all you need to know.' (He was taking Keats's line, you see.) 'Come and say that.' 'But I can say that here without coming to the museum. And besides it wouldn't help you, for the department leans toward archaeology and your tomb could be as beautiful as it liked but if it can't prove it is within a decade of the right period, it will never get out of the cellar!' "

"But don't mistake us," said Mrs. Whitehead. "He is a dear and we are very fond of him."

The talk then veered to the Buchman sect, which was just then coming into prominence, and was articulate, not to say vociferous.

"What is it about that movement," someone asked, "that makes a reticent person wince?"

Whitehead said what it was in no uncertain terms.

"Have you heard," said Mrs. Whitehead, "of Dr. and Mrs. Richard Cabot's visit to the group confessional?"

"No."

"At the proper moment Mr. Buchman, not knowing who they were, nodded, signifying that it was their turn to testify. Dr. Cabot rose and said sternly, 'I am Dr. Richard Cabot, a physician, and professor of sociology in Harvard College.' His wife followed": (she dropped her voice to a mere wisp) " 'My name is Ella Cabot. I am an earnest seeker after truth,' and *she* sat down. That was all."

"It seems to be a kind of upper-class Salvation Army," said I. "A time of social confusion jolts people loose from old beliefs and they catch at straws. Sex-confession is one of the selling points."

"So with the psychoanalysts. Isn't it inevitable that they should develop a taste by all this digging, digging, digging, for unconscious secrets?" asked Mrs. Whitehead. "I should think they ended by digging simply for the fun of digging. And what is there in it for the poor, who must need it as badly if not worse than the rich if there is anything in it? I don't notice any free psychoanalyst clinics. It strikes me that regular physicians are often paid rather meagrely and these psychoanalysts are doing themselves rather well. Isn't it something of a craze for prying into other people's minds and getting you to tell what perhaps you ought to tell, but perhaps not to the prier who is trying to get you to tell?"

Mrs. Dr. Nichols defended the absent profession rather ably, and seemed to know a good deal about it.

"Of all the branches of Protestant sectarianism that I know of," said the philosopher, "King's Chapel in Boston is unique. They will let anybody come there and preach to them—even myself, for instance. It is incredibly respectable. Do you know of any place more respectable," he appealed to me, "even in Boston?"

"None except Mt. Vernon Street. Doesn't Henry James call it the most respectable street in America?"

"I am afraid that doesn't help us," said the philosopher, "for King's Chapel is, as I understand it, owned by people who live on Mt. Vernon Street. It's extraordinarily select. There is a King's Chapel religion, the only one of its kind in existence. I believe it is *the* correct place to be married from."

"You see," explained Mrs. Whitehead, "we went into this venerable place and all sat down, and Altie climbed into a high pulpit, and one naturally expected that we would sing a hymn or begin a litany, but nothing of the sort happened; and then Altie spouted, I must own, in his best manner . . ."

"It's all quite liberal," said he, "almost as much so as Harvard. Did you know that Harvard has an endowed lecture dating back to the eighteenth century, the lecturer being expected to descant on 'the damnable errors of the Church of Rome'? They have even invited a Catholic priest to deliver it."

"How do they get around the terms?"

"Oh, quite easily! Perhaps the lecturer can't discover any damnable errors in the Church of Rome; he then isn't expected to descant on them."

"How that would be relished by one of my old friends. He is now a priest but was formerly a professor of history in Harvard, and with a distinguished career. We were undergraduates together and got on famously, both being from the Midwest and our fathers doctors. He was even then recondite of High Church Anglican lore."

"He must be the man I frequently meet in the library," said the philosopher. "We are just on the point of nodding."

[32]

"Do nod, next time."

"His clericalism dates a good way back?"

"Even thirty years ago I used to wonder, in my theological illiteracy, how he kept his High Church Anglicanism and German transcendental philosophers in logic-tight compartments."

"I fancy," said the philosopher, "that isn't as hard to do as it sounds. We all do a bit of that. The hard thing is to keep them in the same compartment."

II

April 22, 1934

ANOTHER fortnight of spring, and along the four miles from Mattapan to the Whiteheads' a veil of green leaf-buds had been spun over the woodlands of that hill country. My arrival this time was a little before seven, and the taxicab driver was asked, as before, to return at nine-forty, out of regard for Mrs. Whitehead's frail health; an order which was later to be rescinded.

She was just being brought to her chaise longue in the living-room by a wheel chair, Professor Whitehead, in his seventies, performing that act vigorously, and then bustling about under her direction arranging chairs and lights.

They chaffed me for leaving so early the previous time.

"Altie said, 'Have we been too much for him? Has he had all he can stand of us?' I told him you probably had an article to write for the morrow. One expects that when a journalist comes to dinner. But Grace DeFriez tells me you have to go early to bed."

"But Grace DeFriez told me *you* had to go early to bed—or something equivalent. It took all my self-abnegation to order that cab for nine-forty."

"Then don't do it again!"

"I just have done it again."

"Then undo it."

It was undone by telephone.

"The wife of Professor Morgan is coming." She briefed me a little. "(He, poor fellow, can't be here. He is in the hospital. His tuberculosis, as you know.) The others are Mrs. Nichols, whom you met here last time (the doctor is out at Ann Arbor studying), Professor Rosenstock-Huessy, a German, and Mr. and Mrs. Agassiz. He, too, was here last time. She is a dignified New England gentlewoman, the perfection of her type, and he, I tell him (it is a standing joke between us), *looks* like a Parisian *boulevardier* and *is* a correct Puritan Bostonian, and of course, a member of the Board of Overseers of Harvard. His sense of humour is quite equal to the antithesis, and he even improves upon it: 'When I am in Paris I have a Puritan conscience, and when in Boston my conscience is Parisian, but that won't go in Boston. In consequence, I am always at a disadvantage.' "

They arrived presently. Dinner was served to Mrs. Whitehead and Mr. Agassiz at a small table in the living-room; the rest of us went out to the dining-room.

"I understand," said one of the guests to the host, "that you have compared President Roosevelt with Augustus Caesar. I am a Republican. I can't bear the man."

Whitehead turned to the speaker with a look of glistening hesitancy, then replied in his urbane tones:

"I know of only twice in history when there was a gentleman on the throne."

" 'Throne' ought to satisfy any Republican animus," said Mrs. Nichols genially, being a British subject.

"But wasn't King Edward VII a gentleman?" inquired Rosenstock-Huessy, not unmindful of Edward's kinsman Wilhelm, a Hohenzollern.

"Far from it, I should say," replied the philosopher. "He was very badly brought up. He couldn't get on with the kaiser."

"But no one could get on with the kaiser," said Mrs. Agassiz, "and besides he was the kaiser's uncle. It was a family matter. The uncle-nephew relationship made it impossible."

"That isn't the point. It was Edward's *job* to get on with the kaiser. That is what we paid him for, and paid him handsomely, jolly well too much. No, he was ill-bred! When he went out to India as Prince of Wales he blew up an old general who came to a review in the wrong uniform. 'You old fellows out here get into loose habits,' he stormed. 'Including this one, your Majesty!' said the old soldier, tapping his wooden arm with his remaining good hand."

"As if Edward were the one to talk about loose habits," remarked Mrs. Morgan.

"I could forgive him that. After all, his mother *was* a bit stuffy. But he should have minded his manners in public. I'm afraid I didn't care much for him. They knew their royal manners better in the eighteenth century. There was a powerful magnate named Tom Coke, who had great estates and hated George III. At a big public dinner someone proposed a toast to the king, and Tom Coke exploded, 'I won't drink the health of a bloody tyrant!' It was quite shocking and everybody wondered what would happen. But as the throne was just then a bit shaky, all that happened was Tom Coke got a letter from his sovereign saying that no offence was taken because His Majesty understood the *spirit* in which the remark was made!"

Conversation moved to Granville-Barker's production of *The Trojan Women* of Euripides in the Harvard Stadium in 1915, and there was a sudden tacit rallying of the table's talk to shield the German present from the discomfort of what was in every mind at the time, that it had been a contemporaneous performance of *The Belgian Women*, for that was why it was given. Someone said, "The tragedy gave a feeling of the shared guilt of all wars."

"Did anyone here see it?" asked Whitehead.

"Yes. And one of my old professors in the Greek department, who sat next to me, said, 'This is a complete knockdown for me.

I have read *The Trojan Women* repeatedly, and taught it; and if you had asked me this morning, I would have told you that it was full of faults and not really a very good play: and now here it is, overwhelming. You don't know a play until you have seen it acted.' "

"And yet," said Mr. Agassiz from the living-room, "the power of that performance was said to be twenty-five per cent Euripides and seventy-five per cent Granville-Barker."

"I should have put it the other way round," said Mrs. Agassiz.

"Knowing Euripides," said Whitehead, "I should say it was 'fifty-fifty.' "

We adjourned from the table to the living-room for coffee. The talk got headed toward how to get a good government. Someone had been saying that there have been plenty of Power States; indeed, of one sort or another, there has never been any other kind; but why not a Culture State, replacing government by the acquisitive persons with government by the creative people?

"That's so!" said Professor Whitehead. "The acquisitive, being interested in material concerns, do manage to get hold of government."

"Isn't that why they, in general, run it so badly," I asked, "why we get selfish governing classes, why they do such ruthless acts, care so little for the arts, and follow low-minded policies? After all, they are merely expressing the acquisitive instincts. How can we get the creative impulses running a state?"

"It would have to be made amusing," said Whitehead. "I fancy statecraft at present isn't amusing enough to keep a poet or an artist interested. It would need to be as interesting as poetry."

"I know of only one poem that has to do with such subjects," said Rosenstock-Huessy, "and that is by Goethe, and it has never been translated into English that I know of. In it he recites his pleasure in the administrative work he has done at Weimar, the road-building, military reorganization, metallurgy and so on."

"What is its title?" I asked.

"*Ilmenau.*"

"Wasn't it written for one of the Duke Karl August's birthdays?"

"Yes. You have read it?"

"As it happens, quite recently. But there is a difficulty. Goethe enjoyed administration and did it well, but *too* well. He got enmeshed in it to the detriment of his poetizing. That is why he ran away to Italy."

"What I think we want," said Whitehead, "is a head of state reasonably secure, but not *too* secure."

"How about the Antonine emperors?"

"They gave excellent administrations. It was a peculiar system of adoptive successors ratified by a military oligarchy. And singularly enough, the one who has the most credit deserves the least. I mean Marcus Aurelius, for he departed from the rule by appointing his own son Commodus, which happened to be a bad appointment. Marcus would have fared very ill with posterity if he hadn't written those amiable memoirs, which, however edifying and delightful, had nothing to do with the point. His job was to find a good successor."

"How would Pericles qualify?"

"Admirably. There you had the head of the state chosen by means of a political free fight and removable the same way."

"Altic dear, the reason you are down on Marcus is because he intruded into your pet preserve of philosophy where he didn't belong," his wife chaffed him.

"No, I don't say he didn't belong. I should like to venture as far afield from philosophy if *I* had plenty of lifetimes in which to experiment."

"Where, for instance?"

"Well, for one, I would like to be head of a great department store."

"You? Running Jordan Marsh's?"

"Oh. I don't say in Boston. Say London."

"Competing with Selfridge."

"Not necessarily. Mr. Selfridge might be considerate enough to die and leave me to manage the store."

"But, pettie, he *has* died, hasn't he, and here you are not running his store!"

"No. I don't think he is dead. Let me consult *Who's Who*." He went to his study for the volume.

"Oh, you!" Mrs. Whitehead fired after him. "You want to handle silks and satins. You'd *love* it."

"I assure you, my dear, my aspirations to management are much more impersonal."

Presently he returned with *Who's Who*, open to the page.

"He's still alive. Here he is. 'Gordon Selfridge,' " and he read excerpts.

"But that's the son, isn't it?" said Mrs. Whitehead.

"But it *would* be, wouldn't it, my dear?"

"What I'd like to know, Professor Whitehead, is what effect on a public you would try for in a department store?"

"Taste. Household economy. How to get along with fewer things and better."

"Then your shark competitors would devour you."

"I don't think so. That would be part of the fascination— keeping out of their maws."

III

January 24, 1935

THE Whiteheads have moved from Canton back to their former apartment in Radnor Hall on Memorial Drive overlooking the Charles River in Cambridge.

It was the day after a heavy snowstorm. The sky had cleared, an icy wind blew from the north-west, and snow lay heaped in the thoroughfares two and three feet deep. No paths had been shovelled between Harvard Square and the Charles. I waded and floundered, thinking of David McCord's variant of Robert Louis Stevenson:

> *In Boston when it snows at night*
> *They clean it up by candle light.*
> *In Cambridge quite the other way:*
> *It snows, and there they leave it lay.*

Dinner was at seven-fifteen. Only the family were present, Professor and Mrs. Whitehead, Margot, their daughter-in-law (Mrs. North Whitehead), and Eric, the grandson, a blond, blue-eyed lad of thirteen or fourteen years. Mrs. Whitehead was more vigorous and walked in and out of the library several times.

At the table the talk was of their life in Cambridge, England, as contrasted with this in Cambridge, Massachusetts, and of the English stage as they had known it in London. They had seen one of the first performances of Pinero's *The Second Mrs. Tanqueray* with Mrs. Patrick Campbell, who of course *was* Paula Tanqueray, in the title part, and they said that everyone came out of the theatre stunned and almost speechless at what was then considered its outspokenness, and yet, half a dozen years ago when it was revived and very well played by an excellent company, it fell flat and audiences actually laughed. What was all the row about? What was there in the situation that couldn't have been unscrambled in two hours' talk with a competent psychiatrist?

After dinner we separated, the women to the library, Professor Whitehead and I to the sitting-room, where coffee was brought. He talked a little about journalism, and we came to the subject of reputations made by machine publicity, and why fame, which used to be an oak, taking eighty years to grow, should now be a summer squash.

"Is there anything in spiritual law," I asked him, "to

compensate the truly fine pianist for two concerts a year as against the professional showman-virtuoso's two hundred?"

"I am inclined to think that is one of the permanent tragedies of life," said he, "that the finer quality doesn't prevail over the next less fine."

He asked why newspaper headlines are so sensational.

"They are billboards to sell the article."

"Often they give a wrong idea of what is inside the paper."

"Do they? There are days when my impression is that they are our modern substitute of the colosseum martyr-and-wild-beast show."

He looked grave and did not dispute the remark.

We returned to the library. The heavy curtains of black velours had been drawn across the tall windows which looked toward the river and Soldiers Field, and a wood fire burned on the andirons under a black chimney piece of panelled wood in a classic design. The long, wide room, walled with books on three sides, was cheerfully lamplighted. It is the philosopher's study, and his reading chair and writing table are established in a comfortable nook.

As conversation went on there was an opportunity to ask if they had noticed a sterility in the creative arts among the Bostonians. It was soon evident that they had.

"Has their loss of political control something to do with it?" suggested Mrs. Whitehead a shade diffidently.

"Frederic Stimson, a Boston lawyer, novelist, and sometime our ambassador to the Argentine," I said, "has dealt with that in his autobiography, *My United States*. It was published about four years ago. He says that immense wealth had been accumulated in Boston in the first sixty years of the republic, but the wealthy men, instead of trusting their sons and sending them out at their own risks on life's seas as they themselves had done, tied up their fortunes in trust funds so that they could not be squandered by their heirs. The effect was to choke off their initiative."

"Among the few wealthy men I come in contact with," said the professor, "I find a state of funk over what the Roosevelt administration is (quite wisely, I think) doing, and no equipment for understanding it."

"That was evident when the class war struck us in 1912 with the first Lawrence strike," I said. "It was a large-scale revolt and they were too frightened to understand it."

"Their women are timid," said Mrs. Whitehead. "It shows in their houses. Every house is furnished alike. No one dares be different. The monotony is so deadly that every time I go into one more such, I could scream."

He agreed. "In England, the houses would present more instances of vulgar taste, but it would be at least individual. The interior could express the personality. Here the shops do not keep the articles necessary for individual variety. You must take what you can get."

"The notable exception," said she, "is Grace DeFriez. In that house you have taste and individuality."

A question rose whether a common language is a help or a hindrance to Anglo-American understanding. Both Whitehead since he has come to Harvard, and Gilbert Murray when he was last here from Oxford in 1926, have expressed the opinion that it betrays both people into supposing they are alike, when they are profoundly different, and actually promotes misunderstanding.

"I have been reading John Buchan's *Cromwell*," said he, "and the point he makes is that both Cromwell and Charles I were beaten. There was a transition period from 1680 to about 1737 when there is rather a cultural blank; then England finds its footing again and is off into its eighteenth century. But it follows an aristocratic, land-owning tradition which lasts on and merges into the nineteenth-century industrialism, the old aristocracy intermarrying with the new. But your American history stems from the dissenter, the Puritan middle class with a strong democratic tinge. The Cromwellian revolution was undefeated in America, so the two countries have developed along quite different lines. Yet see what a curious science sociology is! In England, owing to the difficulty of individual talents finding their way up through class strata, people stay with their class, bring their class along, and we have a labour movement ably led by working-class men, *so* ably that in 1924, and again in 1929, when we had Labour governments, they were well qualified to carry on all the ministries of empire, including foreign affairs."

"Our labour movement is still a long way from that."

"Yes, and isn't that one reason why your exceptional talents can rise rapidly through the class strata?" said Whitehead. "*They* rise, but they leave their class behind. Thus, English aristocracy is creating a genuine democracy, and American democracy is creating an aristocracy."

He told of being consulted by a young graduate student in the Divinity School, on what early Church Fathers he should read.

"I asked how long his ancestors had been in this country. He replied that he had come here from Norway at the age of thirteen. His father was a country parson, too poor to give him a secondary-school education, so he was sent to Wisconsin or Minnesota, merely to an acquaintance, who got him a place to work on a farm for a year. Then he went to high school, did well, worked his way through a small college, obtained a scholarship, and came to Harvard, and here he was consulting about Origen and Thomas Aquinas. I understand he is being considered for an instructorship in the university. Of course there was some luck in it: there is an enormous element of luck in human lots; but he must also have been treated with great kindness. My point is that I know of no other place in the world where quite such a thing could happen."

He said that he thought the instrumentality of the monasteries in giving the more sensitive and imaginative types of humanity expression by protecting them in the Middle Ages had never been adequately explored. "The outer world was

violent, yet here was this world of thought going on concurrently
and it had enormous influence. Humble and impecunious
scholars found harbourage in them. And then I observe how
institutions run their course. From about the turn of the fifth
century into the sixth, when St. Benedict founded his order, up
until the fourteenth—nearly a thousand years—if any intellectual work was to be done it had to be under monastic protection.
Yet by the time you come to Erasmus, he can hardly mention a
monk without going out of his way to utter an expression of
contempt. And I wonder how long our universities will keep
their edge. Just now they have an enormous vogue and influence. Teaching can be too good. It can perpetuate a tradition
and lose the spirit. I reflect that the University of Cambridge,
which has done best at teaching mathematics, is the one from
amongst whose graduates have come more of the English poets,
while Oxford, which has specialized in the humanities, has
tended to turn out writers who have attained, on the whole, a
high level of mediocrity. I suppose by the time a man has discussed literature with a learned and witty tutor two or three
times a week over a period of years he has rather talked it out
instead of writing it. Then he knows too well how much good
work has been done and how good it is, and is too respectful
toward it: 'Who am I that I should do better?' "

We amused ourselves trying to see whether English poets
derived sectionally, predominating in certain geographical
regions. It seemed to run from the Lakes down through the
Midlands east of a central vertical axis, and over into East
Anglia, focusing of course in London.

He then discussed American universities in their broad functions: "I disagree with Abraham Flexner's idea that there
ought to be separate institutions dotted over the land each
giving a specific kind of training.[1] It seems to me that you do

---

[1] "The University in American Life," *Atlantic Monthly;* May, 1932: Vol. 149.
"Failings of Our Graduate Schools." *Atlantic Monthly;* April, 1932: Vol. 149.
Universities, American, English, German. Oxford University Press, 1930.

much better with a more flexible system in which a man taking a technological training can get cultural courses also if he wants and needs them. Your big midwestern universities seem to me to be doing this passably well. This flexibility gives the student a chance to look around and get his breath. Minds don't classify as easily as some of my colleagues appear to think. I am profoundly suspicious of the 'A'-man. He can say back what you want to hear in an examination, and since the examination is roughly a means of test, you must give him his *A* if he says it back; but the ability, not to say the willingness, to give you back what is expected of him argues a certain shallowness and superficiality. Your 'B'-man may be a bit muddle-headed, but muddle-headedness is a condition precedent to independent thought, may actually be independent creative thought in its first stage. Of course it may get no farther than muddle-headedness. But when my colleagues chaff me for giving more *A*'s than they are willing to do and tax me with tender-heartedness, I reflect that I would rather not have it on my head that I was the one who discouraged an incipient talent."

IV

March 25, 1935

TEA with Professor and Mrs. Whitehead in Cambridge. The sycamores in double row along Memorial Drive are not yet in bud, but there was a goldenly hazed sun of early spring, the air though not warm was still and mild, the river glassy-blue where it was not stirred by college oarsmen.

Tea was served in their living-room. They brought out two old volumes of letters, *Three Generations of English Women*, Mrs. John Taylor, Mrs. Sarah Austin, and Lady Duff-Gordon, edited by Janet Duff-Gordon. The professor said:

"I think you get a truer picture of a period from intimate letters written spontaneously and without a thought of publication than you do from its fiction and often better than from its historians."

"And women write better than men in that vein," said his wife.

"Certainly better than authors writing letters to each other with an eye to future publication," he agreed.

"Edmund Gosse used to complain that while the letters Robert Louis Stevenson wrote him were works of art and literature they didn't tell him what he wanted to know about his friend—which touched off Carolyn Wells to write that ballade with the refrain, 'They *must* look well in print!' "

The professor read aloud a passage in remarkably prophetic vein about Bismarck, written by Sarah Austin to M. B. St. Hilaire, July 7, 1856 (volume 2, page 42):

> *. . . for these small (German) kingdoms, so admirably governed, are destined to disappear, and the reign of armed force inaugurated by the French Revolution and the wars which followed will soon be universal. Your pupil, Prussia, will beat you with your own arms. M. de Bismarck will not hesitate at violence, fraud, or baseness. He will be at least on a par with all you have. Our stupid Liberals insist on seeing liberty in Prussia, despotism in Austria; there is but one word—and name—for such people.*
>
> *Alas, my predictions are being realised. The small independent States will be annihilated and eaten up by the monsters who only know the law of the strongest.*

He laid down the book and said:

"All this has come strictly true, and it is not mere vague prophecy of disaster but a specific forecast of events by a liberal at the very zenith of nineteenth-century liberalism. The reverse of '48 had occurred, but few realized how serious it was."

"Janet Duff-Gordon Ross, who edited these letters, comes in like an old acquaintance," I remarked. "She was the young friend of George Meredith, is the 'lady' in *Modern Love*, Rose Jocelyn in *Evan Harrington*, and Janet Ilchester in *The Adventures of Harry Richmond,* but she had some less amiable qualities than those heroines of poetry and fiction."

"Wasn't there an episode with Ouida?" asked Mrs. Whitehead.

"She horsewhipped that novelist in Bond Street. Evidently she was one of those redoubtable characters of nineteenth-century England who did what they pleased, and were accepted."

"They were by no means rare," said Mrs. Whitehead. "Those great liberal families, though often poor, managed to go everywhere in England and on the Continent and knew everyone in the liberal movement. Ideas were the passports, and that condition to some extent still exists."

"When you get a distinguished liberal," said he, "you generally find nonconformists behind him: often quite humble people, tradesmen and such. To change the subject: we have been reading with great pleasure two articles by you, one signed, in the *Yale Review*, about Sibelius, the other unsigned in the *Globe*, about Hitler's move for rearmament, which we think took a very sensible view of it. I am not a musician, though my wife is; but you managed to interest me in Sibelius to a very lively degree. You took that significant figure and interpreted him in such terms as to universalize him, and your sociology was expressed in such concrete language that it made the whole study alive."

What so touched him off in conversation was that we both knew Eckermann's *Conversations with Goethe* forwards and back. He had gone to that book for help.

"You were doing a difficult thing universalizing a particular figure. It reminded me of how the aesthetic sense in that range of border peoples from the Balkans north, between Germany and Russia on up into Scandinavia, predominates over their administrative sense. They are little in politics but much in art. Finland's political history is brief, yet she produces this great artist. In East Anglia, that part of England where I was born and brought up as a boy, our executive abilities were good but our aesthetic powers were almost nothing. Our coasts face the Low Countries, which were the transmitters of the Renaissance, but more on the side of its political liberties, and it was from East Anglia that most of your New England colonists came. The west of England is more Norman and looked toward France; the tradition was more monarchical and mediaeval, and the Plantagenet kings looked across the Channel to their French provinces of Anjou and Aquitaine. The University of Cambridge was comparatively insignificant beside Oxford for generations after its founding and I do not consider it an accident that Charles I found Anglican and monarchical Oxford loyalist and that Cromwell was a Member of Parliament from Cambridge. East Anglia is largely Dane and Saxon: the west of England, between the Midlands and Wales, was more Norman French, and much more aesthetic in its tastes."

"New England inherited the non-aesthetic strain from East Anglia, then?"

"It was a series of precipitates," said he. "East Anglia, New England, and your Middle West. Midwesterners have something in them which I think New England would be better off if it had more of; and your New Englanders again have something for which East Anglia today would be better."

"How odd. Dr. Harvey Cushing said something almost identical—leaving out East Anglia. One Sunday afternoon in July 1932, over in Brookline before Harvard let him go back to Yale, we were talking about enthusiasm, how the tendency around here is to frown it down. He said, 'Nothing great or new can be done without enthusiasm.' He has plenty, and this community never damped it down, but he comes from the Midwest and can't be understood without that fact. He said he thought that, beginning in colonial times, the 'outgoing' people, who found the atmosphere of the Massachusetts Bay Colony a bit oppressive, moved on to Connecticut and Rhode Island—Hartford, New Haven, Providence—and that in turn those who found Connecticut a bit slow moved on after the Revolution to the Western Reserve in Ohio, where he came from, and he said he had picked up further footprints of this long trek in Bloomington, Indiana, and somewhere else on out in Iowa."

"I think that was it," said Whitehead; "the vivid people keep moving on, geographically and otherwise, for men can be provincial in time, as well as in place."

"When you lived out Milton way they must have told you how one of Cameron Forbes's aunts said—or is said to have said—during his long absence as governor general of the Philippines, that she 'hoped Cam wouldn't get out of touch with Milton.' I'm not suggesting that you are; but how does it seem to be back here in the thick of things?"

"We had exhausted that experience," said he. "It was delightful while it lasted—five years; but we are better off here."

"Near our friends," Mrs. Whitehead added. "To live in the country when you can't walk or go out of doors is absurd."

"I think it is a mistake," he continued, "to cling to a region because it has given you a delightful experience once. You merely accumulate dead possessions. Don't cling to the old because it made you glad once: go on to the next, the next region, the next experience. We have left behind us the most extraordinary succession of delightful dwelling-houses each of which in turn once meant everything to us, but not one of which we now regret having left."

V

April 5, 1935

PROFESSOR Whitehead had had to go to a meeting of the Senior Fellows. While waiting for him, Mrs. Whitehead and I were in her little sitting-room, which overlooks the court of Radnor Hall, and the river, through the sycamores which are now beginning to bud. Her own books are in here on shelves from floor to ceiling.

"Mostly French memoirs," she explained, "in double rows, with Saint-Simon at the top 'for reference.' I have a hook by which I can pull the volumes down. France, as Altie was saying at tea the last time you were here, had the misfortune to lose a large proportion of her potential liberal intellectuals at the Revolution and that, I think, accounts for the low tone of her early nineteenth-century literature. I never could read it, and that is why I took up memoirs and letters."

He came in seasonably before the dinner hour, and we adjourned to the library beside the fire, for the April evening was sharp.

"I am a firm believer," said the philosopher, "in letting guests start off on commonplaces till they have shaken down and got the temperature of the room." He smiled expansively. "Even the weather, or the climate, is an unfailingly good topic."

One of the guests was to be Professor Ralph Barton Perry, a colleague of Whitehead's in the department of philosophy, and the biographer of William James. When I was an under-graduate in Professor George Herbert Palmer's course in the history of philosophy, Perry, a dark, brilliant-looking young fellow, occasionally gave one of the lectures for Palmer. Now past middle life, he has lost none of his edge nor his good looks. He was a little late, and, just before he arrived, our host was saying:

"When other Western nations perpetrate anything especially disgraceful at least they don't boast of it, but Germany seems to be peculiar in that the more atrocious the act the more vehement the Germans are in affirming its righteousness."

We all agreed that just so surely as a liberal in some other country defends them, they let him down with a crash. This happened to us repeatedly at the paper in 1914–1917, until we had had enough of it.

[49]

At table we were the Whiteheads, North, their son, now on the faculty of the Harvard School of Business Administration on the opposite bank of the Charles, and Professor Perry. The talk started on alcohol, since the maid had, to the dismay of the hostess, deposited a huge decanter on the table, *so* huge that it all but elbowed off the bouquet of spring flowers.

"A good many years ago," said Whitehead, "we lived in rather a drunken village, so in the hope of setting a good example we went teetotal, because the cathedral people were running a crusade. The result was we noticed the effects of drinking on others when we went to dinner parties. At last I said to one of my hosts, 'Look here, do you realize that although after everybody has had two glasses of champagne there is a good deal of laughter, the jokes aren't *really* very witty; you only think they are?' His reply quite dashed me. He said, 'Yes, but that's a definition of wit: a joke is funny if you think it is!'"

"Kittredge used to say," I remarked, "that everything is a joke when people are in high spirits."

"Yes," said North, "but isn't there a difference between wit and high spirits? I used to know an old bargee who was never sober but never quite drunk. He discoursed at large on politics, always keeping to the magnificent generalities but never getting down to brass tacks. He wasn't really witty, but when I had had a drink I noticed that his jokes sounded better and his wisdom more sublime."

"Has it ever been made clear why Northmen prefer hard liquor to wine?"

Whitehead thought it was to keep out the chill and damp.

"Could it be because the grape does not grow in the north?"

"I think it might be largely that," Perry agreed, adding, "but the fermentation of juice is as old as civilization."

"Are you suggesting alcohol as a criterion of civilization?" North Whitehead teased him.

"If so," replied Professor Perry smiling grimly, "the United States had a very low form of civilization in the 1920's!"

"The Norsemen were heavy drinkers as long as a thousand years ago," I remarked. "It was a recognized way of disposing of your enemies to wait until they were all drunk then burn their hall and them in it. Saga after saga records this amiable custom, and they even carried it over into Scotland."

"But did they drink at sea?"

"Apparently not."

"But active sailors can eliminate alcohol."

"As they can coffee."

"And there are the rations of rum."

"Don't take them too seriously," said North. "They are quite pathetically small."

"Discipline in that respect on English ships seems quite strict . . . not much drinking at sea, unless it be at Christmas."

By one of those swift transitions which occur in a conversation, the theme moved from the rarity of drunkenness in Latin countries south of the "wine line," to the comparative reliability and seamanship of Latin sailors. Someone said:

"They must have been good once, for most of those daring fifteenth- and sixteenth-century voyages were made by Portuguese, Spaniards, and Italians."

"That was quite a while ago," said Mrs. Whitehead, and she told of being aboard an Italian steamship coming out of Naples. "The pilot, who was disembarking, got into difficulty with the painter of his skiff. The captain, who happened to be standing near a stewardess, screamed and flung his arms around her: she screamed, and a general scream went up from all the crew. The pilot managed to disengage himself, but it was scarcely a reassuring way to start the voyage."

"If you want an example of the excellence of British seamanship, and a very recent one, here it is," I said. "A boy who was saved from the burning of the S.S. *Morro Castle*, a young Phelps from Philadelphia, related the affair to John Richards, who had been one of his schoolmasters at St. Paul's. He got hold of a rope which hung over the steamer's rail and clung to it four hours, wondering if the fire would burn it off, and *then* what? The two American ships steamed up, did little or nothing, then steamed away again. Finally, at daybreak came the British ship, and *three times*, said John, this American boy, without realizing that he was repeating, told of the effect on him of the calm efficiency and discipline of that English crew. The ships were so close that he could hear the creak of davits and the rattle of blocks, then the calm, cold voice of the first officer sounding over the water as he said to the man in charge of one of the lifeboats: 'Mr. Hawkins, your boat is slow. Lower away, damn you.' "

This story seemed to please Professor Whitehead immensely, but he said, "I think perhaps a fiery Latin might have screamed an order that would have got equal results."

Thence the talk moved to the Yankee clipper ships in the nineteenth century and the Gloucester fishing schooners in the twentieth having each in their turn reached a culminating point where they were works of art, only to be superseded, the clippers by steam, the schooners by the internal combustion engine.

"As I remember," said Whitehead, "perfection just precedes a change, and signifies the approaching end of an epoch."

This discussion was carried over from the table to coffee in the living-room, where it was presently being remarked by the host that "American inventiveness is not as primarily originative as it often gets the credit of being, but is frequently in the secondary inventions that diffuse the article into general use. You didn't really lead off with the automobile," he continued. "The French did that. What you did was adapt it to the multitude."

"Yes, and doesn't most of this inventiveness come down in the end to apparatus for the transportation of bodies and the transmission of thought, not thought itself? How about original thought? If these United States were engulfed, like the fabled continent of Atlantis, what would we have left by which to be remembered?"

"Your diffusion of literacy and average comfort and well-being among the masses, in my opinion, is one of the major achievements in human history," said Whitehead. "In previous lands and times, even under the best conditions, the diffusion of culture was to only a small stratum at the top, never more than twenty per cent at the most. I think this extending to the multitude of at least a decent standard of living is an enormous contribution to civilization."

"What is it more than mere material well-being, creature comforts?" I asked, and Professor Perry agreed.

"The real arts," said Perry, "are aesthetics, science and philosophy. The others are secondary achievements, not major ones."

"You Americans!" exclaimed Mrs. Whitehead. "Perpetually denigrating yourselves!"

"It is only of late that we have arrived at the stage of self-criticism," I said. "Perhaps we overdo it. But why, when the comfort was more widely distributed than ever before or since —from 1919 to 1929—did that tone of anger, bitterness, and exasperation so permeate our public prints? Don't you remember what a painful impression it made? Was it disenchantment with the war, or a sense of our temporary political impotency? The well-being came to the average lower-middle-class or worker's household in the form of a radio, a cheap car, a parchment lampshade, cretonne curtains, an armchair, and household short cuts for labour saving. Was it because comfort and leisure came to people unschooled to use them, and were withdrawn before they had had time to learn?"

"They were always looking forward to the time when they would have more material comforts," said Perry, abetting me. " 'Never were, but always to *be* blest': and so remained discontented."

"You are in too great a hurry," said Mrs. Whitehead. "You have only had three hundred years. Europe has had three thousand."

"But the Greeks had had only about three hundred years."

[53]

"Yes, but they bothered themselves singularly little about Egypt and Persia, if you will notice," interpolated Whitehead. "True, they picked up a few principles of civilization from Crete and Mycenae and Asia Minor, and not very much from Egypt —as you will remember, the Egyptian priests in Plato's story told Solon: 'You Greeks are only boys.' The point is, they did it on their own. And like America, they were rather violent. I can imagine the Persians and Egyptians saying to one another, 'I say, isn't it shocking how many murders get committed in Greece? Their society must be fearfully insecure.' But the murders didn't stop things from getting done. I fancy the place I have been in that was most like Greece was a gathering of university scholars at Chicago! The city was disorderly but very much alive. The Greeks weren't studying the best models to be had abroad. They were making their own. That, I fancy, is the most Greek thing a man can do. As for the value of studying the language in the original, I think most of the good can be got out of translations. As a young man I read the New Testament in the original. The Greek, as Greek, was quite beneath contempt and the translation into early seventeenth-century English is far superior. Ninety per cent of good old Herodotus can be got in translation, and sixty or seventy per cent of Thucydides. Even the sainted Plato doesn't lose so much. I have to teach several of his best Dialogues to successive classes of students, and I often ask myself what value there is to the ideas in them that would justify a man for the labour of going to get up the language. It being forty years since I read Greek fluently I now take a Loeb translation with the English on a parallel page, but with the help of Liddell and Scott's lexicon I can generally tell where old Jowett is making a fool of himself, which is about every other sentence. . . ."

"Altie, dear!" his wife stemmed the tide of his waxing eloquence. "Oxford, you know!"

"Yes, my dear . . . What I mean is"—he obediently moderated his pitch—"I question the value to the average student of digging out the niceties of meaning from the texts. The Greeks themselves wouldn't have done such a thing. And when Greek scholars tell me, 'Yes, but what our author *really* meant was . . .' they aren't helping along the thought. They say any other method is anachronistic. I'm not sure the true anachronism isn't the other way round. This backward-looking traditionalism came in at the Renaissance. It wasn't Greek. My own department, philosophy, has been especially a sufferer from it. That is why I have attempted to invent new terminologies for new concepts. There is a jargon of thinking which gets in the way of thought itself. It is as bad as this archaeologizing of American art. In the great period of Renaissance painting the princes bought pictures that were being painted *then*, not centuries before. If your millionaires would spend their money not on collecting old masters but on contemporary paintings, your American art would have a better flourishing. The essence of your life here in America is that it looks not back but forward. If aesthetic history is all you want, then of course it is all to nothing in favour of Europe. But if it is forward-looking creation that you want, then you Americans must rely on yourselves and it is all to nothing in your favour."

A suspicion flickered in my left eye that the good philosopher was leaning a little in the other direction to correct the excess of my Hellenizing zeal, but I was busy laying the lesson to heart for all that, and presently I had a joke on him. He and Perry were talking of the combat in faculty meeting over dropping the Latin requirement for the degree of Bachelor of Arts. The name "Rand" suddenly caught my ear—this would be Edward Kennard Rand, Pope Professor of Latin in Harvard University, who put me through Livy and Horace as an undergraduate.

"Ken Rand made the principal speech on behalf of the Latin requirement," recited Perry, "and a very good speech it was: just the right arguments and just the right seasoning of wit, and, by the by, you came into it," he addressed Whitehead.

"*I?*"

"Yes. He quoted liberally from one of your essays in *Aims of Education.*"

"Then he didn't quote all of my points, for not all of them would have been in his favour."

"Enough of them were in his favour to make a devastating loss in *our* ranks, Alfred. There were a good many members who did not say much, but when it came to vote—young men, too, whom you wouldn't have expected to be on that side— they voted with Rand—and you."

"I say," said Whitehead, "this is extraordinary—and a lecture I delivered years ago."

"It was one of your very best, Altie," said Mrs. Whitehead.

"Yes, but . . ."

"Not so extraordinary, sir," I decided to come out with it, "when I confess. A few weeks ago there was a dinner at Sam Morison's to collect ammunition for the defence of Latin. I found that they didn't know about that chapter in your *Aims of Education,* so I put them on it."

Perry looked startled. An enemy battery unmasked at his elbow! But I had calculated it before speaking and Whitehead's eyes sparkled with amusement. Whether he did or did not relish the result, he could see the fun.

Professor Perry's sense of humour was also equal to the occasion. When we left, he carried me in his car to Harvard Square, where we parted with mutual assurances of continued esteem.

VI

August 25, 1935

TEA and dinner with the Whiteheads in Cambridge. They had read my "Hellas and All Souls" and "Realms of Gold" in the "Oxford Rondo" of *We Northmen,* the typescript of which

chapters had been submitted to Professor Whitehead because
he is quoted frequently and at length, in part from his published
works and in part from the conversation of April 5, 1935. He
had read this typescript, he said, three times, and it precipitated
a general discussion.

"The Jews," said the professor, "are singularly humourless."

"In America, at least, they get off some very good jokes—
including jokes on themselves," I objected, "and some
of the Jewish comedians are among the funniest people on
earth."

"Yes, but their laughter is generally ironic. Heine is the type
of Jewish humour. In that path between the Babylonian and
Egyptian Empires, they were a people in a desperate position,
feeling that they were not getting their rights, and thus from the
beginning to end of their thought there is always a chip-on-
shoulder."

"When all the usual historical explanations have been entertained," I asked, "what, after all, does explain the hold that
this Hebraic thought gained over us Northern Europeans—for
that is what we are?"

"It is peculiar," he said. "I think we must remember that it
was a view of life that came in through the slave and proletarian
populations. It was *their* view of how life may be well lived even
though you are an underdog. And of course that view has
coloured all subsequent European history. It is much more
Paul's than that of Jesus. There is no evidence that Paul ever
saw Jesus, and he seems to have had rather a patronizing view
of his entourage. . . ."

"Like an Oxford don . . ." interpolated Mrs. Whitehead.

"Yes, one would have thought Paul would have gone to the
apostles and said, 'Come now, tell me all you can remember
about him. Just how was it?' But no: instead, he says, 'Now
you sit there and I'll tell you what it all meant.' Jesus would
appear to have been one of those winning persons to whom
good things get attributed, so that when those oppressed classes

were making up a scheme of life whereby existence would be tolerable to them, it clustered round the figure of Jesus. . . . But now curiously the Hellenic element which came into Christianity was an approach to the same problem from exactly the opposite end; namely, that the Greek thinkers had seen that 'the mailed fist' is the vulgar thing. They called it 'barbarian.' They had seen, as aristocrats, that kindness, graciousness, is the true ornament of life. And these two coalesced. But it must be remembered that Christianity came into Europe through 'the lower orders.' "

"Doesn't the chip-on-shoulder signify the state of mind of not having risen superior to your occasion?" I asked.

"Certainly, and you are quite right in your definition of Protestantism in America."

"I said it had no older tradition to temper it."

"That is its difference from Europe. In England, I think, after *The Tempest* got itself written, let us say after 1610, the vivid and sensitive people, the artistic type, got their satisfaction no longer out of aesthetic creation but out of religious experience, at least for the next fifty years. You will notice a distinct falling off in art, architecture, and poetry (Milton's *Paradise Lost* is an anachronism) until after the reign of Queen Anne. The literature is good, even work of genius, but not as good; the architecture has elegance but lacks power. Now I think religious experience lacks something which is got out of artistic expression: it stirs but it does not soothe. Perhaps it is that it lacks the intellectual discipline of artistic expression. When people watch a gorgeous sunset, for example, they are excited but they are also soothed, and when you add to this the element of order which the artist introduces into his creation, which must also be grasped by the enjoyer, there is mental effort required in co-operation with the artist in order to produce the effect. The Catholic Church knows this and has managed its affairs better. The confessional stirs the feeling which is aroused in man by not having come up to his own best

[58]

standards and then soothes it by sending people off reassured and comforted. I don't say it isn't open to grave abuses; but compare it with Calvinism, in which the man undergoing conversion cannot be sure whether he is one of God's elect or marked for eternal damnation, and there is nothing he can do about it. Even good works will not save him, they are 'the filthy rags': the conception is as of God, an omniscient, all-wise, all-powerful Being who has created this world exactly as he wanted it, even with the evil pre-ordained, and although they throw in a few sentences to mitigate its severity, it does not really get them out of the rigid situation they have let themselves in for."

"What, do you suppose, is the difference between religious experience and aesthetic experience which seems so often to make the second—our response to an art-form or to aesthetic feeling—so much more wholesome? (An intellectual discipline is involved, too.)"

"I should say it was just that: aesthetic experience soothes as well as excites: religious experience is more apt to leave one suspended in mid-air, the emotions aroused but not satisfied."

"The preternatural solemnity of a good many of the professionally religious is to me a point against them."

"I have always noticed," said he, "that deeply and truly religious persons are very fond of a joke, and I am suspicious of those who aren't. The strain of solemnity becomes unbearable, because unnatural. The Athenians, you remember, after their tragedies always had a satyr play."

"Yes, and often the satyr play ridiculed the theme, if not the characters, in the tragedy."

"In *Science and the Modern World*, I have dealt with the 'necessity of irreverence.' " He got down the volume from the shelves, and found the passage in Chapter XIII, which we read aloud together.

Is it that nothing, no experience good or bad, no belief, no cause, is, in itself, momentous enough to monopolize the whole of life to the exclusion of laughter? Laughter is our reminder that our theories

are an attempt to make existence intelligible, but necessarily only
an attempt, and does not the irrational, the instinctive burst in to
keep the balance true by laughter?

"It often seems to me," Whitehead resumed, "that European
man was at his best between 1400 and 1600. Since then our
appreciation of beauty has become too overlaid with intellectualizing. We educated people have our aesthetic sense too
highly cultivated and do not come to beauty simply enough.
It is possible that the feeling for beauty is much more true and
strong in unschooled people than in ourselves. The early
cathedral builders—even the Norman and Romanesque—did
not theorize: they *built*; and the poets went to work much more
directly. We of today over-elaborate. The only place I see where
another great flowering of European culture might come is in
the American Middle West, where the start could be fresh and
from the ground up. You, in your chapter, have dealt sensibly
with the problem as between Americans and Europe. Americans must not copy Europe. They must be themselves, must
create *de novo*. These American imitations of Europe will always
lack interest and vitality, as all derivations do. Let Americans
study Europe and see what has been done. But when it comes
to creation, God bless my soul! then forget everything that has
ever been done before, and create!"

"In the deeper reaches of creation, there is nothing else you
can do," I said, "Your learning may help you, but it can't save
you."

"It can only help you, even," said he, "by having been so
assimilated as to have become unconscious and forgotten. As
you have written, there is something backward-looking in most
universities dealing with literature: it is not—'What is to be
done?' It is what has been done: and it is apt to be unctuous
and deferential. I have a horror of creative intelligence con-
gealing into too-good teaching—static ideas: ' *This* is the correct
thing to know'; passive acceptance of polite learning, without
any intention of doing anything about it. Teachers should be

acutely conscious of the deficiencies in the matter taught. What they are teaching may be quite lacking in the necessary ingredients of nutriment. They should be on their guard against their materials and teach their students to be on their guard against them. Once learning solidifies, all is over with it. These college faculties are going to want watching. The danger is that education will freeze, and it will be thought, 'This and this are the right things to know': and when that happens, thought is dead. I am immensely annoyed by the smugness of a certain kind of talk which goes on among my colleagues, scornful talk about no theory being good that is 'only half tested,' and the meticulous assembling of facts. Also, the aloofness of the university from practical life: not only the federal and state governments, but even municipal affairs. There is a great function which awaits the American universities, and that is to civilize business: or better, to get business men to civilize themselves by using their power over the practical processes of life to civilize their sociological functions. It is not enough that they should amass fortunes in this way or that and then endow a college or a hospital. The *motive* in amassing the fortune should be *in order* to use it for a socially constructive end."

"Would a man with so altruistic a motive ever be able to amass a fortune?"

"It would probably be given away as fast as he amassed it. What I mean is, law has been civilized—that was done by the Greeks and the Romans, Justinian and that lot;—medicine has been taken out of magic; education has been getting rid of its humbug; and next it is time to teach business its sociological function; for if America is to be civilized, it must be done (at least for the present) by the business class, who are in possession of the power and the economic processes. I don't need to tell you that there is a good deal of sniffing on this, the Harvard College and graduate schools side of the Charles River, sniffing at the new Harvard School of Business Administration on the opposite bank. That strikes me as snobbish and unimaginative. If the American universities were up to their job they would be taking business in hand and teaching it ethics and professional standards."

He said that he thought the interpretation of history by economic determinism was a singularly deficient method, and that even such an attempt at the unification of the world as Alexander's Hellenization of Eastern Asia, "success though he made, and muddle though he left," was a nobler effort and a more effective agent.

We talked of why the middle class has made such a sorry fist of it, and he thought it is because it was a highly selected group who happened to do well because qualified for the limited function of *entrepreneur* in a given epoch, though not really superior people, but merely that class of talent which changing circumstance throws uppermost. "But in England when that class is sincerely touched by the nonconformist religious feeling you get very valuable people, who have been of great historic significance."

"Is it that the middle class divides into two groups; one, which is accessible to religious emotion, or to aesthetic—which takes some of the curse off their economic function—and, on the other hand, those accessible mainly or only to the 'possessive impulses'?"

"Yes, I think that would go far to explain it. In England the aristocracy and the working class are found to have much more in common, and a better understanding of each other than either of those classes with the middle class. They get acquainted through their sports, and both are closer to the realities and the soil. Here in America I think your middle class is superior, and far more effective than ours. I can't see that your trade-union movement is politically responsible or fit to govern yet, and of aristocracy, in the European sense of a responsible governing class, of course you have none."

"The word 'aristocracy' in this country has a black eye. In

the Midwest, when I was a boy, one generally heard it coupled with the term 'codfish.' That had travelled out there from New England and, in especial, meant Boston. The New England aristocracy, if that is what we are to call it, seem to me to have lost or abandoned their leadership, imported hordes of Southern Europeans to work for them, then, frightened at their numbers, restlessness and potential power, gone into a funk and given up the task of trying to govern. The old stock make good doctors and professors, but a lot of them live on inherited money and social position."

"Any aristocracy that shirks its leadership," said he, "is done for. Its only excuse for existence is that it takes the lead. The Yankee upper classes in Boston and New England are, individually, among the kindest people I have ever met. Personally they are cultivated and charming: but when immigrants began flooding in here from Europe in the nineteenth century, they did nothing for them except in certain forms of philanthropy. The result is that two generations later, when they are now outnumbered and outvoted, they find themselves politically at the mercy of people who feel no loyalty towards them or their institutions." A moment later he remarked, "The nonconformist merchant families marrying into the English landed aristocracy in the nineteenth century brought a moral seriousness into an aristocratic class which I do not think ever quite existed before in history."

Earlier in the evening I noticed an instance of Whitehead's watchful kindness: he was speaking of Catholicism and lowered his voice, saying, "Our maid is a Catholic and we are devoted to her." What he had been saying was:

"The synoptic gospels are the thinking of vigorous people: the disciples pluck corn on the sabbath, and are chidden by the mayor and the village council. They reply brusquely": (he roughened his voice to asperity) " *'What does it matter?'* But the official religion which begins at about the second century, that is, the Catholic theology, is a philosophy of life as of a man who had lived dissolutely, tried everything, had a lot of sexual excitement, and suddenly, at the age of thirty-five, turned exactly around the other way, and thrown it all over."

"Why confine it to official Christianity?" said I. "Haven't you been describing our old friend Leo Tolstoy?"

"Not far off," said he, smiling.

This led into the subject of authorship. He said:

"A man really writes for an audience of about ten persons. Of course if others like it, that is clear gain. But if those ten are satisfied, he is content. A certain amount of encouragement is necessary."

I raised the question why the creation of an art-work exhausts the experience for its creator, but is infinitely potent of repeated stimulations in the enjoyer.

"Perhaps," he said, "it is because all human effort is directed towards the achievement of an end, whether it is satisfied or not, and the artist's end, although never quite the result he hoped for, is largely attained, and therefore finished for him; the point at which he ends is where the enjoyer begins."

"I would accept that, in the main; but I think it likely that Beethoven, Wagner, Brahms, and Goethe felt fairly well content with what they had brought off in the Ninth Symphony, *Tristan*, the Violin Concerto, or *Faust*—not that they didn't wish the work had been better; but did feel that it was as good as they could make it, so there was nothing left to bother about."

At table we talked about the intrusions upon personal privacy by American journalism. He said:

"An English publisher can appeal to a fairly compact public with taste who are easy to get at, so that the people interested in a really notable book hear about it in sufficient numbers to make its publication profitable; but here the discriminating public is widely scattered, the country is still sparsely populated, publishers must send agents in person vast distances to remote places, and in their advertising they seem to feel it necessary to make the book sound more exciting than it is. In America everything has to be 'pepped up,' made exciting. Your potential public is greater than ours; but in proportion to your total population, far smaller: ours is perhaps twenty-five thousand. Yours is bigger but distributed. The result is that the publishers of newspapers especially, instead of appealing to a select group who will take excellence, must dilute and distribute their article so that it will appeal to all classes, and that results in a levelling down to some lower common denominator. Add to that, they have got into a fix where their news is so expensive that they are dependent on advertising to pay for it, and that impairs their independence."

We also talked of the cleavage between youth and its elders since the war. They said it was far less pronounced in England. I asked what he thought it was that had happened here.

"The generation now at the age of fifty or thereabouts," he said, "seems to me to have had its upbringing terribly bungled. When I address an assemblage of youths under the age of thirty, I am aware of feeling a hearty respect for them.

"I think," he continued, "it came from their parents having lost their own belief but going on insisting on the dead formulae of conduct in order to keep their children 'good,' when they no longer believed in these formulae themselves. The children eventually found it out, deceived their parents in turn, and it resulted in deceit all round. They knew their old religion was empty but were not honest with themselves nor with their children about it. Their children, in those years between eighteen and twenty-four, when one is experiencing for the first time vital necessities, emotional and physical, were left in total ignorance of the social consequences of certain types of conduct."

This was said as we were returning from dinner to the library, and when we were companionably settled there, a question was put which had long been pending:

"Why has science kept advancing with such strides since 1900 when so much else has retrograded?"

D

"One reason," said he, "is the great advance of mathematics between 1700 and 1900. Men of science have thus had a delicate and precise instrument with which to explore their new worlds."

"But why such an advance in the past two centuries, when mathematics had been highly developed by the Greeks at least twenty-six centuries ago?"

"Man's earlier discoveries in mathematics were made by observation of his physical surroundings, as contradistinguished from abstract reason," said he, "On the plains of Chaldea he noticed the stars swinging round and round, deduced the conception of the circle, and finally arrived at the wheel. Now the wheel is not such an obvious invention as it sounds. As late as the fifteenth century, when America was found by the Europeans, the wheel had not been discovered in this hemisphere. Geometry, 'earth-measurement,' γεωγραφία, was developed by the Egyptians from their need to redraw boundaries obliterated in annual inundations of the Nile.

"But between these earlier discoveries, deduced from physical experience, and the later ones, only to be arrived at by abstract reason, occurred a long gap. Roman numerals were clumsy, and the Arabic numerals, easier to manage, did not reach Europe until the twelfth century. When they did, their simpler patterns, more readily seized by the eye, laid mathematics within the grasp of a wider variety of minds. By the end of the seventeenth century, this advance, begun at the Italian Renaissance, culminated in Newton and Leibniz—logarithms, trigonometry, and algebra were developed, and the period closed with, if not the invention, certainly the perfecting of the integral calculus. The road was now open, from 1700 onward, for that excursion into applied mathematics which has equipped scientists with a complex and sensitive medium for creating thought-patterns with which to interpret their explorations of sensory phenomena."

"Even when allowance has been made for the historical vicissitudes, the collapse of the Roman Empire, the Dark Ages, and so on . . . it still seems odd that that long lapse should have occurred after such a hopeful start in the ancient world," I remarked.

"You get a lot of hopeful starts," said he, "and then one or another will lead through. It will take two hundred years to follow out into all their ramifications the leads which scientists have started. This can be done by really rather second-rate men, men with nippy minds who can follow assigned procedures within a limited field. But they are not original minds. Their achievement may wear the look of originality yet be so limited that it may not represent one one-thousandth of experience. Science has reached a point where it can transmit this facility of investigation; but it is of secondary worth. It takes no Shakespeare to do."

"Are you suggesting that genuine scientific originators come as rarely as Shakespeares?"

"I am suggesting that a good many of the people, including prominent ones, who are now regarded as scientists are really little more than technicians. Only once in a great while do we get a really swagger scientist."

"How is experience to be brought to the level of consciousness and transmitted into an art-form out of the subconscious?"

"You are speaking too mentally. It is first an aesthetic experience, powerfully felt—emotional experience with mental perceptions—then it demands a definite artistic form. The trouble with creators of today is that they try to substitute a mental idea for the aesthetic experience. They think: 'Look here, wouldn't it be exciting to try it this way: a way no one else has ever tried it before?' But the novelty is of no significance. All that has any significance is the depth and validity of an experience out of which the art comes; and if it comes out of mere consciously clever ratiocination, it is foredoomed. You are dealing in secondary perceptions and relatively shallow experience: it does not bear the stamp of deepest truth."

[67]

"A while back you spoke of our Midwest, something to the effect that . . ."

He took it up vigorously:

"My remark was that the only place I know where European man can still create civilization on the grand scale is in the American Midwest."

"Between the Appalachians and the Rockies?"

"Yes. Roughly, the Mississippi Basin."

"Why not the coastal regions, Atlantic and Pacific?"

"They are rather transmitters of cultures, and their cultures are likely to be more derivative. In the Midwest, climate, soil, and food—those three preconditions to a flourishing civilization —are favourable. Man's earliest essays in recorded civilizations occur in hot climates where food is abundant and clothes and shelter next to needless. Rice, in large part, sustained the civilization of India; in Mesopotamia a civilized society arose on grain; in Egypt the food staple was mainly the date; in Central and South America among the Aztecs and Incas it was maize and the banana. But over-population, made possibly by cheap food, cheapens labour and opens the way to political despotism; and although the wealth, and hence the leisure requisite for culture may result from cheap labour, the consequent loss of liberty stultifies the intellect. Thus it was that in Europe, a colder climate, where food, clothes, and shelter are harder to get, and where proliferation of the human species is not so exuberant but individuality is more pronounced, our northern civilization ventured into rational thought, thought less shackled by religious superstition, and finally produced that energetic and self-reliant creature, European man."

"Nearly every variety of European man is somewhere in our Midwest."

"It has a human soil further favourable to a new civilization: not only is it a self-selected stock; the country people and the people in small towns still hold a favourably large proportion, as compared with the population of cities. Man's best thinking is done either by persons living in the country or in small communities, or else by those who, having had such environment in early life, enrich their experience by life in cities; for what is wanted is contact with the elemental processes of nature during those years of youth when the mind is being formed."

"How often I have noticed that as between country boys or boys from small towns, and city boys or boys brought up in the suburbs," I said, "how much more self-reliant and resourceful the country-bred lads are. Suppose they lose their jobs: the city or suburban boy, who is usually from the white-collar class, is generally upset and feels rather helpless; your country boy will be cool as a cucumber. What of it? He has earned his living by working with his hands, and he could do it again if necessary."

"Urbanization," Whitehead continued, "is a weakness in much of our modern thinking, especially about social problems. Thought is taken primarily for the cities when perhaps it isn't the cities that so much matter. Smart plays are written for blasé audiences in a metropolis; eccentric poetry and clever novels are concocted about dwellers in crowded streets who, poor souls, are cut off through most of the year from contact with the soil, the woods, and the sea, and who perhaps never did a day's hard manual labour in their lives; and to whom the very changes of the weather are but feebly perceptible. They are deprived of that discipline which is imposed by daily contact with the leisurely growth of crops, by the anxiety that those crops should be so at the mercy of nature's caprice, and yet also the reassuring experience of nature's bounty in the long term."

"Not long ago I was rereading the tavern scenes in the two parts of *Henry IV*," I remarked. "Those two plays come in the full flush of Elizabethan England, and I couldn't but keep noticing how gorgeous the sheer vocabulary is, and it comes from the commonest life; much of it from the country, and some of it from the barnyard. Having had a good deal to do with barnyards as a boy, I thought the barnyard smells in Shakespeare's vocabulary very wholesome. Anyhow, as you were saying, such writing had to come out of the countryside. It could have come from no other place."

"Yes," Whitehead assented, "and what is more, I don't believe Shakespeare ever had to grope for a word. Can you imagine him chewing the end of his quill pen until he could think of the right one? There is such exuberance in him that I believe once he had clearly imagined a scene, the words came of themselves, in a rush. You must remember that that immense vigour pervaded the whole of Tudor England. If we ever find ourselves in Cambridge together I would like to take you to the combination room of Trinity College. Here are the portraits of the college officers from the start—it was founded by Henry VIII—first you get the vivid Tudors and Elizabethans, then the dour Puritans, then the animated eighteenth-century people: in the nineteenth century you get the scholar and the gentleman; then in the twentieth century you have the scholar, and drop the gentleman. . . ."

Mrs. Whitehead made a wry face, but he wouldn't take it back!

"The intellectual drill of the Tudor monarchs must have sharpened their minds for ruling. Elizabeth's education was the broadest that Europe could afford. She was at home in Greek and Latin on her visits to the universities of Oxford and Cambridge. She had read Greek every morning with her tutor, Roger Ascham, beginning the day with the Greek Testament and then reading and translating such classical authors as Isocrates, Sophocles and Demosthenes. The afternoons were given over to Latin, and she read almost all of Cicero and a great part of Livy. When the Polish ambassador, wishing to insult her, made her an affronting speech in Latin, which he knew she could comprehend, but to which he did not suppose she could reply in kind, she delivered him a terrific counterblast which lasted half an hour—in Latin!"

VII

March 19, 1936

AT dinner, where we were but three, they asked me what I thought of the European broil. I said: "Not war—at least, not for the present."

"German diplomacy is operatic," the professor said. "They see themselves as romantic heroes. In 1914 they had the world outdistanced without fighting, yet they must try it. I imagine their industrialists knew it was folly, but yielded when the military men were able, as they thought, to show that it would be an affair of six weeks, or of six months at the most. I say, does it occur to you that half a century of Wagner's music may have had a lot to do with the mischief? Plato knew what he was talking about when he said there was 'immoral music.' It is *a*-moral. I was once taken to a performance of *Carmen* by a delightful little girl for her birthday party and when it was over, she stupefied me by asking, 'Was *Carmen* a really nice woman?' The question had never occurred to me. One enjoys the music and discards his moral prepossessions. The Germans are emotional and musically susceptible. Wagner appeals to their pride of race. I venture to think that if you had in England a series of really stunning grand operas with gorgeous music and pageantry glorifying England from the Tudors up to 1914, that in a generation they could wreck the English genius for political self-government."

"The idea is disquieting," was about as far as I wanted to assent to that, but in the interests of candour, went on. "As you know, I was at the festival in Bayreuth in July 1933, the fiftieth anniversary of Wagner's death. 'And Satan came also . . .' Hitler was there. He came for the six performances in eight days, the four operas of the *Ring*, *Meistersinger*, and *Parsifal*; sat in Wagner's box in the *Festspielhaus* with Frau Winnifred, the widow of Siegfried. He had only been in power since January, nazidom was still in its honeymoon; he came and went between the theatre and restaurant between double rows of Germans, any one of whom could have thrust a dirk between his ribs, and had his *hochs* and *heils*. He was a fresh-complexioned, brown-haired fellow. You never would have noticed him in the street. There he sat in the opera house, day after day, at performance after performance, and I wondered at the time what he would be making out of it."

"A year later," said Whitehead, "we saw his first blood-purge."

Since artists are not to be blamed for what is done with their works, Wagner was allowed to drop for the time being.

After dinner we returned to the library. The heavy black velours hangings had been drawn before the windows and a wood fire was burning on the hearth under the black chimney piece. Mrs. Whitehead, dressed in her customary black and white, looked handsome and distinguished.

Whitehead was speaking of how to identify talent, and what to do with it when you have identified it. I said:

"Aren't certain ages and civilizations favourable to the development of a given type of talent? Isn't it desirable to create a civilization that would be favourable to *all* types?"

"The most we can ask of a civilization, I think," said he smiling wickedly, "is that it shall not crush *every* type of talent."

"Aren't we Nordics of the late-blooming variety?" I asked. "Or, if you don't like 'Nordic' (and in the hands of certain people the word has begun to smell), let us say the Northern Europeans—don't we mature more slowly? When we are young, at least, the young Jews seem able to beat us all hollow."

They both agreed, and we discussed precocity awhile.

"But," said Whitehead, "when you meet them as students, it is very hard to know just what sort of handicaps to impose so as to equalize the strains as between the precocious, and the perhaps deeper minds which mature more slowly. You need first to know the student yourself, then you need to know what others think of his capacities, and then you need to know those others to know why they think of him what they do."

"Is German scholarship," I asked, "for all its laborious erudition and its ponderosity, not a little lacking in imaginative insight?"

"Scholarship," said he, "can ask itself three questions: first, 'What exactly did an ancient author mean when he wrote certain words, and what exactly did those words mean to his contemporaries?' (That is what scholarship was doing pretty much throughout the nineteenth century.) Next, it can ask, 'What and where are these flashes of insight in the work of genius whereby he rises out of his own time into all time?'— Such flashes as are always anachronistic, in the sense that they are timeless. (And this is a realm in which scholars do not much move and where scholarship rarely finds itself at home.) And finally, 'How can we perpetuate and propagate these rare flashes of genius in which humanity, as nowhere else, has risen above itself?'"

"In that, English classical scholarship is enough better than ours. Here in Harvard in the first decade of the present century, we had some of our very best, especially in the Greek department. Herbert Weir Smyth was then the authority on Aeschylus. Four years they put me through it, and I was glad to be put through—poetry, history, philosophy, drama; but it wasn't until a dozen years later that I began to understand what the great Hellenic ideas meant, and then the people who told me were Murray, Livingstone, Zimmern, Cornford, Casson, and that group. You may retort that I've thrown my case away, that those Harvard professors sowed the seed, and that I, being an excessively late bloomer had to have another dozen or fourteen years; but the same thing happened to others that I know."

They rummaged for specimens of precocity among the Northern Europeans. Keats and Shelley, of course; then Mozart and Mendelssohn, but Whitehead thought that although interesting specimens, they could scarcely be classed as typical, partly because music and poetry do seem to lend themselves peculiarly to brilliant work by young persons.

Then he suddenly fired at me:

"I say, with all this passionate love of music amongst you Americans, *Where are your American composers?*"

The very form in which the question was asked would have spiked my guns, for if we had had any undeniably of the stature of the great Germans, he would not have asked it. What I did find to say was that this art of symphonic orchestration, which had been developing in continental Europe for the past two or three centuries, has been imported into America at the very peak of its complexities and that our composers, instead of beginning back where the Europeans began, in simplicity, have begun in complexity and tried to make it more complex. It is perhaps too soon to know whether this is a success or a failure.

VIII

May 8, 1936

Dinner with the Whiteheads. The spring is now far enough advanced for it to be a pleasure to walk from Harvard Square down to the river. Elms are budded and the little grass plots are green in front of Hicks House, that white, wooden, gambrel-roofed farm dwelling which was General Israel Putnam's headquarters during the siege of Boston in 1775–1776. Moved from its original site, it is now the library of Kirkland House. Next comes the big, formal, arched gateway of Kirkland House itself and its iron gates in a red-brick Renaissance façade, and after this, heading the corner of Boylston Street and Memorial Drive, another Renaissance façade, the library front of Eliot House, its tall westward-facing windows flanked by white pilasters.

"Blossom by Blossom the Spring Begins"

The river banks, too, are now green, and the double row of sycamores along Memorial Drive is in bud. The river is glassing in a breathless calm, stirred only by a single crew who have just landed at the Newell float and swung their shell overhead for the march up the ramp into the boathouse. From the river comes a cool exhalation with the pleasant smell of fresh water. One begins, in the language of Schubert's song, to have *Frühlingsglaube.* . . .

Dinner was at seven, which means six, since we are now having what the farmers call "daylight-wasting." The other guests were North, Margot, and Sheila, son, daughter-in-law, and grand-daughter respectively, and Dr. Walter B. Cannon [1] and his wife Cornelia.[2] He is a rugged, ruddy Midwesterner with a hearty voice, simple, direct, and no nonsense. An authority in his subject, he is freighted with honours which he wears invisibly. His wife is a good deal like him, full of humour and kindness, learned, clever, witty, but sees no reason for putting on side. There was no need to waste time over social preliminaries.

Yellow rays from the westering sun, streaming over roofs, and spires and treetops of Cambridge, shone on the table making a glitter of silver, sparkle of glass, and lighting brilliantly the stalks of yellow iris in a tall vase at the centre. Mrs. Cannon was placed at one end of the table, Mrs. Whitehead at the other.

Dr. Cannon talked of Russia, Germany, and China where he had been on tour and in medical conventions last summer.

Ivan Pavlov, the Russian scientist ("conditioned reflexes"), was one of his old friends. During the early days of the revolution, he said, Pavlov, as was his wont, before beginning his regular series of academic lectures, commented on world events.

[1] Dr. Walter Bradford Cannon, physiologist. Born Prairie du Chien, Wis., 1871. A.B. Harvard 1896, M.D. 1900. George Higginson Professor in the Harvard Medical School since 1906. Died 1945.

[2] Cornelia James Cannon (Mrs. Dr. Walter Bradford Cannon), author. Born St. Paul, Minn., 1876. A.B. Radcliffe 1899, L.H.D. Wheaton 1928. Married June 25, 1901.

He was called before the Cheka. After they had questioned him awhile he drew out his watch and said:

"Gentlemen, you must excuse me. I have a lecture to deliver," and walked out.

"You can do that if you are a Pavlov," said Whitehead. "Otherwise you go to Siberia."

"Foreign diplomatists and consuls in Russia," said Dr. Cannon, "have no Russian friends. The Russians dare not be seen talking with foreign officials. A British consul in Leningrad, who cultivates gypsy lore, was rejoiced at the prospect of going there because the Russian authority on gypsies lives and teaches in that city, but in two years he has not been able to meet him. Friends of the Pavlovs, a young scientist and his wife, were arrested by the Cheka while their little boy, a seven-year-old, was asleep, and they were jailed separately incommunicado. The concierge saw them being taken away and notified the Pavlovs, who took the child. By acting through Moscow they obtained the release of the parents a week later, but the woman was shattered and probably will never recover. The boy is of necessity being brought up in an utterly abnormal atmosphere, goes guarded to school, and can have no playmates."

"The hounding of scholars," said Whitehead, "is one of the symptoms of social decay, it keeps cropping out in Western Europe as well. The dread must be always upon them."

"It is," said Dr. Cannon, "and they bring it with them. When Pavlov visited me here in Cambridge, it was a sultry day in July. My family was in New Hampshire and I took him down to Harvard Square. 'But where is your watchman?' he asked. 'I have none.'—'Your house will be robbed?'—'Oh, I don't think so.'—Then seeing my old Ford car in the back yard, he said, 'But your beautiful car will surely be stolen!'—'Oh, no.'— 'No? Then how superior is the morality of Boston to New York!'"

Poor Pavlov had been robbed of twenty-three hundred dollars in the Grand Central station in New York, wanted to go home to Russia then and there, and was only persuaded to stay as guest of the Rockefeller Foundation.

"He 'conditioned' a word for me while he was here," continued Dr. Cannon. "We were going down to Woods Hole on the train, when he saw in the seat ahead of us a man reading a newspaper whose headline had in large type the word 'fizzle.' 'Fitzel?' quoth he. 'Was meint das? Fiasco?'"

Presently the doctor was describing an incident in Russia: he had seen a huge crane operated by a woman. "She lifted tons of metal about as though she were putting her baby to bed." He had obviously been more open-minded about the Soviet state than a good many who have gone there of late—conceded that it had improved the lot of the common people.

Of Germany he said that, meeting a professional friend of his in Munich, he was told that the spirit of the German universities, their intellectual freedom which had been built up through centuries, had been crushed. "A sadder man I never saw."

"A young Jew," he recounted, "—an eminent man—was removed from his professorship. His post was offered to a young friend of mine, a German. He replied that he would accept it only with extreme reluctance. His punishment was to be excluded from every library and every laboratory in Germany. . . . The idea of the Nazis seems to be that the universities exist not for intellectual advance but to foster 'comradeship.' This is the expressed dictum of Bernhard Rust, Reichsminister of Culture and Education, who governs them."

"How does this arise in Germany?" asked Whitehead. "Does a house-painter express the Germans because he *is* a house-painter? (They have plenty of house-painters!) Is this regimentation an utterance of the military spirit, or of the undermen? If there had been a glittering Napoleonic dictator as successor to the Hohenzollerns, it might be understood as militarism. This seems more like a revolt of the unintelligent."

"I think," said Dr. Cannon, "it is the young people, who see in Hitler a chance to get what they want in life, and they little care how or what higher values perish in the process. In fact, they do not know that such values are higher. The higher-minded men in the universities often resign on account of what they see being done around them. . . . We are getting a similar group of young people here, and for the same reason—chafing from denial of economic opportunity."

"As in Denmark," said Mrs. Cannon, "where Ph.D.'s sell shoestrings on the streets."

"I don't see why Ph.D.'s shouldn't sell shoestrings," said Whitehead. "They can also meditate on philosophical problems."

". . . like Spinoza polishing lenses!"

"That was rather a better job: but people are better schooled than unschooled, selling shoestrings or no."

"The trouble is," said Dr. Cannon, "that so many Americans want an education not for its own sake, but in the hope of getting a better job."

"Couldn't we rear up a generation," asked Mrs. Cannon, "which would see its value in and for itself? In six years the whole tone of the young people we meet has changed, from the Jazz Decade of the 1920's to a serious interest in social questions."

The talk veered to the excessively long time it takes to train a doctor. Cannon said it was due to Eliot's fiat of ruling pre-medical studies out of the liberal arts course, though, by taking science, the student could to some extent defeat the veto. Men coming from western universities with a B.S. can anticipate the first two years of medical school.

"Our boy," said Mrs. Cannon, "at the age of twenty-eight, an A.B. and a skilled surgeon, is now as an intern earning his first salary, the munificent sum of fifty dollars a month."

Whitehead thought that a boy should be able to begin his medical practice at twenty-six:

"Between the ages of nineteen and thirty-five the imagination is most active," he said, "and we mostly keep going thereafter on whatever 'fizz' we have experienced then. He ought to begin while his imagination is effervescent."

"Wasn't Eliot's purpose—as Mr. Lowell's was—to save the liberal arts college from nibbling from above by preprofessional studies?" I suggested.

"In Europe," said Whitehead, "much of the liberal studies is given in preparatory-school work. Here in Harvard the freshmen are still treated like high-school students, examined once a week to find out if they are working."

"Do you remember William James's definition of such 'tests'?" asked Dr. Cannon. "He said it amounted to little more than applying the stomach pump!"

There was a gale of laughter.

The discussion swung to whether the Philistine hostility of students to faculty is dissolving at Harvard. There is still a good deal of it, but it is relaxing.

"The students seem to take the position," said North, "that they have a 'cheek' to trespass on their instructors' time—as if that weren't our job!"

"Or," said his father, "to put it bluntly—what we are paid for!"

"We can only get them to our house twice a year," said Mrs. Cannon.

"Do you have a regular time?" asked Mrs. Whitehead.

"No. But poor Mr. Conant does, and the Conants think they have had a big party if they get thirty out of a group of six thousand."

"Of course the president can't expect to meet the six thousand," said Whitehead. "His teas are a gesture, a useful one, I grant you, but a gesture it must remain."

"They come better in the evening," said Mrs. Whitehead, "when their day's work is past."

"In other colleges," said North, "we hear that students who are friendly with their instructors incur the stigma of suspicion that they are 'sucking up' to get good grades."

"It is a primitive taboo and dies hard."

"Is there such a thing as 'voodoo death'?" asked North abruptly of Dr. Cannon, knowing evidently that he had investigated it.

Then followed learned discussion of "controlled" experiment, whether the medicine man secretly poisoned the victim. Examples were adduced from Australian and from ancient literatures. After this came the question of how the American aborigines reached this continent from Asia—via Behring Strait or across the Pacific from island to island. Mrs. Cannon recounted having been shown a newborn baby in Mongolia with the Mongolian "blue" patches (peculiar to that stock) on its little buttocks—said baby having been picked up at random by a nurse in a maternity ward—and Mrs. Cannon added that a Dane who had a baby by an Eskimo woman in Greenland observed the same phenomenon on his own offspring. It disappears soon after birth.

Since no one present seemed to know which way our American aborigines came, the sequel was provided some days later by Dr. Alfred Vincent Kidder, the archaeologist who explored the cave-dwellings in the American Southwest and the Maya ruins in the jungles of Guatemala.

"There is no question whatever," said he. "They came across Behring Strait about twenty-five thousand years ago, either dry-shod at the end of the glacial period, or on the ice or in boats. All sorts of animals crossed on foot. 'The Mongolian spot?'" He took up that question with relish. "I was at a dinner party in Guatemala, when someone asked about it. 'My cook,' said the hostess, 'has just had a baby.' She clapped her hands (the way they call servants there), and said, 'Ask Maria to bring in her baby.' The baby was accordingly brought, the hostess turned him upside down and exhibited his little rump. Sure enough, there was the 'spot'!"

★　　★　　★

In the library the window hangings had been drawn close and the candles lighted. The place was gay with vases of apple twigs in pink and white blossom, and in this simple but beautiful study of a scholar, I enjoyed watching Whitehead's serene and luminous face. He looked a little tired.

Here, over coffee, Dr. Cannon talked of his sojourn in China. One of his former pupils is Minister of Public Health in the Nanking government and induced him to speak to two hundred students who understand English.

"At the sight of those expressionless bronze Buddhas my heart sank, but I tried a funny story, they all laughed, and my saliva began flowing normally again. The Chinese laugh at the same jokes as we do but what the Japanese laugh at no one but a Jap knows."

"You Americans," said Whitehead, "have done a great service for the English language by your return of the Boxer indemnity."

"So I found! Our colleges are sending a steady stream of English-speaking Chinese back into China."

"English is destined to be the second world-language."

"Would Shakespeare have been able to understand the language of our advertising signs in the subway trains? 'Vitamin,' 'germ' . . . and so on?" asked the doctor.

"He would have picked it up in no time," said North, "and would have positively revelled in American slang."

"Especially the expletives," put in his father. "Can't you fancy him writing a scene of Falstaff bursting into the Boar's Head tavern shouting, 'Gee Whiz!' " Some of us thought the slang would have been stronger.

The doctor asked:

"What is the taboo on the word 'bloody'?"

"Because it is short for 'By 'r lady.' "

"The taboo," said North, "is not universally operative."

Dr. Cannon returned to the point of what the Chinese laugh at, saying, "When Howard Lindsay was playing *Life with*

Father in Philadelphia, a young Chinese came back after the performance to thank him 'for a delightful evening.' Lindsay's curiosity was aroused. What would there be in the life of an American family that would strike a Chinese as funny? Lindsay said, 'Do you mind telling me just what it was about the play that you enjoyed so much?'—'Why,' said the Chinese, 'my father used to fuss just like that at breakfast.' "

IX

April 19, 1937

THREE novels about Boston have appeared within a year. The latest of them, *Ward Eight* by Joseph Dinneen, is a study of municipal politics, with a lifelike portrait of Martin Lomasney, who was something between guardian and czar of the West End. It deals with the other three-quarters of the city not coped with, although noticed, in John Marquand's *The Late George Apley*. Santayana's *The Last Puritan*, of a wider range, ends with a period two decades earlier than the other two.

The Whiteheads had been reading *Ward Eight* and asked:

"Do you know the author?"

"Certainly. He is a reporter on the *Globe*."

They pounced: "Tell us more about him. How old is he?"—"Fortyish."—"Born in Boston?"—"Yes, and knows it well, from the inside."

"We gathered as much," said Whitehead, smiling amusedly. "But we were wondering if he had been made to feel uncomfortable in consequence of his book."

"Well, encountering him yesterday upstairs in the reporters' room, I asked him just that. He said, 'In certain places that you can guess I am made to feel as though I am an advanced case of leprosy.' Not that he looked at all downhearted."

"How well he understands his own people," said Mrs. Whitehead, who is Irish.

"That is part of the case against him. The verdict is not unanimous."

"Could you bring him to see us? Would he care to come?"

"One can't undertake to produce him, but I can try."

It proved easier than anticipated. We went. Both Whiteheads were in top form: perfection of handling: genial, considerate, interested, but uncompromising. It was amusing to see Joe shaken out of his attitude of indifferentism. He began with a general defence of the system; they demolished it by Socratic questioning: What service does the Boss perform? Employment agency? Yes. Humanizer of the ward? Yes. But isn't the tribute he exacts excessive? And how about selling their votes after they have paid him for jobs and the employers have paid him for getting the labourers? Is it finally defensible?

Dinneen took it gamely. Besides he knew that Mrs. Whitehead was emotionally in sympathy and that both of them admired the novel. He explained the graft all through society—in the labour unions, the unions expecting to be sold out by their elected agents who openly justify their having done so on the score of policy; then in business, finance, journalism; it is an enveloping climate.

The discussion moved to a comparative view of the two social systems, American and English.

"We in England," said Whitehead, "have a bad system inherited from mediaeval feudalism which oughtn't to work but which, as a matter of fact, does work rather well; whereas you, here in America, have an excellent system which ought to work very well but does, as a matter of fact, work rather badly."

"Your system," said I, "keeps the individual of the class in the class, but by so doing provides it with able leaders, which gradually elevates the class as a whole; ours allows the individual to rise, but by so doing deprives the class of its natural leaders and so tends to leave the class as a whole down."

"That's striking," said Dinneen. "I never thought of that before."

"Neither had I, Joseph, until Mr. Whitehead pointed it out to me a year ago, since when I have been thinking of it."

Resuming, Whitehead said of the class system in England:

"There, where awareness of it is more precise, along with relative homogeneity of race, people know that at a pinch they will be taken care of. I am speaking now of the village and country where squire and gentry adopt a definite responsibility for illness and disaster. After the reforms of 1830, for example, when the middle classes, newly come to power, stiffened the poor law and made it harsher, it was the Tory squires who resisted violently, although the new law would cost them less than the old. Here, wages may be higher and there is more comfort while things are going smoothly, but the consequences of a break in luck or of disaster are frightful. The fate of the poor seems to be nobody's business. . . . In England, class lines may be stiff in major social relationships, but are softened in minor ones . . . the farmers' sons play cricket with the squires' sons. Here, our superficial fraternizing between classes dulls our perception of the profound cleavages between them until the clash occurs."

"In the sit-down strike in Michigan," said Dinneen, "what do you think of the owners' appeal to legality?"

"As the law now stands, the sit-down strike is probably illegal. If they stay on the premises but won't work, they are trespassers. Whether that is how the law *ought* to stand is another matter. Strict application of the present conception of property rights ('doing what I like with my own') may work well enough with small units like shops on Mt. Auburn Street employing a few people, but when you come to great corporate industries which affect the lives of hundreds of thousands of people, it seems to me that the state must step in, if necessary, to direct that they be so managed as to serve the interests of the greater number. The best way to do this, I think, is to leave the actual management to private initiative so as not to destroy that motive, and let the government exercise a general supervisory

[84]

authority. To do this is the one chance that I see for the capitalist system to survive.

"It isn't, you know, very old: only about three hundred years at most. And it often seems to me that Adam Smith did us a grievous disservice in emphasizing the economic motive. It is important of course. We must eat. But it isn't so important. Think what could be done by stressing the aesthetic motive. I can imagine a state of society, even under our existing system, in which parents wouldn't need to be so anxiously concerned that their children should earn a great deal of money—as they are now. I mean that nervous struggle of American parents to lift their children at all costs into a higher income class than their own, which is called, 'giving my children a better chance than I had': but a chance at what? At more money, or at the things of the mind and spirit?

"I can imagine a society, even under capitalism, in which it wouldn't greatly matter whether a family had much money: music—free concerts; the radio. (I know the radio isn't as good as a concert hall, one wants the music not coming at him from one direction out of a box: one wants it all round him; still, the radio does give access to good music.) Then halls where people could give their own plays; and lectures, and discussion groups, a radio speaker perhaps stating the question, then the group carrying it on; or state-provided moving pictures on a really grand scale, free to the public; and playgrounds for athletic sports; and public libraries such as we already have. Mind you, I don't mean that all this should be heavy and dull. There could be light music, and informal games, and amusing plays. But under such conditions the average person, without much money, would have access to the good life."

At ten hot chocolate was brought, and at ten-thirty we left. Dinneen had to go back to the *Globe* office, and, as he had brought me over to Cambridge in his car, he carried me back to Beacon Hill. On the way, at intervals between a discussion

[85]

of *The Late George Apley*, which we had both been reading, we counted up our takings from the evening.

"Anything farther from the Apleys," said Dinneen, "I wouldn't know where to look for in the city of Boston."

"All the same, they are warm friends with a lot of Apleys, and respect their good qualities."

"That may be," assented Joseph, a shade absent-mindedly; then, as we drove along he came out with it: "What I bring away is this: more than anyone else I ever met, he seems to have the answers. You say his subject was originally mathematics?"

"Yes."

"He is a Higher Mathematician," said Dinneen.

X

May 24, 1937

THE afternoon was clearing after rain and the drenched turf and foliage of Memorial Drive along the river bank, fresh in May green, smelt delicious.

In their apartment at Radnor Hall the Whiteheads were waiting in their library. Their maid had been out for the day and they laughed over having enjoyed the privilege of doing things for themselves.

". . . doing them on the whole rather badly, and getting thoroughly tired doing them."

Mr. Whitehead wore formal afternoon dress, spike-tailed black coat and starched collar; probably there had been some academic function. Tea was brought. Conversation was on the subject of tolerance.

"There is no tolerance," said he, "unless there is something to tolerate, and that, in practice, is likely to mean something which most people would consider intolerable."

"Do you suppose that the persecuting temper is peculiar to

religions, or only to some religions? Hellenism, for instance, was not a persecuting religion."

"Religion carries two sorts of people in two entirely opposite directions," said Whitehead; "the mild and gentle people it carries towards mercy and justice; the persecuting people it carries into fiendish sadistic cruelty. Mind you, though this may seem to justify the eighteenth-century Age of Reason in its contention that religion is nothing but an organized, gigantic fraud and a curse to the human race, nothing could be farther from the truth. It possesses these two aspects, the evil one of the two appealing to people capable of naïve hatred; but what is actually happening is that when you get natures stirred to their depths over questions which they feel to be overwhelmingly vital, you get the bad stirred up in them as well as the good; the mud as well as the water. It doesn't seem to matter much which sect you have, for both types occur in all sects. . . ."

"Does the fact of certain religions pretending to a closed system, one which sets up to have an answer for every question, have anything to do with it?"

"Wouldn't that be more or less included in my previous definition: that when people do feel strongly on a subject, they consider such questions closed?"

"Is impartial aloofness from such controversy (supposing it is tolerated) an effective position?"

"It depends on what you mean by 'effective.' In general, the 'effective' people are expected to act, and action lands you in conflict."

"Then here we are, at the question of violence. I remember you to have said in your *Adventure of Ideas* (one of the few books I was ever able to read on shipboard) that the only justification in the use of force is to reduce the amount of force necessary to be used."

"If there is a young fellow," said he, "who makes an infernal nuisance of himself going up and down stairs drunk in this building, annoying the twelve families who occupy suites in tihs entry, we either write a letter to the newspaper about it or telephone for the police: one is a mild form of persuasion, the other is potential force. If he then persists, we have him put away. That is restraint." He grinned engagingly.

We got into the question of non-resistance: does it make its appearance except as the last weapon of otherwise defenceless people: Czarist Russia, British India, the American anti-slavery agitators, pacifists in wartime?

This was taken by Mrs. Whitehead as a challenge to British imperial policy in India, which she proceeded to justify till I explained that the subject was adduced purely on its psychological merits, and quoted the chapter in Webb Miller's *I Found No Peace* on the clubbing of non-resisters in India as showing that non-resistance seems to increase the brutality of the attackers. As this topic was not especially congenial (which I might have known beforehand) it was dropped in favour of another, namely, how fares talent in different types of society.

"Aristocracies," said Whitehead, "welcome talent. Burke had neither money nor birth, yet they were glad to have him and he always had a seat in Parliament, for they knew he was a genius. The monarchy was, as the house of Hanover has been all along, healthily unpopular, allowing the government to be run by a committee of parliamentarians who could always hold over their kings the threat that if they didn't behave they could be sent home where they came from. Consequently a career was open to talents. Even the middle classes were privileged up to the time of the World War; we didn't realize it, but we were. My father was rather well off for a country parson. Yet my education was virtually paid for by scholarship funds up to and through my university training, not because we couldn't have paid, but because we weren't asked to. That is now changed. The scholarship funds, I believe, are supposed to go only to students who need them."

The telephone kept ringing. Mrs. Whitehead kept rising and

going into her sitting room to answer it. Finally, returning she seated herself on the arm of her husband's deep chair to say:

"Altie, it's the (she named the dean of a men's college in Massachusetts, and his wife). They 'must' see you. How about Thursday night?"

"For dinner?"

"No. After. It mustn't be for dinner. You must have your rest."

"Then let me look at my book."

He produced a tiny black-leather engagement book with gilt edges from his pocket and peered into its pages.

"Thursday will do."

"He will entreat you for lectures next year. You must be firm."

"I know."

"Remember he is a German. He will talk and talk and talk. You must just sit still, and not be talked over."

"I shan't be talked over."

She looked at me and smiled over this domestic duologue. He was quite unperturbed.

Again the telephone rang. This time it was a secretary in the School of Business Administration, whose father, a country parson from Maine, "dearly wishes to call," Mrs. Whitehead grumbled, "as if you were deity itself! (Imagine you, as deity!)" It was decided to have them, but the girl herself couldn't be persuaded to come.

" 'Why not?' "

" 'I have nothing to bring.' What nonsense! How sad it is. Where does this self-denigration come from?"

"It is the 'sense of sin,' " said Whitehead. "The worst blight that ever fell on man."

This domestic interlude being disposed of, we resumed a discussion of the correspondences between the principles governing diverse art-forms; various devices resorted to by artists to comment on their themes, the choric odes in Greek drama for one, and for another those symbolic figures on the Medici tombs by Michelangelo.

"It is human history speaking in the four recumbent figures," said Whitehead, "and the Medicis are rather lost out of it."

"Apparently Michelangelo knew it at the time," I said. "When it was complained that the statues of Julian and Lorenzo did not look like them, Michelangelo replied, 'Who will see that ten centuries hence?' "

"As for the choric odes in Greek tragedy," said Whitehead, "there it is as though the poet ceased and human nature, the great elemental truths of life, began speaking through him."

"Is it fair to say, as so many do say, that there is more milk of human kindness in Hebraic thought than in the Hellenic?"

His answer was in *oratio obliqua*, so blandly given, so disarming:

"I think there should be an Eleventh Commandment, *'Always make friends with people who do you a service.'* "

XI

March 17, 1938

THE usual holiday celebrating the evacuation of Boston by the British; but no holiday for a newspaper since there is always a big parade in South Boston, where Washington's cannon from Fort Ticonderoga were planted.

Evening with the Whiteheads. It was just after the Germans' seizure of Austria and they were feeling glum. He said he thought the situation was very bad, and she that it meant another war sooner or later. We talked about the composition of the British Cabinet. He said:

"Foreign policy has been run by a Tory group who wanted peace, it is true, but wanted it for the wrong reasons—in order that they might keep their havings. I'm not suggesting that they were treasonable."

"They wouldn't need to be," I said. "Classes identify the interests of their nation with those of themselves."

"That," said Mrs. Whitehead, "is as true of Labour as it is at the Tory end."

"The Labour people," resumed Whitehead, "have been shouting against rearmament whenever anybody mentioned a gun, and directly we began to come into collisions—as with Italy in the Abyssinian affray, they cried, 'This wouldn't have happened if we had been armed.' "

"I often wondered what Labour would have done had they suddenly been given the responsibility."

"Tories and Labour, both have been following one half of a wrong policy," he replied, "Labour opposing rearmament, Tories trying to conciliate dictators."

"It begins to look as though the one thing democracy has that is worth saving is the freedom of the individual."

"I would say," remarked Whitehead, "two: the freedom of the individual is one. But your knowledge of history will remind you that there has always been misery at the bottom of society: in the ancient world, slavery; in the mediaeval world, serfdom; since the development of machine technique, industrial proletariates. Our own age is the first time when, if this machine production is sensibly organized, there need be no material want. Russia has relieved the suffering of the masses at the price of the individual's liberty; the Fascists have destroyed personal liberties without really much alleviating the condition of the masses; the task of democracy is to relieve mass misery and yet preserve the freedom of the individual."

"Are aristocracies, so-called, of much use to us?"

"If they are kept alive. I would have inheritance taxes high enough so that a family of lazy aristocrats wouldn't survive. But I wouldn't have a dead level of income. Families with wealth are free to experiment. And the rich man's fad of one generation becomes the poor man's necessity of the next; from Rolls-Royce motor-car to the Ford car. Without rich families you couldn't get your privately endowed universities in America, and it is Harvard, Yale, Princeton, Chicago, and such places, that set the pace for the state universities, without which they might be badly stagnant."

At nine the doorbell rang and Grace DeFriez arrived, animated and handsome, gowned, like Mrs. Whitehead, in black, which becomes them both. The week before, being in Nantucket, I had gone up on the moors' edge to the grave of her young husband, Thaddeus, who had been managing editor of the *Globe*. Nantucket, having been a family home of the DeFriezes for four generations, was mentioned briefly; the talk shifted to sea fogs which beset that island, and thence to the "dew ponds" of the Wiltshire Downs, where the Whiteheads had spent their summers for many years. When the conversation had regained momentum, I brought up his remarks of a year ago about grand opera. He corrected my memory:

"I don't say that Wagner isn't magnificent or that I didn't enjoy him. What I say is that an ideal of power and glory appealing to racial saga is fatally easy to misconstrue and has, as a matter of fact, *been* misconstrued. Struggle, ambition, heroic energy—these are noble, as potentially noble as anything in man; but when they decline into a mere love of domination they are evil."

"When I try your remark that such a series of music dramas could have wrecked the political genius of the English people in a generation, they say, 'Shakespeare!'"

There was a good deal of laughter and I got chaffed. In fact, I chaffed myself.

"Last summer they got me into the Memorial Theatre at Stratford-on-Avon for a performance of *King Henry V* and, at the end of three hours, three centuries of history had been so obliterated that I didn't care whether I was an American or an Englishman. You may say that it is the music that repeals the ethical sense, but I say Shakespeare's poetry can be just as insidious."

[92]

For a while we talked of small-town, suburban, or country people as desirable human types. Mrs. Whitehead described a Seattle woman who has brought up four handsome, manly sons:

"She talks platitudes—*and* yet she is the salt of the earth."

"How has she done it?"

"By being kind, and full of fun, and keeping them at home. She comes here and we talk platitudes—you should hear me grind them out—but it doesn't matter. The woman is as good as there is."

"How I would like to hear you talking platitudes!" cried Grace, laughing delightedly.

"I wouldn't want you to. It couldn't be true then. But vis-à-vis her only, it is perfectly genuine. We don't say a thing, and yet we understand each other perfectly."

"There you are," said she, "at your very best; and you couldn't be better!"

At ten, in came a tea cart with whisky, soda, ginger ale, and ice. A light fire of logs was burning on the hearth.

In a discussion of war, Whitehead said:

"The absolute pacifist is a bad citizen; times come when force must be used to uphold right, justice, and ideals."

This struck me as rather extreme. Is it as simple as all that?

Grace left at a little before eleven. Mrs. Whitehead had told me that she would, and had asked me to stay a little longer. At eleven they turned on the radio to hear the news:

"One must take the advertisements along with it," said he, "for it is a flash of news and advertisements alternately. They have got us quite depraved. We no longer mind it much, if any. Ask us and we can tell you all about Hecker's ale and somebody's toothpaste which is far and away the best."

They turned it on. Sure enough! A voice came out of the void:

"Snoodledicker's ale is made of toasted barley . . ."

"There," said Mr. Whitehead, grinning, "that's new! I didn't know that before."

Then came news; it was ghastly enough; the bombing of Barcelona; nine refugee Austrians arrived by plane in England, and, denied admission, one took poison at the airport. . . .

They looked at me inquiringly—as though I knew any more about it than they did! All I could find to say was:

"Allow for distorted emphasis. Mornings, as I walk downtown, the headlines fill me with dismay, old hand at it though I am; but at the office when I sit down to the papers for a careful reading, the scares seem to evaporate. This has been going on for the last dozen years, time after time it has looked like another explosion—only it didn't explode. Of course the danger is that we may grow desensitized."

XII

April 28, 1938

ONE of those spring days of sudden summer heat, the thermometer only half a degree under ninety, steam still on in office buildings, and effect, general exhaustion. Nothing and nobody could have induced me to go out for the evening except the Whiteheads, and even there I arrived in a state of wilt at eight o'clock.

The formality of last names has been discarded, and dinner is now a removable feast; conversationally we move faster and farther by ourselves. With windows open to the spring night, we forgot all about the oppressive day.

They talked of their life at Grantchester when Whitehead was a Fellow of Trinity College, Cambridge. They lived in the old Mill House and showed me a coloured picture of it in the *National Geographic* magazine for September 1936. The life of the village went on in all its Chaucerian looseness and in bland indifference to its near neighbour, the university; a bastard child was merely "a little mistyke." The easy-going, good-natured people relied instinctively on the gentry, as they had done for centuries, and the gentry did not fail them—or, if they did, lost caste; and when a liberal candidate for Parliament made the error of denouncing the local squirearchy, there was a storm of anger and he had to be bundled out to avoid unpleasant consequences. The Mill House was charming and picturesque, all but one drawback, rats. They were resisted in various ways, but at times would stage a come-back and have "terrific fights" inside the walls of the ancient dwelling. One got the idea that life there was exciting. They told it with huge gusto, and we had a good deal of laughter.

Later we got on to what Whitehead called "Asking ourselves 'historical riddles' ": whether the Spaniards had maimed their intellect by expelling the Jews and Protestants. He added:

"The gold they brought from the Americas demoralized them. And the armies they sent over Europe drained off more of their best blood. No doubt the soldiers produced their proper number of babies—but not in Spain. The blight, however, did not extend to the arts."

"Did the expulsion of the French Huguenots postpone the French Revolution?"

"Perhaps *caused* it," said he.

"That suggests the German 'forty-eighters.' After the failure of their revolutions, multitudes of Germans got up and came over here."

"You Americans have been fortunate in them. I fancy you got the Germans who could not go it in a stuffy political atmosphere. Note that emigration is always selective, in *some* sense: people must have a strong reason for moving. The reasons may vary from high moral grounds to steamship agents importing cheap labour from southern Europe. . . . If we English had found gold mines in North America instead of arable land and trade, it might have ruined us. Even as it was, after the vivid people had been drawn off by emigration in the seventeenth century, our eighteenth-century people, compared with those of the sixteenth, were a dull lot. . . . And, since we are asking ourselves historical riddles, here is one: didn't the younger Pitt, instead of letting Europe's worn-out dynasties tumble down when they deserved to, promote the present collapse of Europe by getting up a war to beat Napoleon and put them back in power for a hundred years during which things got too bad to manage? Didn't Pitt have one of the greatest decisions to make in the history of humanity, and make it wrong? . . . listening to Burke and that lot, instead of to the liberals?"

Later in the evening he said, "I have been meditating on the relation of technique to art, and have a theory; whether it can be sustained I am not sure. It is that in the early stages of an art, technique comes in as a means of expression for the burning conviction that is in the artists. It is often ragged. Take the cathedrals: you get something profoundly moving, and, at elbows with it, something clumsy but which does not detract from it. Then as the art matures and the technique gets established and transmissible by teaching, the bright boys are picked out who can learn the technique readily, to the neglect of the boys who have magnificent dreams. The work is clever and finished but lacks depth."

We started rummaging among the arts to test it. He thought Raphael was one of the clever technicians who appear at the moment when the profundity begins to be lost, and Milton another; and the flamboyant style in Gothic a further example.

"English Gothic," said he, "runs through about four centuries, 1100 to 1500, and through four successive styles— Romanesque, Early English, Decorated and Perpendicular— each style lasting, roughly, about a century, up to the sixteenth when it begins to peter out. What was happening in those four centuries was that new aspects of the idea of Gothic architecture were being discovered and developed. Its possibilities of novelty looked endless, but by the 1500's they began to look used up, I don't say that they *were* used up. Then you get a complete break. Builders go back to the architectural style of Greece and

Rome, 'Renaissance': they adapt that style for every usage in the modern world from church to railroad station, so that in London you get instead of a Gothic abbey, St. Paul's Cathedral, and in New York, the Pennsylvania railroad station, which is modelled after the baths of Caracalla in Rome."

We tried this theory on the art of Greek tragedy, and sure enough! here was the same life cycle: Aeschylus has burning moral convictions, his technique in *The Persians* is little more than that of a cantata or an oratorio; but in the *Agamemnon* it is highly advanced. In the extant plays of Sophocles you have the balance of a middle period: there is still strong conviction, the ideas are expressed with tremendous force, and at the same time with a technical mastery which releases their power to the full. In this group are the *Antigone* and the two *Oedipus* plays. By the time Euripides arrives, technique is so well understood that it can be juggled; but while there is still strong conviction and the ideas are powerful, the spirit is one of sceptical criticism.

We found that what we were discussing in terms of techniques were the life cycles of art-forms. Such cycles can be traced in Greek sculpture, in Renaissance painting, and in modern music, beginning three centuries ago and coming on down to the twentieth, when the technique of symphonic orchestration is so well understood that it can now be taught to the bright boys. . . .

"Some of these bright boys," Whitehead's theory had let in a flood of light, "put on dazzling shows of technical fireworks, brilliant flashes and bangs; they can astonish the natives with previously unheard-of combinations of sounds, can shock the daylights out of the old folks by using the naughty four-letter words of harmonic dissonance and atonality; but believing in nothing they have nothing to say, and the once-powerful idea is stone dead."

"Yet it may have a resurrection," cautioned Whitehead. "There are ideas which have lain in their tombs for centuries, then rising again, have revolutionized human society. Some boy who is more than merely bright gets hold of an idea which has long been supposed to be dead, and it comes to life in his hands. For when a young man is all in a glow over the discovery of a great idea, it is not so much the particular idea he has discovered that is important, as it is his glow over it. There you have the sense of adventure, of newness, the old idea has been seen freshly in some new aspect. For the vitality of thought is in adventure. *Ideas won't keep.* Something must be done about them. When the idea is new, its custodians have fervour, live for it, and, if need be, die for it. Their inheritors receive the idea, perhaps now strong and successful, but without inheriting the fervour; so the idea settles down to a comfortable middle age, turns senile, and dies; but the institutions organized around it do not stop; they go on by sheer force of acquired momentum, or like the dead knight borne along on his horse."

He did not particularize.

XIII

January 17, 1939

WHITEHEAD is now professor emeritus. He is in his seventy-ninth year, and since his retirement, owing to reduced income, they have moved from Radnor Hall to a four-room apartment in the Hotel Ambassador on Cambridge Street. On the fifth floor, their windows look out over the treetops southward, and westward to green dooryards and shade trees, and the delta where stands that red-brick, secular cathedral, Memorial Hall.

Most of his library had been fitted in here; a study where books are shelved from floor to ceiling on four sides, interrupted only by one door and one large window, and in the dining-room three more walls of them, where they have been treated so decoratively that one is hardly aware of them as an intrusion. The living-room is fairly spacious, and here the arrangement of furniture is so skilful and the effect so pleasing that although there is no fireplace, it is not much missed, and when conversation starts it is not missed at all. Again, as at Radnor Hall, the walls are tinted a shade just off black, and instead of being gloomy, it is restful.

Since it is no longer practicable for them to give dinner parties, guests are invited in after dinner for conversation. Robert Cunningham had driven down from Exeter, and we were dining in evening dress at Durgin-Park in the market district, which is nothing unusual since men and women go down there to dine before the opera in full regalia, the attraction being that you get a better dinner than you would in a swagger hotel, and at marketmen's prices.

One of Cunningham's former pupils at Exeter, now a freshman at Harvard, seeing us, came over and spoke. Here was his schoolmaster all dressed up and dining in the market, where was he going? The boy was all excitement and devoured with curiosity.

"Is it a date?" he asked.

"Yes," said Cunningham, "heavy."

He was aching to know. Finally Cunningham said:

"We are going to Professor Whitehead's for conversation."

Nick was as wise as before.

With the Whiteheads we found Mr. and Mrs. Richard Gummere, he being chairman of the Committee on Admissions for Harvard College. They were Philadelphians, Quaker in their religious sympathies, and he was formerly headmaster of Penn Charter School. Presently we were joined by Mr. W. G. Constable, curator of paintings at the Boston Museum of Fine Arts, whither he had come from the National Gallery in London. He is an Englishman of wide experience, learning, and cultivation, and such pleasant company that one always rejoices to see him. Last came Grace DeFriez, in black furs and black velvet, her usual sparkle of geniality and high spirits a little heightened by having just come in out of the winter night.

Whitehead talked of the differences between the seventeenth and eighteenth centuries in England. He thought the seventeenth-century Englishmen had more depth: "Their dominant interest was religion, as against the 'debunking' of the eighteenth-century rationalists. 'Debunking' is a good thing to have done, but is comparatively shoal water. Johnson, a sturdier figure, was still in essence of the seventeenth century. If he and Voltaire had met, they wouldn't have had much to say to each other. One trouble with the eighteenth century was that so many of the earnest people had emigrated to the colonies, leaving only the other kind to predominate. They had pale monarchs, shadowy figures from the Restoration till the Guelphs, whose dynasty was that of tame kings holding tenure at good behaviour, the country being managed by a committee from the aristocratic class. George III, the only masterful one, bungled badly our affairs with the American colonies; and we never should have fought Napoleon. What had we in common by that time with continental monarchism? We should have kept quiet and watched them."

"How much of such epochs, do you think, are caused collectively, and how much brought about by exceptional individuals?" asked Cunningham.

"The surrounding social conditions for a great age have to be present, but much, if not all, depends on the chance of there being a powerful personality to set it going. Lacking that, the occasion peters out. John Wesley was such a figure. He ignited two others, and they roused the serious part of the nation. But in times which are ripe, when such dynamic personalities do not appear, the opportunity is lost. Much depends on the chance production of a great man whose powers are adapted to the needs of his age. He voices those needs."

"Who would you say," asked Cunningham, "are the ablest people in England today?"

"The upper artisan class."

This did not surprise some of us, but Cunningham, a former

Rhodes scholar at Queen's College, Oxford (by way of Princeton), wanted it a little more precise:

"Not the intellectuals then?"

"I never can sufficiently get my friends to understand that the intellectuals do not speak for the country," said Whitehead. "If you want to hear that voice and watch it act, wait for the back streets, the quiet people of the middle and working class. When they act, the intellectuals are brushed aside."

"They are the 'respectable,'" said Mrs. Whitehead lightly. "And I honour them for it. Their religious life is lived once a week."

"But does religion cramp the style of the artisans?" asked Richard Gummere.

"Quite the contrary," said Whitehead smiling blandly. "They are nonconformists, 'chapel people,' and the first thing they think is that the Church of England should be disestablished. That makes them aggressive!"

He asked me where I thought American liberals mainly come from. I postponed the question, but asked why doctors are so reactionary in their social thinking.

"When I was in Cambridge, at Trinity," said he, "the question came up whether to award degrees to women. On the one side were men who worked in laboratories, and on the other, including physicians, those who worked with human beings. Almost to a man those in favour of granting degrees to women were the people who dealt with lifeless matter, while those who dealt with women as living creatures were opposed. In London I saw a good deal of physicians. After their day's work when they picked up their book or paper they were too spent to think on what they read."

"In this country," said Mr. Gummere, "doctors are scientifically acute and humanely sympathetic, but you must not expect them to understand social questions."

"Does a doctor see all of a human being?" asked Grace.

"No," said Whitehead. "When a man is full of beans he

doesn't say, 'Look here, let's go and see a doctor.' The doctor is the last person he is thinking of. He only sees us when we are a bit off our feed, and with the psychiatrist it is even worse; he only comes in when our friends are beginning to be worried about us. Taken as a whole, I think the professional classes are bad judges outside of their professions."

"This brings us back to your question about American liberals. Before the war, and perhaps still, many of the best of them came from fairly comfortable middle-class families where there had been good schooling and religious instruction. Then they either saw poverty by living in some social settlement house, as Jane Addams or Lillian Wald, or encountered some dynamic personality like Brand Whitlock, or as Newton Baker did in Tom Johnson of Cleveland. Then there were the radical journalists who became authors, the group which included Ida Tarbell, Ray Stannard Baker, and Lincoln Steffens."

"What happened to their religious faith?" asked Grace.

"It turned to social service."

The question was raised whether any equivalent class is in prospect now.

"When I first lectured in American colleges," said Whitehead, "—roughly, from 1924 to 1929—in those five years, I soon saw if I used a quotation from the Bible that not one of my students had ever read it, ever intended to, or had the least idea what I was talking about, and if they sensed that I was speaking of religion they leaned back until I should have got on to something else; but in the years from 1929 to my retirement, the last seven years of my active teaching, this attitude changed, and when I spoke of religion there was an attentive leaning forward."

"I see it among the young men I encounter at the museum," said Constable. "Their work, with them, is passionately felt as a religious mission. This acts irrespective of income; the sons of the wealthy feel it the same as those who have hardly enough money to get along on."

"Might this mean," I asked, "that the religious spirit of our time, which seems to be subsiding from the churches, may be going to reincarnate in the form of artistic and creative activities?"

No one cared to pick this up. For a diversion the talk veered to the subject of interior decoration. Mr. Constable said:

"One of my duties at the National Gallery in London when estates were being broken up was to go and see if they contained anything of national importance. Often I went into rooms where the masters themselves had never been; it was not only my right but my function. One found the oddest things. In a great house where the top story of a wing had been partitioned off for maids' rooms in the eighteenth century, I went along the corridor and found a complete dozen of Chippendale chairs, two in a room (the rooms were six), where they had been apportioned perhaps a century before. All I had to do was set the chairs out in the corridor. Down below, in the mansion's rooms of state, was Victorian black walnut."

"When I see English furniture," said Whitehead, "it looks as though its origin had generally been a comfortable but not pretentious house somewhere near the middle of the social scale. From there it might move in either direction, up or down; but generally kept its distinctive quality of comfort. In France . . . (My wife, who has lived there, will correct me if I am in error." —"Not publicly, my dear," said she, rising to pass the sandwiches.) ". . . wherever I see furniture," he resumed, "it always strikes me as an imitation, good or bad, of something in a palace."

The three English people fell whimsically to comparing their impressions of the British royal palaces.

"I have never been at Buckingham," said Mrs. Whitehead to Constable. "Have you?"

"Yes. Much of it is about what you might expect, pretty awful: lambrequins, and long fringe around the bottoms of the chairs; but even in the big rooms of state there is always some concession to comfort, some suggestion of human beings making themselves at home there."

Mrs. Whitehead laughed, "Exactly the same at Windsor."

Conversation veered back to the subject of religious enthusiasm.

"Religion in England," said Mrs. Whitehead, "isn't a thing to be enthusiastic about. That wouldn't be respectable!"

"No," said Mr. Whitehead, "we get our enthusiasm done for us by the Welsh and Scots."

"And the religious spirit of both gets into politics. Lloyd George, for example, came out of a Welsh chapel."

The death of Yeats had been announced and it led to a discussion of the Celtic revival.

"I think the attempt to revive the language itself was a mistake," said Whitehead. "The Irish have made a distinct contribution to English with the sounds they give it and the Gaelic is something only a few would understand. It resulted in many being taught Gaelic but remaining illiterate in English."

"When the Abbey Theatre first came on tour to Cambridge," said Mrs. Whitehead, "I had Alfred give them lunch at the college. Yeats was the *poseur*; tousled hair, adoring females in attendance, one permitted to carry his muffler, another his raincoat. He had written some splendid poetry, but certainly was conceited. There was one young man, shabbily clad, who said almost nothing and coughed dreadfully. After lunch someone took them the rounds of the college, but this young man stayed behind with Alfred and me. And then! Three hours, he talked brilliantly. We hadn't got his name. But after they were gone, we told each other, 'No matter who he is, the man is extraordinary.' At that time he had published nothing. Later we found out that his name was Synge! We hugged ourselves that we hadn't had to be told."

The group broke up at about eleven. While Cunningham and I stayed to replace the chairs and carry off the plates and tumblers, we talked of Celtic dialects in Breton and Irish, about Celtic racial types and of where the most beautiful human beings are to be seen. Northern Italy, they thought, especially the blond Italians up into the Italian cantons of Switzerland. English? "No," said Whitehead. "They are wholesome and rugged but seldom beautiful." There was another vote for certain parts of Southern Italy, where the people still seem to look like the old Greeks of Magna Graecia.

They were in high spirits. The evening had gone well. Before leaving, Grace DeFriez had said to me privately:

"A dinnerless party that went better than most dinner parties."

XIV

February 27, 1939

IN the *Atlantic Monthly* for March, which was already on the news-stands, was Whitehead's "An Appeal to Sanity," occasioned by the excitement over Czechoslovakia; but Whitehead's discussion so transcended the immediate issues that one finished it feeling in a larger world. An editorial précis of his essay had been published in the *Globe*.

That evening he said genially:

"We have been reading each other."

"Mine is only to advertise the existence of yours. Also, I have sent a copy to Barrington-Ward of the London *Times*."

"It was written last November," said he. "Everybody has forgotten Czechoslovakia by now."

"That is precisely its value. The immediate occasion may be fading, but the historical processes you relate it to don't fade at all."

"Originally," said Mrs. Whitehead, "it was started as a letter to Felix Frankfurter. He was pressing us on the subject, and rather vigorously."

E*

"With his keen sense of justice these times must be peculiarly painful to him."

"Then, too," she said, "there is a strain of the crusader in Felix."

"The way he spent himself trying to get a fair trial for Sacco and Vanzetti," I said, "strikes me as something more abiding than mere crusading zeal."

"I always think of him as a Viennese," she said affectionately. "He has their gaiety, although, God knows! there hasn't been much to inspire it in the past half-dozen years."

"The day his appointment to the Supreme Court was announced," said Whitehead, "Evelyn and I happened to hear it on the radio broadcast. We called a cab and drove over to congratulate him. A few of his students from the law school were already there. It was quite charming: they were immensely pleased and one saw in them what young men are at their best, gracious and kindly."

From here the discussion detoured to a discussion of crusading zeal, and Whitehead remarked of professional crusaders that "their old age is likely to be a melancholy affair; they go from 'cause' to 'cause.' "

"Where, precisely, should a man's crusading zeal abate?" I asked. "When his blood cools?"

"With the professionals," said he, "it never does."

"Your spirited vindication of the Jews in the *Atlantic* prompts me to ask why they are, as you have remarked, so often unpopular."

"They are acute, and their acuteness often takes a form which excites envy, namely, the form of doing well in trade. It is not always depth. In picking men you must guard against the brilliancy of the young Jew. They mature at nineteen or twenty and can seem dazzling, but they do not always fulfil the expectations of them based on their superiority to others at that age."

"Furthermore," added Mrs. Whitehead, "they have not

had the experience of ruling other peoples, or even a state of their own."

"That gives them," said he, "a certain helpful preoccupation with the ideal. They are singularly deficient in humour, or were till they lived among the Europeans. The Bible is quite humourless. After their tragedies they never seemed to have a farce by Aristophanes."

"Situated as they were between military empires, perhaps there was nothing to laugh about."

"The Jew is naturally melancholy," said Whitehead. "And they don't get credit for their enormous achievement, the influence they have had on the development of Europe. Allowing for three centuries to get going, the Bible has been a best seller for fifteen hundred years, and is still. But the Jews get no credit for having produced the most influential book on earth because they insisted that every word of it had been dictated by God."

We discussed their achievements in the creative arts; for example, in music, since that is the dominant art-form of our epoch, or was until the 1920's. In music they give us some first-rate composers, from Mendelssohn to Ernest Bloch, and a great many executants, brilliant performing artists, especially in the past few decades, violinists, pianists, orchestral conductors. Whitehead said they produced good mathematicians.

Watching my chance I asked him how he thought the future would appraise the achievement of Lawrence Lowell.

"His predecessor, what was his name . . . ?"

"Eliot."

"Eliot did a very useful thing; he broke up the classical tradition in the American college. It never could have had the meaning here that it has in Europe because you are too far away from its sources; not only have you no direct geographical contact with the ancient Graeco-Roman civilization, but also none with the mediaeval world which transmitted it. Besides, the humanities, as taught in universities and derived from

Greece and Rome, have a divorcement of the life of contemplation from the practical world that comes of a slave society. The
slaves did far too much of the manual work; the hand and
brain need to be trained together. Eliot opened the whole field
of study for choice, and left it open for quite a while. Finally,
in due season, came Lowell, to give it some co-ordination. He
came after about the right interval. What he did was very daring
and difficult."

"President-emeritus Eliot 'is said to have said,' " I told him,
"that after he had devoted his life to turning Harvard from a
college into a university, President Lowell was devoting his to
turning it from a university back to a college. He may never
have said it, and probably the antithesis isn't fair."

"Lowell also," said Whitehead, "took good care of the
graduate schools, and did something else that wanted doing;
there was the matter of housing the young men."

"Mr. Lowell once told me with pride," said Mrs. Whitehead,
"that when he was a boy of sixteen here in Harvard, walking
down there on the then undeveloped river flats, he told himself,
'If I ever get power here, I shall do two things: bring the
college down to the river, and break the Gold Coast' [1]—and
he added, 'I have done both.' "

"In the nineteenth century," said I, "we modelled our
university system after the Germans': in the twentieth, we
appear to have begun copying the English. I wonder what our
own is to be. . . ."

"I am not one of those who look down on what is being done
at the big state universities in the Mid and Far West. There you
get more attempt at co-ordination between learning and practical life. I think Hutchins, at Chicago, was quite wrong in
ridiculing them for their courses in practical techniques. Some
of the courses he named 'household techniques' may have been
silly courses—that I don't know—but the principle is not. Here,
in the East, the sciences do better than the humanities because

---

[1] Dormitories on Mt. Auburn Street for rich men's sons.

there is laboratory work, something to be done, tested, made accurate, not left hanging in the air. . . ."

"Mr. Lowell's pronounced fostering of the 'Department of History and English,' is, as I understand it, an attempt to do something of the sort Oxford does in 'Greats,' in English. But the question remains, how to relate it to practical life."

"Mind you," said he, "I don't say that Greek and Latin aren't excellent for those who can catch hold of their meaning; but I do say that, in America, where you are so removed from immediate contact with the ancient and mediaeval civilizations, it takes more imagination—to get the substance of those older worlds out of books—than all but a few students have. Your friends in Oxford—Sir Richard Livingstone, for example —read Greek and Latin always with an eye to 'How does this affect our life of today? How can we utilize it for the modern world?' "

"Sir David Ross, who was here at Christmas, was speaking of someone's strictures against the American universities— Abraham Flexner's I think—and said that he wrote and thought as though universities exist for research scholars alone, or, if not that, then to produce them—whereas, said he, the number of students who come to a university who are qualified to become research scholars or scientists are very few; and is the whole university system to be designed for the few?"

The question of Mr. Lowell's deficiencies arose.

"He has defects," said Whitehead. "I have known him very well for years and I can see them. One is, that he doesn't understand timid men. He thinks timidity is cringing."

". . . and barks at the man," supplied Mrs. Whitehead. "Altie, tell Lucien that experience you had with a certain modest gentleman who wanted to lay a case before Lowell. . . ."

Fearing that he would not, she did. The man had come to Whitehead saying, "I can't take this to Lowell. He will shout me down. Could you?" "No," said Whitehead, "but I will go with you." He did. Three times, Lowell, irritated by the visitor's timidity, began bawling at him, and thrice did White-head raise his hand and say, "Wait!" The visitor finally got his case stated, and, the mentor being Whitehead, Lowell did not take offence.

"He is the queerest of democrats," said Mrs. Whitehead. "He cannot practise democracy personally but he does believe in it passionately."

"And," continued her husband, "his judgments are states-manlike."

This led into a discussion of Boston as a dwindling Yankee island in an Irish sea.

"They don't mix—these Yankees," said Whitehead, his eyes twinkling with inward amusement. "Only this very afternoon I was in a group of them, including Lawrence Lowell, Lawrence Henderson, and John Livingston Lowes—the last a New Englander at least by assimilation—and you never would have imagined, *you never would have imagined*, from a single word they uttered that they were living in the midst of a community of a million and a half people, at least seventy per cent of whom are Irish Catholics."

I told him how Brüning, sometime Chancellor of Germany, had said during a conversation at Dr. Hans Zinsser's that education should be reserved for an elite.

"Until fifty years ago in England," said Whitehead, "it was confined to a small upper layer, and no one thought it amiss that the mass of the people should be illiterate. Now we take literacy for granted. My father had the running of the village school when schooling was first made compulsory. He encountered the stiffest opposition. The villagers had not been educated and they did not want their children to be educated."

"There was a sudden and immense trek to education in this country after the World War, which has continued ever since," I remarked. "By 1926 it was unmistakable, and it kept right on through the depression. With it has come a higher regard for the teacher."

"In the early nineteenth century in America, as I understand it," said Whitehead, "the teacher, and scholar, and professor were looked up to. They were Unitarians and had a nimbus of religious awe. But as the century wore on, that wore off. Unitarianism was a religion not of 'one God,' but of 'one God at most,' if not of 'one God, if that. . . .' "

"And also," said I, "as the continent was opened, the feeling was at the turn of the century that if a man was what he ought to be, he would make a fortune. This was what made William James call success the 'Bitch Goddess.' That worship is not as prevalent now."

"There are still 'escapists' in your faculties," said Mrs. Whitehead.

"I don't deny that. But men of first-rate ability now not only go into teaching, but are respected for so doing."

A paragraph in Whitehead's "Appeal to Sanity" prompted me to ask again if any state had ever permitted adequate expression to the creative impulses of man. Time and again we see the heads of states, themselves humane men, acting on behalf not of a society's creative impulse but its possessive instincts:

"Herbert Hoover, a Quaker, fed milk to Belgian babies; Herbert Hoover as President of the United States had the war veterans of the Bonus Army bombed out of Washington by tear gas. What is this profound dichotomy?"

"The milk for Belgian babies didn't necessarily imply humanitarian sentiments on his part," said Whitehead. "It was merely an organization job which the sentiment of his time had adjudged had to be done and he was engaged to do it. Quaker, yes; but unimaginative. In his original function as an engineer, his job was to get minerals from mines somewhere in the interior down to tidewater. Such men don't think in terms of human values or human well-being; those items, if they enter at all, come in incidentally to the main object, namely: that of taking up the metal from one place and laying it down in another. They keep their minds fixed on that. . . . When it came to getting the Bonus Army out of Washington, there you had a situation that wanted to be handled very delicately, and he showed how heavy-handed he really was. . . ."

"Then let me cite another instance. In 1914, we had an 'incident' with Mexico. Something provocative happened in the harbour at Tampico, first a squabble, then a dispute over an 'insult' and a demand that the Mexicans apologize and salute our flag. The affair kept worsening, the North Atlantic fleet was ordered to the coast of Mexico, public feeling was inflamed (or, at least, the press vociferated) and President Wilson ordered the Navy to attack and capture Vera Cruz. They did, and seventeen boys were killed, sixteen marines and one sailor. (Two more died of wounds a few days later.) Only half a dozen years before that, Mr. Wilson, instead of being President of the United States, had been a college president, at Princeton, a humane gentleman, like any of your colleagues here, who would have been distressed if seventeen boys in his freshman class had died of an epidemic. The bodies were brought to the Brooklyn Navy Yard on an armoured cruiser, and the coffins each covered with a flag were rolled out on the parade ground on caissons. The President came from Washington to deliver the funeral speech. He said he envied those dead young men. It was Wilson the official who had given the order for them to attack; it was Wilson the man who had to look at the seventeen coffins. Remember, this was in May 1914, and next to no one foresaw the World War; our world hadn't then been calloused by years of mass slaughter; such events were still felt normally, and Mr. Wilson was heartbroken. My point is that as President he was required to act on behalf of collective property interests in a manner which, as a man, he never would have entertained. Only a part of the man was acting, as President, because only a part of man is organized in the state."

Whitehead replied that inside the state men pursue numerous

corporate enterprises which do express other aspects of their natures: educational, charitable, creative, artistic, social; and that perhaps the function of the state thus far is to provide conditions of sufficient tranquillity within which those more varied forms of activity can proceed. Already many of them, such as science and education, are international, and supervene the state boundaries.

What he had said in his "Appeal to Sanity" was:

> *Each human being is a more complex structure than any social system to which he belongs. Any particular community life touches only part of the nature of each civilized man. If the man is wholly subordinated to the common life, he is dwarfed. . . . Communities lack the intricacies of human nature. . . . War can protect; it cannot create.*

Later, in our discussion of this, he said:

"The task of government is not to satisfy everybody, but at least to satisfy *somebody*. If it satisfies one reasonably influential class, or perhaps two, they will try to keep it in power; and the more classes it can satisfy the solider it will be. . . . Civilization doesn't break up when only one major activity, or two, go awry. But in our age economics have swollen into these huge corporate enterprises which bring a new form of oppression that wants coping with; and nationalism has got out of hand; and religious faith has gone to pieces . . . and between the lot of them our civilization does seem to be in a bad way."

"The Emperor Domitian's reign gets a bad press from Tacitus, and no doubt deserved it," I said, "but although it is clear that the emperor's ferocity paralysed Roman thought for nearly a generation and none of the patricians could be sure of their lives, still the wheels of common life were kept rolling. Perhaps it was none of his doing, but it was done."

"Tacitus," said Whitehead, "who so abhorred him, I have always suspected of being a conservative who, on behalf of his class, resented Domitian's raising to positions of administrative authority a lot of social nobodies, clever Greek freedmen and the like. . . ."

"If the Jews have done little laughing until comparatively modern times, how about the Romans? One doesn't hear them laughing either, at least not until the second century B.C. In the earlier centuries they were for ever fighting, now with the Celt, again with the Carthaginian; and when the laughter does come; that is, when you begin to get it in their literature, isn't it satirical, or '*Schadenfreude*'? "

"The Romans"—began Whitehead—"They were a queer people . . ." He thought of it, then decided to give it up!

"The Greek gift for laughter, including laughter at themselves," I said, "begins to look the more remarkable, since there was apparently so little laughter in the ancient world."

"But there is less occasion in America," said Mrs. Whitehead, "for you to study the Greeks, for you are like the Greeks yourselves—creating a new world."

"Quite so," said Whitehead. "The last thing the Greeks would have done would have been to read about what another people thought, or said, or did."

By way of a little laughter for ourselves, we fell to recalling our earliest conscious memories. Hers was of "Biting my father's ear and getting well thwacked for it"; his was as a child of three at a Swiss table d'hôte, being very thirsty and drinking glass after glass of water, till an old gentleman sitting opposite said, "Little boy, you shouldn't drink so much water."—"Whereupon I picked up a spoon, threw it, and hit him in the mouth! My father, quite sensibly, did not punish me. Partly he was amused, and partly, I suspect, he thought it served the old fellow right." Whitehead instanced this as an example of "false memory." "It was being retold in my hearing as I grew up until by the time I was nine I could picture the whole scene perfectly, and thought I remembered it."

I told them they must have been violent children.

XV

July 17, 1939

As respite from the sultriness of midsummer in Cambridge, the Whiteheads were staying with Mr. and Mrs. Edward Pickman at Dudley Farms in Bedford. Trained in the law, a naval lieutenant in the war, Pickman is of the family of the historian Motley and has himself turned to the writing of history, *The Mind of Latin Christendom*, published two years ago.

Dudley Farms has belonged to the family since before the Revolution. There is a brick farmhouse, hip-roofed and with the usual four tall chimneys, two each in the end walls, dating from 1795, and the simplicity of the building has been retained although wings and guest houses have been added. The drive to it from the highway is through seemingly interminable woodlands and meadows, a pine grove here, a pond there, and what Concord people call a "bog garden," all amounting to a New Englandish wild park. Up the river to Concord are similar estates almost boundary to boundary along its bank. These neighbours are known as "the river families."

Theodore Spencer was there. This tall, fair, mild-mannered scholar had just figured in an adventure story typical of our time, when anything can happen to anybody. Along with several other members of the Harvard faculty he was suddenly informed by President Conant that his assistant professorship in English, which he had held on a three-year appointment, would not be renewed. Feeling ran high. One of the ablest academic heads in the country had said, "I may not know much about administration, but I doubt if you can break ten men's lives in a forenoon and expect your institution to go on as before," a doubt which events in the next three years justified. The sequence was dizzying. Professor Spencer had been appointed visiting lecturer in English of the University of Cambridge for 1939–1940. When the second world war began, that university, having a visiting lectureship to fill at Harvard, reappointed Spencer to fill it. Back in the bosom of alma mater. Tableau! At the moment, however, this comedy, known to Spencer's friends as one of Life's Little Ironies, had progressed only to the end of Act I. His sense of humour was quite equal to it, though at moments he found it a bit grim.

There were a dozen of us at dinner. The dining-room is an eighteenth-century kitchen, cavernous fireplace and brick ovens. On its outer side the room opens to a lawn, a garden with a round pool under elms, and a peaceful vista of pastures sloping to the placid current of the river, which Whitehead said he was never tired of contemplating.

Conversation was brisk, but since there were many speakers and it went so fast, it can, at the start, only be summarized. What was being said was that in any assemblage of alleged eminence hereabouts you were likely to find that most of them owed their prestige to being not so much creators on their own account as administrators of cultural institutions—a college, a university, a publishing house, a museum, a conservatory of music, a state government, a library, a hospital, a religious society—and the question was raised whether civilization in America had reached a point where it could identify and utilize administrative ability, but not yet genuine "power of origination," Whitehead's phrase.

From here, since the household is musical and there were musicians at the table, the discussion moved to the singular but little-regarded fact that so many, if not most, of the European composers of first rank, from the youth of Bach to the death of Brahms, a span of two hundred years, were men who not only wrought for the most part outside of institutions, but also owed little to formal institutional instruction. This was the more striking since music is the one art-form in which our world, since 1700, has excelled every other epoch. In consequence, well, what? Apparently, that the spring may decline to bubble up through the marble basin prepared for it, and that the wind of creative spirit bloweth whither it listeth.

At this point someone remarked that the year 1859 was a climax of the nineteenth century. The table started rummaging for verifications and brought out quite a list. Darwin's *Origin of Species*; an essay on political economy by Karl Marx; Dickens's *Tale of Two Cities*; George Eliot's *Adam Bede*; George Meredith's *Ordeal of Richard Feverel*; Thackeray's *The Virginians*; Tennyson's *Idylls of the King*; Fitzgerald's *Rubáiyát*; Wagner's *Tristan und Isolde* . . .

(Pause, while the twentieth century tries to match that score.)

Then ensued a discussion of something which seems to fascinate the people of this country—namely, the superiority of uneducated persons. Pickman, from his experience in the navy, had been immensely struck by it, but thought their three weak points were, generally, an inability to see a long way ahead, to take a line and stick to it over a period of years, and a tendency to confuse public questions with personal ones.

"The mass of people probably determines the general direction of society, but its great men give that direction its precise aim," thought Whitehead. "I put it in the metaphor of a ship; the masses are vessel and crew, genius is captain. . . . The supply of babies in any one year in a land as large as the United States must cover a spread of all the potential talents necessary for any kind of cultural development."

"Any *one* year?" asked Mrs. Pickman genially.

"I'll say five," replied Whitehead smiling. "That will make my argument stronger. . . . But obviously conditions may prevent certain types of talent coming to fruition; that of a musical composer, for instance, in the western states during the past century. Clearly, a general has no chance in peace times."

"Grant," said Spencer, "was a failure, addicted to drink, and living in a log cabin outside St. Louis as late as 1859, in that same climacteric year of the nineteenth century. Four years later he was hero of Vicksburg, and nine years later President of the United States."

"There was more than luck in it, though," said Pickman, addressing Whitehead. "Alfred, you have often spoken of the element of luck in careers. . . . Lee had been an honours man at West Point; he had studied the same textbooks as the Northern generals, knew what moves they were likely to make, and beat them. But Grant was unpredictable."

The dinner-table session adjourned to the living-room. This is contrived a triple debt to pay, being also music room and library. It is quite large and high, open beams supporting a stucco ceiling. Draperies are few, so as not to deaden the sonorities, and there is a grand pianoforte. The bookshelves are well-populated, about four thousand volumes. At the inner end is a large fireplace with the usual assemblage of settees, armchairs, and small tables on opposite sides of the hearth; while the walls east and south open to the grounds by large French windows.

Conversation had moved to why nineteenth-century England should have been a time peculiarly favourable to writers of prose fiction, and what a powerful influence they had in imparting to people the unwritten laws.

"*Middlemarch*," said Spencer; "was the first novel I read as a youth which gave me the feeling that I was being treated as a man and paid the compliment of being talked to without sentimental deceit."

"What parts of it?" asked Mrs. Whitehead.

"The Lydgate-Vincy theme, that disastrous marriage."

"We knew them in Cambridge," said she.

"*Knew* them?" (It was a knockdown for me.) "I never heard that she had taken those characters from life!"

"Oh, but didn't she!" Mrs. Whitehead named names. "Everybody knew it."

Spencer raised the question whether George Meredith's one-time pre-eminence is destined to last.

"I think not," said Whitehead.

"What will defeat him?"

"He lived in a high-grade literary set, rather out of the current of events, and evolved those figures out of his cogitations. When a good writer fails, it is likely to be from too great preoccupation with clever literary ideas to the exclusion of the broad common human themes. Take Shakespeare, there is hardly an idea or a situation that isn't commonplace, but the language and imagination make them into something that is superb. There should be broad human subjects of interest to everyone, vividly treated."

"We read aloud in our family," said Mrs. Pickman, "and I find that my young people aren't interested in Meredith, but are in Henry James. They don't find his involved sentences difficult to understand and do follow the involutions of his thought. Within the limits of the smaller field that he tilled, evidently he delved deeper. He explores the individual."

"When first," someone asked, "in history does the individual begin to be prized for his own sake?"

"I would have thought our old friends the apostles," said Whitehead. "But no, that won't do, they were subordinated to a theology."

"Can the Greeks serve us here? That remark of Pericles in the Funeral Speech, 'We have no hard words or black looks for people who enjoy themselves in their own way.' Where does the concept of liberty first arise?"

This flowed into a general discussion, but without much agreement, perhaps because too many disputants were in it. Whitehead remarked that among the eighteenth-century thinkers there was a clear prevision that the tyranny of a majority might be more onerous than that of a despot.

Continuing, Whitehead said, "Historians never sufficiently credit the man who *averts* a catastrophe. I am thinking of Augustus Caesar. It has always been a marvel to me that Rome could produce, just when they were most wanted, two such men of genius as Julius and Augustus. People must have wanted order and civilization in their hearts, for the legions were mostly at the frontiers. Not many troops were required to suppress . revolts at home."

"The Romans had had more than enough of that in the hundred years of civil war," I remarked. "People were in despair; they had been caught in those terrific duels, first between Marius and Sulla, then between Caesar and Pompey, and finally between Antony and Augustus, and it was by no means certain that they could ever be stopped."

"The effort was risen to and they finally were stopped," said Pickman to Whitehead. "I have heard you say, 'Because the Romans were not yet bored with their civilization.' "

"I stick to that," responded Whitehead. "That we are seated here, in the clothes we wear, and uttering some of the thoughts we do, is in part thanks, I believe, to Augustus. He found a way to keep the empire in being by the principate. He gave men of all parties responsible tasks to which they responded. Gaul was quiet, but Germany" (he smiled), "then as now, was the problem."

"They never did pacify it," I said, "and no wonder. The German forest was nine days' march from one end to the other —dark, damp, no roads, no towns, and the tribesmen always ready to pounce. Gaul was culturally centuries ahead of the Teutons. . . ."

"Had the Gauls a literature then?" asked Whitehead.

"I don't remember any. Unless you want to credit the Gauls with Caesar's *Commentaries*. The difference was that in Gaul, Caesar had roads to travel, crops to live on, and cities and property which the inhabitants were forced to make a stand and fight for; but in Germany, the legions had to make their own roads, and carry their own provisions."

"And then," said Whitehead, "came that fearful disaster in Germany, Varus had perished and with him three of the best legions of the Roman army."

" '*Quintili Vare, legiones redde*,' " Pickman quoted the despairing cry of Augustus ("Quintilius Varus, give me back my legions.") and added smiling, "We are still suffering from the loss of those Roman legions in Germany by Varus?"

"I should think it quite probable," replied Whitehead gravely.

XVI

July 18, 1939

THIS morning at ten the Whiteheads were to return to their apartment in the Hotel Ambassador in Cambridge for a night until North came to take them to "Battleship Island" in Lake Sebago, Maine.

Before leaving, Whitehead, coated and hatted, wanted to step out into the field slope above the river for another look at the scene which he has grown so to love. Pickman and I went with him. Standing in the field and looking across the placid landscape, to the sleepy current of the Concord, conversation turned to the question of a poet's rewards.

"It lies in getting down his thought," said Whitehead. "Something which was unformulated, formulated into a stanza, and he thinks, 'There! I have it!'"

"Is applause of much value to the poet?"

"They must have it, I suppose," said he. "How else are they to know if they are effectual? It is idle to pretend that a man lectures as well if half his audience are drowsing. The response is necessary."

"It can also be an intoxicant."

"It is necessary for the secondary artists; the performers and executants," rejoined Whitehead. "But the poet has his in the doing of it. He *knows* when it is good. . . . And how miraculous it is! Even in common speech. I do not mean thoughts we have first carefully formulated in our minds and then given words. I mean quite unconscious thoughts which spring instantaneously from the unconscious into words without any intermediary process being operative that we know of; that is the most amazing thing. It has never been explained, no one knows the connection between these unconscious meditations and their sudden translation into speech."

The talk turned to Goethe:

"It has been occurring to me of late," said Whitehead, "that Goethe's thinking is too special, and that the world would be better off for the sound, sane, sensible, second-rate sentiments of Schiller. They never rise beyond a certain level but they are safe and serviceable."

"Our friend Livingstone," I remarked, "once said to me that he did not care for Goethe because 'he was not a gentleman.' Three years later, in Oxford, I taxed him with it; he burst out laughing, 'Did I say that? I wonder what I meant.' "

"Goethe uncommonly indulged himself in romantic emotions," said Whitehead, "for which specifically I doubt if the world is much better off."

The drive to Cambridge was through a radiant summer morning. They spoke of their regret at having had to give up their Sunday evenings for the students.

"When we first came to Harvard," she explained, "Altie's colleagues in the department said, '*Don't let the students interfere with your work!* Ten or fifteen minutes is long enough for any conference with them. . . .' "

"Mind you," he supplied, smiling with relish, "they were mostly graduate students, with complex psychological problems to discuss."

"How did you get around it?"

"Altie replied in his most mellifluous tones, which always come out when he is particularly determined to have his own way, 'My habits are too formed. I'm afraid I am too old to change my ways. You will have to be patient with me.' "

"I heard of your Sunday evenings years before I knew you, and longed to come."

"Why didn't you?" said she. "We were told no one would come. And the first time no one did—except one Chinese, who stayed till after midnight. We nearly perished! But then they began coming in squads of six, for mutual protection, I suppose. Finally one night they heard me dispute the oracle—on a point where I knew Altie was wrong. We had it back and forth, and finally Altie admitted he was wrong. For some reason —we never knew what—the fame of that travelled. They began to come. I never had more than ninety-odd on any one evening. Next, the Jews heard of it and came in droves. The gentiles stayed away. This lasted two years, we and the Jews having a good time without the gentiles, then the gentiles came again and all was as before. Felix was a great help. He did not talk, but made everyone else talk. My friends couldn't believe that I would not forgo our Sunday evenings for their dinners to famous foreigners, but we never once failed our students."

We had reached the Hotel Ambassador.

"You will come in, won't you?" they asked.

The apartment was in curlpapers for the summer; literally, for during their absence the faithful Mary and John, who have been with them, she for nineteen years, and he for nearly a decade, had dusted all the books and put them back on their shelves covered over with newspapers. Everything smelt fresh and clean. They went around sniffing and exclaiming their pleasure.

"You will stay and have a chop with us?" she asked.

Getting back from the country to an apartment on a July day which by now was sultry turned into a festive occasion. While the promised chops were being cooked by Mary, we sat in his study, a light breeze blowing through.

Europe's fever chart grows steadily worse, and we fell to comparing the behaviour of the fascist dictators to the mad tyrants in Greek tragedy:

"Hitler never would have heard of the Greek doctrine of 'Hybris' and 'Nemesis,'" I said, "and it would mean nothing to him if he had, but the other man has read."

"He has read Machiavelli," said Whitehead, "and

Machiavelli wrote the rules for a short-term success, of from five to fifteen years."

This led to a discussion of the life span of institutions, and he said:

"The universities are now having a great period, but universities may make themselves as great nuisances as did the monasteries, and for much the same reasons."

"They already have the choice sites," said his wife.

We talked about the abuse of "research" and I cited John Burnet's address on March 12, 1904, at St. Andrews; that the people who talk most about "research" are not those who have done any; it has vulgarized the word and made it offensive to many people. We hear of the "environment of research," "research scholarships," and the like, as if it were all a question of money, but he doesn't suppose that any of the greatest discoveries have ever been paid for at all, and certainly they have all been made by men who had no thought of being paid for them.

"You have heard me criticize the timidity of scholars," said Whitehead. "I think the value of textual criticism is about used up—the immense labour that has gone on since the Renaissance to clear up the classical texts. That has been done. We know now about what the man said. But they will go on re-re-refining, when there is no more value in it."

"Why should science be able to take such leaps, as it has done in the last century, even the last forty years, when the humanities advance so slowly? Are we really much ahead of Plato and Aristotle there?"

"In the eighteenth century," he answered, "(I speak of England where I know what I am talking about) you could follow Rome and Greece of their best ages. The social structures were similar enough for historical precedents to be of some practical value: you still had the mob and the aristocrats. If it was a question of governing a colonial empire, India, you could still follow your Roman model; if a colonial governor was

brought to trial for maladministration—Warren Hastings—
you had Cicero's orations against Verres for his rapacious
governorship in Sicily. . . . Even in the nineteenth century
the Graeco-Roman model could still be fairly closely patterned
after. But now, in the twentieth, this new technology has so
altered the moral values, or the social relationships, that a
much more searching and subtle readjustment of the traditional classic models to modern needs is wanted."

"Well, what is the effect of these scientifically schooled men
on governing the British Empire likely to be?"

"We are sending out as colonial administrators men trained
not in the old humanistic tradition, but products of the scientific schooling. They are just as good intellects, but is their
training as happy? I doubt if they will bring as sensitive an
understanding to the emotional set-up of the peoples they
must rule."

"The Roman Catholic Church is an instance," said I, "of
an institution with an immense experience in governing which
has profited by the learning of the ancient world."

"It is an institution which has learned how to manage
successfully in a monarchical society ruled by an aristocracy,
and when it is proposed to alter that society, to liberalize it on
the side of republicanism or democracy, the Church is generally
found resisting the change. Just now, when certain European
governments are off their heads, the Church sees, or thinks
it sees, an advantage on the side of the fascist dictatorships
as against the kind represented by Stalin. I think they are
mistaken."

"A sociologist of my acquaintance (he is distinctly on the
socialist side) has told me that he believes Catholicism will
survive communism either by adjustment with it or by winning
over it, and this largely because the Marxists wilfully blind
themselves to the emotional needs of average humanity, which
the Church does gratify."

"Catholicism," said Whitehead, "is successful in producing

rather a fine type of woman, but is not so happy with the men. The men have a need to shake off something which the Church hangs on them, and unless they do, they are ineffective as thinkers. If they remain within the Church dogmas they are always fearful of thinking some thought that will conflict with them. The Church, I think, could safely be more venturesome with its list of permitted books than it is. Emerson would really do their people no harm."

XVII

December 15, 1939

MEANWHILE, the second world war had begun. This was my first evening with the Whiteheads since that event in September. One still approached the subject cautiously with anybody, for feeling ran high and unpredictably. Not here, however. We came to it at once:

"I am firmly convinced," said he, "that America should keep out. You need about fifty years to settle and adjust certain domestic problems which you now seem well on your way to do. If you came in and were deeply involved, it might result in a permanent injury to the future of the world. If we won through your help, as the last time, the settlement arrived at through your presence might lose equilibrium after your withdrawal; it is better for Europe to find its own equilibrium."

"But if we are beaten," said she, "you are bound to come in, for otherwise you will have the Nazis in Canada and South America."

"I doubt," said he, "if the world has ever had suffering on such an enormous scale as this."

"You surprise me. Not Rome under the bad emperors?"

"The suffering and anxiety there were largely confined to the upper classes; but, well, yes, I suppose the suffering of the immense slave population on which that society rested must have been enormous."

"The historian Priscus tells of his visit to the camp of Attila's Huns, passing through territories where whole communities had committed suicide at their approach, arrived at their camp, finding those selfsame warriors full of enthusiasm and singing songs about their own virtues. . . ." (I had intended to relate this to the quantitative aspect of human suffering, when my mind lost the thread. I said so, and said it had been happening to me frequently of late.)

"I am relieved to hear you say so," said he, "for mine does the same and I was attributing it to my age."

"It is fatigue, rather, I think. The consciousness of the war is always there; we are forced to rethink ordinary thoughts with reference to it; often we do this unconsciously, but the effort after a while is exhausting. It is a subconscious drag."

"For a while after the war started," said he, "I was able to do nothing; it was constantly in my thoughts, but now of late I have absorbed it into my mental processes, and I am beginning to work again."

"Scott Nearing, who breakfasted with me this morning (he is one of the war-horses of American liberalism), says the problem of our time is how to live well in a decaying society. I am not so sure. Certainly we do live in a contracting economy, but may not the impact of this scientific technology, and the violence and confusion engendered by it, bring about a re-integration of our society? Better not despair prematurely— not that I suggest that any of us are likely to do so. But every great age, fifth-century Athens, Augustan Rome, the Renaissance, the Reformation, the French Revolution, was preceded or accompanied by violence and upheaval; Persian war in Greece, Roman civil wars before Augustus, and so on. . . . Isn't it too soon to judge? And can we be surprised at what has happened when we think of the mechanical and intellectual changes since the turn of the century?"

"I have lived three distinct lives in this single span," said Whitehead; "one from childhood to the first world war; one from 1914 to my residence in America in 1924; and a third here since 1924. The first seems the most fantastic; in those years from the 1880's to the first war, who ever *dreamed* that the ideas and institutions which then looked so stable would be impermanent?"

"Although I was a little boy when you were already a man grown, that world of the 1890's seems to swim in a golden haze of mythological idyl."

"Fifty-seven years ago it was," said he, "when I was a young man in the University of Cambridge. I was taught science and mathematics by brilliant men and I did well in them; since the turn of the century I have lived to see every one of the basic assumptions of both set aside; not, indeed, discarded, but of use as qualifying clauses, instead of as major propositions; and all this in one life-span—the most fundamental assumptions of supposedly exact sciences set aside. And yet, in the face of that, the discoverers of the new hypotheses in science are declaring, '*Now at last, we have certitude*'—when some of the assumptions which we have seen upset had endured for more than twenty centuries."

"Is that a reason why you are at pains to use a new terminology for your own concepts?"

"You have noticed that, then?"

"I have noticed that I can understand the first third and the last third of your *Adventures of Ideas* and of your essay on the Harvard Tercentenary, but that in the middle third I bog down. Is the middle third over the head of a layman who is willing to keep rereading it?"

"No. I don't think so. I write for the layman, and in so doing I avoid the technical language usual among philosophers."

"The philosophers don't like him for it," said his wife, "though they have been very sweet about it."

"But I am convinced," said he, resuming, "that what

philosophers should do is relate their thoughts to the needs of common life. And there is another thing they need to do. When you consider how at pains men of science are to base their hypotheses on carefully criticized assumptions—how they set up tests to control experiments—then consider how the fundamental concepts of even the greatest philosophers in the past must have been largely conditioned by the necessarily ephemeral environmental relationships in which they lived. The scandal is how unhesitatingly later thinkers have accepted their conclusions without pausing to re-examine them in terms of changed social conditions."

"A striking example of it," said I, "is Aristotle's *Politics*. They must have been based on the fundamental assumption that the city-state is the regnant political form, and that, too, in an age when it was already being outmoded and about to be supplanted by military monarchies on a model derived from the conquests of Alexander the Great, his own pupil."

"That is an excellent example of what I mean. There is an enormous need for philosophics to be rethought in the light of the changing conditions of mankind."

"How much of this can be done by intellect alone?"

"I doubt if we get very far by the intellect alone. I doubt if intellect carries us very far. I have spoken of direct insights. The longer I live the more I am impressed by the *enormous*"— he urged his voice into emphasis, and narrowed his eyelids— "the unparalleled genius of one philosopher, and that is Plato. There seems hardly an insight that he has not had or anticipated; and even after you have allowed, as I was saying a moment ago, for the modifications introduced by changed social conditions since he thought and wrote, and the consequent variations which must be made, still in essence the most of it stands. He came face to face with these realities, truths not directly apprehensible by the average man, then by a marvel of subtlety and dialectic, whittled them down to a form in which they could be grasped by the educated Athenian of his day."

It was by now about half past ten. The tray of hot chocolate was brought in. We got on the question whether English Methodism had had any economic determinant.

"Not a bit, I think," said Whitehead. "In John Wesley you had that very unusual combination; a man of spiritual insight coupled with great organizing ability. He organized as naturally as he breathed. I owe to my friend Elie Halévy one of the most penetrating observations on English history that I have ever heard; namely, that the French revolutionary ideas, especially Jacobinism, were prevented from crossing the English Channel by the religious idea of the Wesleyans, who looked upon the Jacobins as godless. The revolutionaries were, as you remember, deists—Robespierre, Saint-Just, and that lot—but to a Methodist that was as good as nothing at all. Then when, at the development of the industrial age, the rich middle-class families began to marry into the aristocracy, it did a singular thing—that mixture gave an aristocracy, almost for the first time in history, a religious tinge which coloured the whole of English political life in the nineteenth century."

"Romain Rolland in *Jean-Christophe* [1] makes someone say that what has made the English so formidable is that they have been for centuries a nation of Bible-readers."

"That sounds more like a literary idea than a historical force." He considered it doubtfully, then said, "The Bible excels in its suggestion of infinitude." Suddenly he stood and spoke with passionate intensity, "*Here we are with our finite beings and physical senses in the presence of a universe whose possibilities are infinite, and even though we may not apprehend them, those infinite possibilities are actualities.*" He remained standing a moment,

---

[1] "England makes me shudder when I think that her people have for centuries been nourished on the Bible. . . . I'm glad to think that there is the dike of the Channel between them and me. I shall never believe that a nation is altogether civilized as long as the Bible is its staple food."

"In that case," said Christophe (a German), "you will have to be just as much afraid of me, for I get drunk on it. It is the very marrow of a race of lions. Stout hearts are those that feed on it. Without the antidote of the Old Testament the Gospel is tasteless and unwholesome fare. The Bible is the bone and sinew of nations with the will to live."—*Jean-Christophe: The House*, Romain Rolland.

absorbed in his own thought, then reseating himself continued, "The trouble with the Bible has been its interpreters, who have scaled and whittled down that sense of infinitude into finite and limited concepts, and the first interpreter of the New Testament was the worst, Paul."

"Do you happen to have read Nietzsche's *Antichrist*?"

"No."

"It sounds more violent than it is, though it is vigorous enough. To my astonishment, he is rather tender toward Jesus, says there was only one Christian and he died on the cross. But Saint Paul certainly does catch it."

"One has to speak of the end of Christianity in terms of a thousand years," he said, smiling, "but it has assumed so many forms in its history that I often speculate on its taking a new and perhaps final form here in America, coalescing with your democratic idea of life. With all its limitations, life in America is better and kinder than anywhere else on earth that I have ever heard of in history. But the clergy have lost their hold. In America a man in trouble now goes to his doctor, he would not think of telling his parson, saving here or there when his parson is an exceptional individual. In England the man people went to in trouble was the old family solicitor; you get that in English fiction; he is a familiar figure there. The problem in religion is to link finitude to infinitude. It is significant that people no longer believe in heaven."

"What would *you* find to do in a Christian heaven?"

"I would far rather go to Limbo, where I could meet the Greek philosophers and Roman statesmen and exchange ideas."

"How," asked Mrs. Whitehead, "could a person beguile the mortal tedium of heaven? At least as it is generally depicted, an oratorio in costumes."

"Something needs to be found to take its place," said he.

"Might not some form of creativity be what is wanted?"

We discussed that. He said:

[131]

"Sir Richard Livingstone wrote me that to him the most significant sentence in my *Aims of Education* was the one that says the common man needs to be convinced of the importance of the work he is doing."

"Of his function, not the importance of himself," said Mrs. Whitehead.

"Similarly, the central problem in modern philosophy is how to relate the one and the many," Whitehead resumed. "Plato talks about that. He was right about so many things and sometimes also dreadfully wrong. The modern tendency is to say, 'I am happy *now*. The future does not matter!' but the 'now' is meaningless without a significant future. What is wanted is to relate all the 'nows' with the future."

"What," asked Mrs. Whitehead, "is the distinction between intelligence and ability? I have the idea that we are all delighted to find intelligence in a child or an adolescent but that if we are still admiring it in an adult there is something wrong."

"Isn't there a character in one of Dickens's novels who is always, to the end of his days, spoken of as 'a promising young man'? I suggest that intelligence is quickness to apprehend as distinct from ability, which is capacity to act wisely on the thing apprehended. But what I have been burning to ask is, What do we mean when we say that a person has depth? We know what we mean but can't put it into words."

"Precisely not," said Whitehead, "for depth is the power to take into account all those factors in a situation which cannot be adequately verbalized."

"When they are verbalized," said she, "they flatten out. It is the ability to see around things, and to see them in all their relationships."

"Are we to suppose that it is inherited or acquired?"

"Acquired? No," said she. "Inherited, yes; but developed."

"You get the best ability," said Whitehead, "from children reared in an economic status without luxury, which admits them at an early age to the society of people responsible for a community. The community may be a big one but needn't be; merely responsible persons doing public work. That is one. The other needn't even be in a comfortable economic position, but the child must be born with or reared in ideas strongly moral or religious."

"Your moral and religious senses are what have served you, Altie. You got them from your parson father."

"America," said he, "was founded by people of both these groups, with social responsibility and moral sense. It has often seemed to me that that was why the eighteenth century in England was so flat, the vivid people had come over here in the seventeenth. France did better in the eighteenth. And the principal result of the French Revolution was the American Revolution. It failed in France but in America it succeeded."

This led to a remark about the lack of enthusiasm in Harvard, as distinguished from the tone of the Midwest, and especially among Harvard undergraduates, where enthusiasm was socially bad form. He said it was lacking from the Boston and New York sons of prosperous families and in one-third of the undergraduates, that another, the middle third, are neutral as always, but that the final third have it, boys largely from smaller towns and more remote places. As for the faculty he admitted that the tone of many of them was set up by the upper-class boys. He thought they do not have voice enough in the government of American universities, but they never have had, in contradistinction to England, where they *are* the governing body. Here, it is every professor for his department; at Trinity you had some of that too, but at the bottom they were all one in wanting Trinity to be a place of lively educational value. When London University was being assembled from schools widely sundered, one of the stipulations was that the faculty have a voice in the management of the institution.

"England has evolved its university system. I often wonder how long will it take us to evolve one peculiarly adapted to our own needs."

"The university system in England has changed momentously since 1900," he said. "Before that, you had Oxford, Cambridge, Edinburgh, Glasgow and St. Andrews. Since then all these others have sprung up." He named half a dozen.

Into the discussion then came the question of how to keep thought from freezing into static ideas, and how easy it is for scholarship to wither into dead learning. When the Senior Fellows were last choosing from among the candidates for the Junior Fellowships, he said a young archaeologist had read a learned paper to the committee on whether a certain excavated pillar was dated wrongly three years one way or the other!

"(And Ferguson sat chin-on-left-hand scowling concentration, (and Chase sat chin-on-right-hand scowling concentration, (and Lowes sat chin-on-both-hands scowling concentration, (and all the while it didn't matter one way or the other.) But a young fellow named Charles Moore [1] presented a paper on Sophocles which was so good that if it wasn't true of Sophocles, it *ought* to have been."

"How old is he?"

"About twenty-two, I should say."

"That seems young to understand so much about Sophocles."

"Perhaps he doesn't; but two of us said he should get in if over our dead bodies."

From here Whitehead turned the subject to Boston newspapers:

"The *Herald*," said he, with a slightly heightened sparkle, "gives the point of view of the prosperous businessman admirably—perhaps too admirably—but if you want to know what New England of all classes is thinking—and I do want to know —it is the *Globe* that you must read. We hazard a guess that a good many of the editorials on foreign relations, especially those about British foreign policy, are written by an irate Irishman."

---

[1] Mr. Charles Moore did understand some very remarkable things about Sophocles.

"They are."

"He is quite within his rights; only he gives undue importance to a phase of Tory influence which annoys him."

"His grandfather was knocked down and beaten by British troops in Ireland. The memory was still vivid with his grandmother when she told him about it. He is a man of extraordinary ability, with high principles which are kept in daily working order."

Without asking who had written it, they spoke of the editorial on music published November 24th. In it I had said that great music, even more than great literature, is intelligible to children, since it speaks directly to the emotions, the imagination, and the intuitions, faculties which in childhood are often more acute than they are when we have grown up, and that no blunder could be more stupid than to suppose children do not sense grandeur in the arts. While agreeing with it in the main, he said:

"Not all children respond to music. About fifty per cent, I should say. It would have been better to qualify. Mind you, I agree with your main contention, that all children have a right to be presented to these major experiences, in literature, the arts, nature; they can then select those which will be fruitful to them. I was especially struck by your remark that the charm of good music is that it surprises the ear by the unexpected interval, and that the element of surprise is permanent, no matter how familiar the music may become. It is a principle which carries over into other affairs of life; what we crave is the element of freshness, and some of the most vivid experiences seem to have in them an element of freshness which is perpetual. This carries over, too, into related areas of experience, so that when we are freshened in one area it freshens us for others."

"My home environment," I said, "a small town, was so aesthetically barren that we were forced upon books and music (apart from friends, and what beauty of nature there was) in order to keep our souls alive."

"His, too," said Mrs. Whitehead, "a country parsonage, was a milieu where the aesthetic was not only absent, but held in contempt."

"Your saying that this freshening of the whole nature by a novel experience, of which music is an example, carries over into other affairs of life reassures me after what Bliss Perry [1] said about this same subject: 'I don't see how you can transform sound-patterns from music into moral concepts.' "

"But that is exactly what music does do," said he, "revivifies the whole nature."

"How can anybody be the same person after a close knowledge of Beethoven's last quartets that he was before?"

This led Whitehead to speak of the striking difference between the seventeenth-century poets in England and those of the eighteenth. "With the eighteenth-century men you never find anything in their poetry that you don't think you could have written yourself; but the charm of the seventeenth-century English poetry is that you come upon something totally unexpected and say, 'There! It is inconceivable that I could ever have thought of this!' "

It was growing late, and for a little while by tacit consent we let the conversation drift.

His *Aims of Education* is out of print in America, and I told him that people I know keep complaining to me that they cannot obtain it. He said it was not out of print in England, "But Macmillan burned their unsold copies without offering me an opportunity to take them off their hands, a performance which made me indignant."

"For a distinguished firm, they certainly do some strange things—the mud-coloured binding, for example, of the *Cambridge Ancient History*, whose English edition is nobly bound.

[1] Bliss Perry, university professor, author. Born Williamstown, Mass., 1860. A.B. Williams College 1881, A.M. 1883. Professor of English at Williams 1886–1893; Princeton 1893–1900; editor *The Atlantic Monthly* 1899–1909; professor of English literature Harvard 1907–1930.

I bitterly regret not having bought mine in the English format."

"I am considering republishing my *Aims of Education*. Tell me what you think of omitting those last two chapters."

"Considering that I couldn't understand them I am a poor one to ask."

"On the contrary, you are just the one."

"The first eight chapters are electrifying. How many of my friends have told me so, Livingstone, for one. Why not omit the last two and substitute your essay on the Harvard Tercentenary?"

"I had thought of that, too; but would the book be long enough?"

"Haven't you something else that would fit in?"

"I have a good deal of unpublished work. . . ."

Mrs. Whitehead suggested various papers that might fit.

"I also have an idea of a volume of reminiscences," said he.

We discussed format, and that it might be wise to keep an eye on publishers about cover designs, in view of some dire experiences.

"When the cover Macmillans were going to put on his *Adventures of Ideas* arrived," said Mrs. Whitehead, "I was aghast."

"What was it?"

"A moon, and stars, and rays of light."

"What was the notion?"

" 'Adventures,' I suppose, and cosmic space."

"Jazzing Whitehead!" said I. "Do you suppose the designer had read the book?"

"Probably no more than heard the title," said she.

As the evening drew to a close he returned to the influence of the Bible, and to its interpreters:

"Two strains seem to run through Hebrew thought; one, mild, gentle, gracious, sympathetic, and full of insight: Isaiah, Amos, Jesus; the other, harsh, vengeful, humourless, treacherous: the very characteristics of the oriental despot. Both are in Paul, but the second comes out strongly. The Semites are harsh. I often wonder if there wasn't an infiltration of Hellenic blood in the Galileans to account for the graciousness of those peasants and Jesus. For if you follow the interpretation of the Gospels in their first four or five centuries, you will find that the Christian thinkers on the African shore of the Mediterranean and on to Spain, who were mainly under Semitic influence, are gloomy and harsh; but that the Italian and Gallic interpreters, Gregory the Great and Martin of Tours, were remarkably tolerant. When the issue of persecution of their own sectaries was first raised, these men saw and said that persecution would do more harm than heresy. These two strains in the Hebrew are greed for material gain, and gentleness of spirit; sometimes, in great Jews, you find both strains in one nature. It is the *interpreters* of Christianity that have been its misfortune."

XVIII

April 22, 1940

WHITEHEAD had asked me to one of the regular Monday evening dinners of the Junior Fellows at Eliot House. On the drive down there from the Hotel Ambassador in a taxi, I asked if he had read the narrative by the British seaman from the destroyer that was sunk at Narvik.

"No," said he, "in a time like this, news that is a week old might as well be about the battle of Marathon." He said it genially, but the remark shows how keenly aware he is of situations affected by changes wrought through time.

At Eliot House we crossed a court and entered by a side door under a bracket lamp held in a wrought-iron lantern. The spring evening was mild and a fine mist was falling, borne in by an east wind off the sea. The forsythia shrubs were in golden blossom.

President Emeritus Lowell and Lawrence Henderson [1] were already there in the common-room with Sam Morison,[2] who considerately let me read a list of the twenty-four Junior Fellows and their subjects of study. Twenty-four names and twenty-four subjects of study are not memorized at a glance, but some of it at a pinch may come back.

"Go easy on the preprandial sherry," Morison warned me *sotto voce*, "it's not much good. Go strong on the Burgundy during dinner. Henderson chose it and he knows wine. Shun the after-dinner port. Lowell gave it, and he knows nothing about wine. It is merely a fortified California port, but the Fellows must drink it up. There are two views about it: one is to drink it up at once and get it over with; the other is to go slow, because Lowell might give us some more."

Mr. Lowell is of course quite deaf, and, as he finds it easier to speak than to be spoken to, conversation with him is, if he likes, allowed to become a monologue.

He was discussing how the English manage their political opposition:

"Party lines are much stricter there, and if you are in the government you must vote with it. The historian Lecky told me, 'I am perfectly free to vote against the government of which I have been a member for eighteen years.' I asked him, 'How often have you voted against it?'—'Twice,' said Lecky."

Continuing the subject of a political opposition Mr. Lowell adduced the Report on German Atrocities in Belgium headed by Lord Bryce which, by a singular coincidence, was made public by the British government on May 12, 1915, five days

[1] Lawrence Joseph Henderson, biological chemist. Born Lynn, Mass., 1878. A.B. Harvard 1898, M.D. 1902; Sc.D. Cambridge 1934. Lecturer biol. chem. Harvard 1904–1905, instructor 1905–1910, asst. prof. 1910–1919, professor since 1919. Senior fellow, Society of Fellows, Harvard since 1933. Died 1942.

[2] Samuel Eliot Morison, historian. Born Boston, Mass., 1887. A.B. Harvard 1908, Ph.D. 1912, Litt.D. 1936; M.A. Oxford 1922. Instructor and professor of American history at Harvard since 1915. Author, *Maritime History of Massachusetts*, 1921; *Oxford History of the U.S.*, 1927; *Tercentennial History of Harvard Univ.*, 1930–1936; *History of U.S. Naval Operations in World War II*, 1947——Rear Admiral U.S.N. (retired).

after the sinking of the S.S. *Lusitania* by a German submarine, when public opinion in the United States was acutely inflamed. He said the report was an example of the mischief that could result from not appointing "an *advocatus diaboli*. . . . You don't get at the truth without a cross-examination of the evidence," he concluded.

(Mindful of Sacco and Vanzetti, I thought, "Nor sometimes with it.")

He moved on to the advisability of due postponements before naming avenues and public places after the illustrious. One of the young men said:

"Didn't the French have a rule not to name a street after a personage until he had been dead ten years?"

"The Catholic Church," said Mr. Lowell, "is even more deliberate: before canonizing it may wait a hundred. . . ."

A gong was struck. It was a signal to go into the dining-room.

The rooms are rather sumptuous. I had first seen them when they were being built, in 1930, but at that time their destined use was not allowed to be known, since the money was not yet available for the foundation of the society. (When Mr. Lowell died in 1943 it was revealed that he had endowed it: ". . . there being no visible source of the necessary funds, I gave it myself, in a kind of desperation, although it took nearly all I had.") As organized on December 8, 1932, there are two-dozen Junior Fellows and nine Senior Fellows. The Junior Fellows are men between twenty and thirty years old, chosen by the Senior Fellows from among the recent graduates of American universities for their promise of exceptional ability to enrich knowledge and thought. They are elected for three years, with prospect of renewal for another three. Given their board and lodging, they are paid a stipend and set at liberty to pursue any intellectual adventures that they find interesting and important. The plan [1] originated by a species of spontaneous combustion

[1] It is fully explained in *The Society of Fellows* by George C. Homans and Orville T. Bailey, published by Harvard University, Cambridge, Massachusetts.

with Lawrence Henderson, Alfred Whitehead, and President Lowell, and it derives somewhat from the prize Fellows of Trinity College in Cambridge University and at All Souls College, Oxford, and the *Fondation Thiers* in Paris.

Both rooms are panelled in oak from floor to ceiling, their tall windows flanked by fluted Ionic pilasters and draped with heavy brocades in a colour to harmonize. The chimney-pieces are similarly framed in pilasters with overmantel panels and ornate carving. The oval table from which sherry is served before dinner is the Breakfast Table at which the Autocrat presided, and on the walls hang oil portraits of eighteenth-century worthies, one by John Singleton Copley.

The dining table is *U*-shaped and, with ease of conversation in mind, narrow enough to permit of give and take across its candle-lighted board. The silver candlesticks are of a design which Lawrence Henderson found at Névache, France, at the time when he first began thinking of the plan of such a society. Mr. Lowell, as chairman, sits at the head of the table in a high-backed chair of carved oak, the other diners have arm-chairs of the traditional Harvard design. The port coasts along the board in two decanters set in a little silver wagon, suggested perhaps by the silver galleon which sails laden with port over the mahogany at All Souls.

One of the unwritten decrees is that guests and Senior Fellows do not sit side by side. This mixes the Junior Fellows with the older men. Thus in Whitehead's immediate group were Harry Levin,[1] George Homans,[2] Conrad Arensberg,[3] and George Hanfmann,[4] a young German who has been through two revolutions and said it was not until he had been in this country two years that he could believe he was actually safe in saying what he thought.

---

[1] Professor of English, Tutor in the Department of English, and Senior Fellow of the Society of Fellows, Harvard University.
[2] Associate Professor of Sociology, Harvard University.
[3] Associate Professor of Sociology, Columbia University.
[4] Associate Professor of Fine Arts, Harvard University.

The five of us, who were within speaking-range of Whitehead, were discussing whether it would ever again be possible for a single mind to grasp the sum of human knowledge, at least to the extent that Aristotle, Da Vinci, or Goethe grasped that of their own time.

Whitehead said he thought such a grasp necessitated too much reliance on the reports of others and brought it down to a mediocre level:

"Aristotle did harm by allowing people to suppose they knew and understood all about the subjects he discussed, and he certainly didn't help Plato."

"Gilbert Murray said something highly similar about Aristotle—especially when Aristotle came to drama," I recalled. "He was talking about the ecstatic element in the *Bacchae* of Euripides, the Dionysian 'possession,' and said, 'After all, isn't μηδὲν ἄγαν (nothing too much) the motto of a Philistine?'"

"That is it," said Whitehead. "To get really into a subject takes more energy than 'nothing too much,' and a man has to ignore much to get on with something. A certain element of excess seems to be a necessary element in all greatness." And, as an example of the opposite he quoted a remark about someone "who knew forty-one languages and had nothing to say in any of them."

Then he and two physicists fell to discussing the alertness and intuition necessary to a good experiment—how it is "competent work plus a 'happy chance,' or even being aware that something is wrong with the result, the discovery following from having asked, 'What?'"

"The heavy hydrogen," continued Whitehead, "was on several men's plates before another man discovered it. Error itself may be the happy chance."

It was suggested that we were here in the problem of how to keep thought active and living, as in his essay on the Harvard Tercentenary in the September *Atlantic* for 1936. He said:

[142]

"I put the things for the rather simple people at the start, and repeated them at the end, but the serious matter in the middle. And the best thing in it came by accident. The editor sent it back saying that it was a little too short for the run-over page and would I add about a hundred and fifty words? With a transitional sentence I found I had added one hundred and sixty-eight words, about the length of a sonnet, and it was the best in the work. I wonder if you could identify the passage."

"Do you challenge me?"

He smiled and nodded:

"Yes."

"Meanwhile, until I shall have had a chance to re-read it, what do you think of Robert Hutchins's reply to it in the following November issue?"

"Hutchins—whom (mind you) I admire—nevertheless treated me like a lawyer, separated certain of my remarks from their context, and then attacked them. I had admitted that a lot of vocational rubbish is taught, and dismissed it."

There was a lively discussion of how long a man can sustain various forms of mental labour effectually. Evidence came in from first and secondhand. Some of the tall tales about scholars working all hours suggested mere acquisitive learning, since certainly most creative artists seem obliged to content themselves with three or four at a stretch.

One of the Junior Fellows (I think it was George Homans) steered the subject to the writing of history. "Gibbon," said Whitehead, "had the best education of any historian excepting Thucydides; he had belonged to a regiment, captain of Hampshire Militia, and knew what that felt like; he knew the London literary set, Johnson and that lot; he had travelled and knew the Continent; and had been in Parliament and heard the talk of men who governed."

"But they didn't govern very well," said Homans. "The prime minister was Lord North, who lost the American colonies."

"I submit," said Whitehead smiling, "that a man who lost a war was the very most valuable acquaintance for a man who was going to write the *Decline and Fall of the Roman Empire*."

A question arose of what is the difference between active and static thought.

"Static thought," said Whitehead, "is knowing exactly where Shakespeare bagged all his plots, and identifying all his borrowings from Plutarch and Holinshed."

Anxious glances swept round toward Professor Livingston Lowes, as Whitehead had humorously intended they should. Lowes had withdrawn. Then Homans discreetly observed:

"Exit Kittredge!" and everybody laughed.

Kittredge is, of course, the autocrat of that Shakespearean breakfast table, and I have heard Bliss Perry,[1] who knew him for years and liked him, say, "I never knew anyone whom words interested so much and ideas so little."

From static ideas the debate moved to that besetting question, whether the modern world is utterly at the mercy of its novel technological inventions.

"I believe Europe would have got on about as well with its inland waterways and canals as it has with railways," said Whitehead, "but for America the railway came at exactly the right moment to enable you to subdue the continent."

"We had not got very far with it before that," said Homans.

"The railroad was your decisive factor."

"How about the airplane?"

"It will revolutionize life in the backward regions, like interior Asia, the east of Africa, and places like that; your American far north. A new technology first destroys half of an old society then assists at its rebuilding into a new. Its first effect is, however, violently destructive. . . . I say," he broke off, "what do people mean by talking about the future being obliged to pay for the wars of the present?" He drew into it a

[1] See footnote on page 136.

handsome, blond young fellow named Paul Samuelson,[1] of whom he was obviously proud and fond. They went into a learned and fascinating duologue on it, but much too fast to take down by memory.

"It is a metaphor, no more," concluded Whitehead, "and if one were writing a poem on economics, as Lucretius did in *De Rerum Natura*, the metaphor would be superb; but in any economic connotation all that you are saying when you refer to the future as paying for wars of the present is that you are bequeathing to posterity a changed form of society."

The group had lingered until nearly eleven o'clock. One of the Junior Fellows, who drives Mr. Lowell home to Boston, where he is now back in his own town house on Marlboro Street, carried Whitehead and me to the Hotel Ambassador. Lowell got out and assisted Whitehead, a bit officiously, I thought. Evidently someone else thought so too, for when we were back upstairs and settled in our chairs over a pitcher of hot chocolate, Whitehead remarked to his wife, with the faintest twinkle of a smile, and in his most demure tones:

"Lowell helped me out of the car."

"Yes?"

"Do you suppose he thought I needed it?"

"No," said she, with genial asperity. "He was trying to prove that he is a better man than you are, and he's not!"

XIX

November 2, 1940

EVENING with the Whiteheads at the Hotel Ambassador. There were no other guests. The strain of the war had been wearing them. When I arrived, at eight-thirty, Professor Whitehead was having a nap in his study. Mrs. Whitehead told me they had had occasional cablegrams from North, who is in

[1] Professor of Economics, Massachusetts Institute of Technology.

the Foreign Office at Whitehall and has been bombed badly twice.

"We live a double life," said she; "when guests are here, we live in this country; when they are gone, we live in the war."

A few minutes later Whitehead came out. He looked a little dim at first, more bent in figure, and more frail, but after about half an hour's conversation was burning as brightly as ever. I told him:

"Since last September the readers of the *Boston Globe*, though they don't know it, have been getting *Science and the Modern World* morning, noon, and night."

"Tell him how you wrote that book, Altie."

"All my life, from young manhood at Cambridge, then in London, I had been a lecturer on mathematics. At the age of sixty-three in 1924, I came to Harvard to lecture on philosophy for the first time. Of course in all the intervening years I had heard and participated in the philosophical discussions at Cambridge and London and read an occasional paper before the Royal Society; so it was mostly in my head. Then in the autumn of 1924 I was asked, in addition to all my regular lecturing which was in a sense new, to deliver the Lowell Lectures. Three-fourths of the volume as it stands are those lectures; they were written at the rate of one a week as wanted for delivery. . . ."

"At white heat," interjected Mrs. Whitehead.

"And I was never more than one week ahead."

"Do you rewrite much?"

"No. But I write very slowly and elide a good deal."

"Am I right in thinking that such sentences are written only by a mathematician? Your prose is totally unlike anyone else's."

"I do not think in words. I begin with concepts, then try to put them into words, which is often very difficult."

"A corresponding effect is had on the reader; after the meaning of the words has been grasped, their content next seems to lead an existence independent of the printed page, and almost a palpable one. But how had you in your head such material as that striking galaxy of great men in the early 1600's —your 'Century of Genius'?"

He laughed. "Ever since I was a young man, and still, as you may have noticed, if a great name is mentioned which is unfamiliar to me, I look it up, memorize the dates and his form of activity, and thus for any period of history I have an accurate image of the sort of activity which was going on in that time and place. Mind you, it had better be accurate; you had better know exactly whether Marlowe was older than Shakespeare and how *much* older. I discovered, for example, that five of the principal figures in English history overlap in lifetimes: Elizabeth and Cromwell; Pitt, Wellington, and Victoria. . . ."

"Altie, show him your little book," prompted Mrs. Whitehead.

He went into his study and returned with a small volume bound in brown calfskin, the back cover of which was missing. This was presented with an expression of whimsey:

"I picked this up at a bookshop in Cambridge when I was a young man. My only criticism of it is that it includes too many second-rate Englishmen."

I read: *A Brief Biographical Dictionary*, by Rev. Charles Hole, Macmillan & Co. 1866. Its pages presented merely the full name, calling, and dates of birth and death. From it he produced sheets of yellow paper on which he had listed the philosophers from Ionia to modern times, the Roman emperors, "and here," said he, "is a table of the English kings."

"Do you people buy books from catalogues or by seeing them?"

"One goes into a bookshop," said Mrs. Whitehead, "and comes out with a book."

He told of an episode early in their wedded life when they had read a great many books on theology. This study went on for years, eight of them, I think he said. When he had finished with the subject, for he *had* finished with it, he called in a

Cambridge bookseller and asked what he would give for the lot. The figure the bookseller named was so handsome that they felt quite affluent until, at the door, he said, "I shall, of course, credit them to your account." So they went on an orgy of book-buying, and discovered after a while that they had spent about twice what their credit was!

This bookseller was one of those oddities which academic towns still harbour. He was very able, but amusingly conceited, and once told them:

"I have been in Oxford recently and don't think their book-shops are up to ours. I went the rounds and looked them all over —*incog* of course!"

"Nowadays when people have quirks," Whitehead took it up, "they are locked up and the quirks diagnosed by pseudo-scientific names, but we used to have just as many queer people and we called them 'characters' and were proud of them. Take old so-and-so who used always to walk along the street side-wise, hop up, pluck a leaf off a tree, and go on nibbling it." Rising, he impersonated the ancient worthy doing that very thing. "If he had been locked up we should have lost one of our best astronomical textbooks."

This led into the subject of the unsuspected powers in common people.

"As you know," he said, "I admire your American democracy and believe our class-lines in England are a great evil. However, they work in unexpected reversals. I believe there is more genuine respect as between persons of different classes in England (excepting the commercial middle-class pusher, or the social 'bounder') than in America, for there you *know* that your gardener or housemaid hasn't a chance in the world to rise, but here you are so accustomed to the idea that everyone has equal opportunity, whether they have or haven't (and mostly they haven't), that unless you are imaginatively on your guard, you automatically assume, when thinking of a supposed inferior, 'If he were any good he would have done as well as

I have,' which doesn't follow at all. What lets a man up to what is popularly known as the 'top' is often a very narrow range of ability which happens to be wanted in a particular place or time and which is compensated accordingly, but this may have little or no relation to the higher capacities of the human being or even the better powers of the individual so elevated. . . . Very few people are adequately drawn out—some are never drawn out at all, and remain, to all purposes, idiotic; though no one knows what their latent powers might have been. Others are about half drawn out; some happy encounter, some favouring condition elicits their peculiar abilities, but the waste of undeveloped faculties must be tremendous. For the powers of the individual are unique and unpredictable. This has been one of the great discoveries of the human race and it is still proceeding very slowly. It was dimly in the mind of Plato, it was being made by the ancient Hebrews and came into articulation by Christianity. But the Christians did not do much with it for a thousand years, because they thought so many people would be going to hell in the natural course of events that it didn't much matter, and they thus failed to grasp the full implication of the idea."

"In speed and force," I remarked, "a great idea suggests a glacier."

"The average length of time it takes, I think," said he, "for any great discovery in the realm of ideas to pass into general currency or to receive any practical effectuation is a thousand years. This idea of the unique value of the individual hardly obtained any political expression until the eighteenth century and it was then given by the framers of your American Constitution, and has become, I believe, the basic unifying idea of your nation. Writing was an invention which took about two thousand years to make its effect felt. Do you recall how, even in Plato's dialogues, the discussions are seldom if ever about what the participants have 'read' but almost invariably about what they 'remember'? The amount of memorizing must have been tremendous, and one reason for the popularity of verse was that the rhythmical cadence is an aid to memory. But for a long time after writing had been invented it was little more than a keeping of accounts; a business of kings and bankers, promulgating orders and computing moneys. Only when men began putting down their thoughts did the effect of the written word begin to be felt on the intellectual progress of mankind."

"The terrific blackout after the fall of Rome suggests how dependent on written words we had become. It took nearly a thousand years to get some of them back."

"That textual criticism of the classics had to be done from the Renaissance on if the modern world was ever to repossess the culture of the ancient one," said Whitehead, "and done it has been in the five hundred years since 1400 . . . whether Sophocles wrote 'he-she-or-it.' But as to transmitting that possession, I used occasionally in London to go to meetings of the Royal Society, and for dogmatism I may say that I thought them the modern equivalents of the mediaeval Schoolmen."

Somewhat later in the evening when speaking of the Roman Republic in the period of the Civil Wars Whitehead said, "To all appearances that was a society that was going to pieces. If a man, not knowing what the issue of the event was, were to want a period to study in which a civilization was disintegrating, that one would appear to have all the symptoms, and yet there came an Augustus who was able to pull it together. He saw the one class which still had the integrity to administer its affairs, namely the small squires. It wasn't easy to enlist them or to get them accepted by the old patricians, but he was able to effect both."

"Isn't it singular," I said, "how little there is culturally to show for the more tranquil centuries which followed? Isn't Tacitus almost the last great name? Under the Antonines probably the world was better administered than it has ever been before or since, yet in creative achievement it was poor. I suppose there wasn't much liberty."

"Periods of tranquillity," said Whitehead, "are seldom prolific of creative achievement. Mankind has to be stirred up."

At eleven or thereabouts we had chocolate. At parting they said, "Do come often." For a whole evening we had been interested and not thinking of the war.

XX

June 17, 1941

A RADIANT morning in late spring. The windows of their apartment in the Hotel Ambassador were opened wide and a scent of fresh greenery from lawns and foliage swung in on a light breeze. We sat in Whitehead's study, where sunshine poured in cheerfully. Keeping off the subject of the war had gradually become a tacit manoeuvre by common consent. Otherwise, it occupied us throughout most of our waking hours.

He said that the Frankfurters had been there yesterday.

"Whose idea do you suppose it was, the Oxford degree for President Roosevelt?" I asked.

He reflected, "I suppose it was the Halifax-Frankfurter connection."

"Tell him the joke about Halifax that is going around Washington," suggested Mrs. Whitehead.

"Halifax," said he, "is very pious, and they say he spends three days a week with the Almighty, but comes back misinformed!"

A turn of the conversation brought up the topic of what valid basis we have for our concept of human equality. We know that mortals are unlike and unequal, yet we crave that sense of equality.

"It is founded on the infinite potentialities of human beings," said he. "In many the powers are never elicited, or only partly elicited. Yet they are there and we never can be sure what they are. I will give you an example: our maid's husband. He is of

[151]

Scots Highland stock, was a highly skilled workman in the General Electric, some skill which required a most delicate manipulation of machinery, and, as such, one of the highest-paid manual workers in America. Suddenly an invention which could do the same task reduced him to the lowest. He came to us. We discovered that he also had remarkable aesthetic sense."

"When we lived in the house at Canton," said Mrs. Whitehead, "I could send him in town to select draperies and fabrics for me. He worked in our flower garden until ten at night, when I had to forbid him on pain of discharge. He always arranged the flowers in my vases."

Whitehead took it up:

"These qualities are latent until circumstances bring them out. Mind you, I don't say there isn't a lot of stupidity—but imaginative people in the presence of those infinities of possibility prefer to reserve judgment. The combinations haven't been explored."

"The way I phrase it to myself is, that the things we, as human beings, do not have in common, are as nothing to the things that we do have in common."

"That glances in the same direction," said he.

"Coming from a small town to a metropolis, when my bewilderment had subsided, I observed two main facts; one, that the first-rate people were all through society, at bottom and middle as well as top, and regardless of education; and the other, that if they had not been at heart peaceable, there were and are not enough police in the United States to keep them from mutual extermination. Doesn't it suggest that most are men of good will and ask only a set of rules to go by?"

"Men of good will is well put in, for there is a vicious element, both in men and in societies," said he. "It is puzzling enough to know what to do with the individuals; it is enough worse when a whole society becomes infected with evil and runs amuck. Even in a peaceable state we all live under police protection, and force is used to restrain evil-doers. But you notice that when we want to word the issue we resort to extreme cases: the poor girl who is kidnapped and outraged by some ruffian. But who shall say in the borderland cases exactly where the force shall be applied, exactly *where* along the series the police shall be called in, exactly where the law shall be invoked?"

"I have seen my own clan, the middle class, foully in error on that point."

"In England, we get our best morality, our better standards, class for class, from the upper strata of the workers and from the conscientious or the gifted members of the aristocracy. In between, a good many in the professional and commercial classes are unkind, unjust, greedy, crass, and inferior in any true sense of morality. I am very proud of the way England is standing up to this ordeal. North writes me that when the news placards appeared in London saying that Roosevelt's speech of three weeks ago would 'strengthen British morale,' people on the streets merely looked at one another and grinned . . . as if a speech by the American President could affect it. They are fighting either Thermopylae or Marathon: they don't yet know which, but in either case there is not a thought of yielding. And when it is over I think you will see the middle-class morality replaced by a fusion of the other two and a result vastly superior."

"If you asked me where our American morality comes from I would have hard work to answer; we are so diverse of races and traditions."

"I will tell you one thing you do have here," said he, "kindness. The presumption is that all people will treat one another kindly. I have never been in a place where kindness was so general, and I do not know of any society ancient or modern where a similar state of things existed. I would not hesitate to say that the United States is the finest society on a grand scale that the world has thus far produced."

"Let me dispute that: Gilbert Murray said much the same thing to me down here by the Charles in the fall of 1926, and

Livingstone said it to me at New Haven in 1934. To both I made the same reply: we are not under the population pressure, and hence not the economic pressure, of Europe. Kindness costs less here. It is no especial credit to us."

Whitehead replied smiling:

"I state it merely as a fact.

"One mistake I think your Protestant sects did make," he continued; "they were too anxious that nothing be taught that was not so. Now of the thirty-odd sects that have come down to us in the form of religions from the Graeco-Semitic origins, I would take vigorous exception to certain elements in all of them; nevertheless there would remain solid substrata, or, if you like, confluent streams which, blended into a general ethical code, would be invaluable to teach the young. I think the moral unity of England today is based on a few such simple concepts, which are accepted by everyone. The school does best when it inculcates moral precepts which are also accepted and taught in the home. They don't need to be very many nor very complicated; hardly more than rules of thumb so they are basically sound. And that, I think, for the time being has been lost here."

"There is no doubt of it," I said. "One sees it in two obvious ways: the generation now growing up does not recognize either quotations from or allusions to the Bible; and the classical tradition is equally on the wane."

"Poor things," said Mrs. Whitehead, "they know so little about what has happened in the world before them, what people have borne and put up with and lived through, and conquered, that when something goes wrong in their own little lives, they think the universe is shattered and that the only remedy is suicide, however much misery that act may spread around them. . . . A moment ago when you two men were discussing the bases for our craving for human equality, I wanted to exclaim: 'I love you both, but you are both miserable sinners. And it is the usual male sin against the Holy Ghost of trying to reduce the infinite to a neat intellectual formula.' Oh, you strange creatures; will you never learn that our craving for equality comes from the sense of the pathos, the grotesquerie, the humour, the tragedy, the inexplicability of human nature? It won't reduce to a formula. It is simply *there*. We can do nothing about it. We *are* fantastic, we *are* pathetic, we *are* comical, we *are* tragic, we *are* human; and all we can do, if we have an iota of sense, is recognize the fact in a sentiment of equality."

"But that is just what I *was* saying, Evelyn."

"Yes, in your precise logic—when there is nothing logical in it." She shook her head at us severely. "That's how we are all at bottom equal!"

XXI

June 28, 1941

S UMER *is icumen in*, and, going over to Cambridge I had taken to the Whiteheads, for her, two boxes of roses from a neighbour's garden in Marblehead, and to him Sir Richard Livingstone's newly published *The Future in Education*, in which his *Aims of Education* is admiringly quoted.

He was seated in his study. They had been out, over to Harvard Square, to buy a *winter* suit, on the hottest day in June, "and could not get one."

When I confessed to having got one last month, "not a minute too soon," the tailor assured me, he said genially:

"We were a minute too late."

They leave for the month of July with the Pickmans in Bedford. Mrs. Whitehead remarked:

"The atmosphere of the place just suits me, a Catholic household where something is being done about religion, but not by me. It is like that in which I was brought up in Brittany, among Catholics but not a Catholic myself."

"It sounds a little like going to church by radio."

"There must be a place in the next world *in between*," said he, "for such people; not too hot nor too cold; nor as melancholy as Limbo."

"You must mean Laodicea, abhorred by the zealots as 'neither cold nor hot.'"

Returning to church-by-radio, he thought the sonorous voices came over best, though divested of all the ecclesiastical trappings which do lend impressiveness.

"The two most impressive religious services I remember," said he, "were, one, a Low Mass in a cathedral in a city—how bothersome it is to forget names!—on the edge of the Black Forest in Germany. There was an immense concourse of devout people, you couldn't hear a thing that was being said, and it was perfect. You had a sense that the religious office was going on, and you shared it with all those pious people. The other was Quaker; only that service must not go on too long. It was at a school near Birmingham. Several of us had gone down there to deliver lectures, which began at nine o'clock, and every morning for a quarter of an hour before nine, the head of the school gathered us in his study, which was commodious, we had a time of quiet meditation, then, just at the end, he spoke briefly. It had exactly the right effect."

"You are not including the Anglican."

"It is admirable for its purpose; the beautiful ritual, the music, the architecture, the good voices—it has everything except religion. It is not religious, it is sociological."

"Ralph Emerson was exceedingly annoyed by it. He says why in *English Traits*."

"Mind you; I think the Protestant sects lack even that. The Anglican service is a symbol of the aristocracy's responsibility for governing a nation. It was not originally in Christianity. The Jewish peasants, out of whose profound moral intuitions Christianity came, had no idea of managing a complex society. Even Christ himself said practically nothing about it, except,

'You had better pay your taxes,' but that is not a civil constitution exactly."

"The rest—responsibility for a scheme of society—was a later
accretion?"

"Yes. And the paradox is that this idea, so new in the world
at its inception—the worth of the individual—which you still
see so strikingly affirmed in any Catholic church by the sight
of a solitary worshipper kneeling in the shrine of a saint—has
been fostered by an institution, namely the Catholic Church,
which has done so much to suppress individuality. There is
always in religion an element of brutality, and it is generally
the work of sincere men trying to conserve a state of society. I
suppose it has seldom been any worse than the Inquisition in
Spain or the persecution of the Huguenots in France. It is
surprising that the separation of the English Church in the
sixteenth century under the Tudors was accomplished with so
comparatively little brutality. There were, of course, burnings
and beheadings but nothing like the quantity you would have
had on the Continent in a similar situation. Whatever the
reform was, however, it wasn't religious. I don't know what
Henry VIII or Elizabeth had to do with religion."

"Trevelyan's pages on the dissolution of the monasteries
make close reading," I said. "The issues weren't as clear-cut
as we of today are prone to suppose."

"The expropriations," said Whitehead, "were harsh, but not
half as harsh as the wars of religion that devastated the Continent. I know of only two occasions in history when the people
in power did what needed to be done about as well as you can
imagine its being possible. One was the framing of your
American Constitution. They were able statesmen, they had
access to a body of good ideas; they incorporated these general
principles into the instrument without trying to particularize
too explicitly how they should be put into effect; and they were
men of immense practical experience themselves. The other
was in Rome and it undoubtedly saved civilization for, roughly,

about four hundred years. It was the work of Augustus and the set around him. He saved Rome from the Romans—I mean the city Romans—from the bankruptcy of the republican form of government, and the desiccated ideas of the old patrician class. Somehow, he found a way to call in, first, the Italian country squires, the 'new men' of new ideas, then, as the centuries went on, came the provincials, people like the Spanish Caesars. It prolonged the life of Rome up to the middle of the third century A.D.—about the time when it began to go to pieces. He left the senate enough power to preserve its self-respect, and, for the rest, the government was in the hands of civil authorities plus the military. It was one of the great achievements in human history and I doubt if, after all the legalistic analysis has been done, anybody quite understands how the thing was accomplished."

He was presently saying that historically the best civilizations seem to come from racial mixtures: the Normans with the French, the Norman-French with the Anglo-Saxons, the Dorian invaders in Attica with τοῖς αὐτόχθονες "the people sprung from land itself."—"Where the racial strain is 'pure' they are likely to be pretty stupid people until their blood is mingled with a more vivid strain. I suspect there was a largish mixture of Semitic with Ionian, which produced that brilliant mainland culture.

"Behind all this," he continued, "is the problem of how to keep a society from stagnating. It is the hardest thing in the world to do. You might have a social system that would run along smoothly enough for centuries, but if it lacks the element of novelty, of progressivism, it is a dead thing. I dare say the ants and the bees have smoothly working systems, but they do not change. This element of novelty is what makes the difference between man and the animals. Man sees a future in the present; there is a vision of what can be done with the materials of what is. A dog sees the present as a present and nothing else. And, mind you, I don't say that it isn't quite possible for man to come to the end of his powers of origination. Not that those powers themselves might fail, but that he might get into a planetary situation of static society where they would have no scope—and 'there an end to man.' His society, creature for creature, would be of no more worth than the ants."

"Artists" (it had occurred to me while he was speaking) "seem to recognize this power of origination as something which they do not command, but which commands them. It is true, they develop a technique through which it can work, but technique no more creates than a mechanical tool—it merely aids creation. Goethe is quite explicit about this to Eckermann; he as good as says that a masterpiece is a gift from on high when the artist has had 'a good day'; but that the force acts from outside himself."

"I suggest," Whitehead took it up, "that that society prospers best which can provide the conditions necessary for artists to give freest scope to their capacities for novelty—not eccentricity, not the bizarre—but origination in the furtherance of an artistic tradition; a carrying forward of what has been its new achievement."

"And Plato, in *The Laws*, the work of his old age—wasn't he very severe about the admission of novelty in the arts?—at least in the art of tragedy."

"Look here: let me show you a passage in Plato. . . ." He rose, peered along his shelves, and finally chose a volume in the Loeb edition, opening to Chapter 51 of the *Timaeus*. The translation was amended here and there by his own pen: he spoke of it: "This translator turns φυσέως into 'substance.' "

"But it means 'nature,' doesn't it? Or more exactly 'growth,' or 'the process of growth.' "

"Yes. Now here Plato is speaking of 'the receptacle'; the idea is vast, and a little vague." He went on through two or three pages summarizing as he read, until he reached Chapter 54. "And now here, you see, he reduces the idea to *commonplace*—to geometry!"

"But wasn't that often his method; to take the infinite, which he alone was capable of tackling, and reduce it to a finite form which average mortals, 'the educated man of ancient Athens,' as you once said, could understand?"

"This relationship between the infinite and the finite is what I was coming to. Our minds are finite, and yet even in these circumstances of finitude we are surrounded by possibilities that are infinite, and the purpose of human life is to grasp as much as we can out of that infinitude. I wish I could convey this sense I have of the infinity of the possibilities that confront humanity— the limitless variations of choice, the possibility of novel and untried combinations, the happy turns of experiment, the endless horizons opening out. As long as we experiment, as long as we keep this possibility of progressiveness, we and our societies are alive; when we lose them, both we and our societies are dead, no matter how externally active we and they may be, no matter how materially prosperous they and we may appear. And nothing is easier to lose than this element of novelty. It is the living principle in thought, which keeps all alive."

"How much validity do you give that sense of oneness which we sometimes have—that sense of our individuality being merged into the all? One is anxious not to talk moonshine about this, the more if, like me, he is neither a metaphysician nor a psychologist. And yet I know that those moments are so memorable, the sense of it is so strong, that years later, ten, perhaps, one can reach back into it as if it were only yesterday or today and create out of it something living and new."

"Mysticism," said Whitehead, "leads us to try to create out of the mystical experience something that will save it, or at least save the memory of it. Words don't convey it except feebly; we are aware of having been in communication with infinitude and we know that no finite form we can give can convey it. . . ."

"Music," I ventured, "may come nearer it than words.

Sometimes, during a good performance of the very greatest music one has a sense that he is in the presence of infinitude somewhat similar to what the composer must have felt when he was having to choose between one concept and another in the hope of expressing it. The definite concepts are there, in tones or phrases, but all around them hover the infinitudes of possibility—the *other* ways in which this vastness might have been expressed."

"Out of this effort to save the mystical experience," said Whitehead, "in the hope of creating a form which will preserve the experience for ourselves and possibly for others, comes clarification—in a thought or perhaps an art-form; and that clarification is then turned into some form of action. . . . Mysticism, clarification, action; I have never put it in that form before; but that is the order in which I would state it."

He said that a static quality appeared in the Buddhist religion as evidenced by the history of India and China, that their rate of advance retarded or stopped, and that since the year 1800 B.C. very little change had come in China until modern times, except minor ones in small living arrangements. He was illustrating how subtle a possession dynamic thought is, and how easy it is to lose.

This led to a discussion of the vitality of thought in the medical profession in our own time, how rapidly their science is moving, and yet they will tell you they know very little. He said:

"One of the most advanced types of human being on earth today is the *good* American doctor."

"Because in him science is devoted to the relief of suffering?"

"I would place it on more general grounds: he is sceptical toward the data of his own profession, welcomes discoveries which upset his previous hypotheses, and is still animated by humane sympathy and understanding."

"But for their advance," said I, "I would have been dead twenty years ago, of appendicitis. In 1892 the victims died. Now it is rated a 'minor' operation."

[161]   G

"But for a discovery in medicine only three years old," said Whitehead, "I would have been dead six weeks ago." He had had pneumonia and been saved by the new drug.

Mrs. Whitehead brought in some of the roses arranged in a glass bowl. So I then produced *The Future In Education* by Livingstone.

"I have a high respect for him," said Whitehead, "I once served on a royal commission with him to study the place of the Graeco-Roman classics in English education. I liked him immensely."

Turning to page 30, I indicated the passage quoted. He read it:

In one of the really good books on education, Professor Whitehead has spoken of the danger of

> . . . inert ideas, that is to say, ideas that are merely received into the mind without being utilised or tested or thrown into fresh combinations . . . Education with inert ideas is not only useless; it is, above all things, harmful . . . Except at rare intervals of intellectual ferment, education in the past has been radically infected with inert ideas . . .

★   ★   ★

For good measure I added that Livingstone had written me months ago that *Aims of Education* was one of the few books he had ever read on the subject which struck him as having been written by someone who knew something about it.

In the little time remaining they talked of the newly published biography of *Catherine of Aragon* by Garrett Mattingly, which Whitehead praised highly.

"It makes historical figures human and alive," said he. "The descriptions are quoted from intimate family letters, and you hear such things as how Henry VIII looked on a particular morning. . . . I say, what tortures mediaeval medicine inflicted on dying monarchs! Everybody thought they were doing their best and nobody knew much of anything. Of course the tortures of the common people were just as bad, only no record of them remains. You get, too, from this volume a very different idea of Cranmer than the usual one of martyrdom. He was perfectly willing to recant to save himself, but when he found he was going to be burnt anyhow, he recanted his recantation."

"We used to think that life in those periods was exposed to fearful risks. And *now* look at us!"

"I know it. One is almost ashamed to say that the day is hot, or the soup is cold, it seems such a trifle to endure. The world is so upset, that even our most platitudinous concepts, things that would once have been accepted by everyone, require to be looked at a second time."

XXII

August 30, 1941

A GOLDEN summer morning. By previous appointment, as always with the Whiteheads, my arrival was timed for eleven-thirty. By now Professor Whitehead was well recovered from his bout with pneumonia, and he looked uncommonly well. I said so.

"People tell me that I do," said he, "but the effects of the illness still linger."

"That should teach you not to have pneumonia."

"Yes," he assented to the chaffing, "there must be a lesson to everything."

"Nietzsche, who specialized in disagreeable remarks, has an observation that suffering may deepen a man but doesn't make him better."

"Anxiety," said Whitehead, "may give one an aspect of brightness, purely because it sharpens all the faculties. It makes all one's impressions more intense. . . . I have been thinking, of late, about custom; how it varies with time and place, but comes, in the end, to much the same thing. Now in England if something goes wrong—say, if one finds a skunk in the garden—he writes to the family solicitor, who proceeds to take the proper measures; whereas in America, you telephone the fire department. Each satisfies a characteristic need; in the English, love of order and legalistic procedure; and here in America, what you like is something vivid, and red, and swift. . . ."

"And noisy! One day in State Street I watched the fire apparatus pass; about six pieces. The streets cleared; the traffic policeman flexed his knees with the tension; the crowds stopped to watch; the speed and din were terrific—everybody was quite happy—and, after all, there wasn't any fire."

"That is my point," Whitehead took it up. "One method works just as well as the other, and the reason is that ninety per cent of the difficulty is psychological. As soon as we are assured that the properly constituted agents are taking the necessary measures about skunks in gardens, we go along contentedly about our business."

"Since 1910," I said, "in this country at least, we would have to admit a new agent, called psychiatrist. But how much of the psychiatrists' knowledge is actually new?"

"Some of it the Catholics have had all along in their confessional," said Whitehead. "I have been reading, or rereading, E. J. Boyd Barrett's *The Jesuit Enigma*. He criticized the order for what he calls their 'false psychiatry.' I looked him up in *Who's Who*, and find he has some achievement to his record, but he concedes very little good to the Jesuit order. My opinion is that it must have more in it than he concedes to have flourished as it has."

"Wouldn't that be an instance of the two-sidedness of nearly everything, from a truth to an institution? Phrased one way, it is intolerable; phrased another, it could be accepted gladly."

"It is the rigid dogma that destroys truth; and, please notice, my emphasis is not on the dogma but on the rigidity. When men say of any question, 'This is all there is to be known or said of the subject; investigation ends here,' that is death. It may be that the mischief comes not from the thinker himself but from the use made of his thinking by late-comers. Aristotle, for example, gave us our scientific technique (he also did some useful work in ethics); but in the main, it was he who devised our methods of scientific investigation (and of observation, too); yet his logical propositions, his instruction in sound reasoning which was bequeathed to Europe, are valid only within the limited framework of formal logic, and, as used in Europe, they stultified the minds of whole generations of mediaeval Schoolmen. Aristotle invented science, but destroyed philosophy."

"Would you say that Plato's distinctive contribution to the technique of thought is the willingness, as he makes Socrates call it, 'to follow the argument where it leads'? This sounds so simple, yet how few people understand how to play the game. In his *Dialogues*, for example, a question is beaten flat and round, several people have a go at it—"

"The German scholars who worked on Plato in the early part of the nineteenth century, to my mind, missed the point," said Whitehead. "Their view seems to have been that a lot of rather foolish people put forward somewhat nonsensical opinions until finally Socrates steps in and sets everything right. I do not believe that is it at all. When you get a group of diverse professional people in a discussion, their experience is so varied that you are sure to get novel contributions to the idea. None of them may be final, some of them may not be valid, but all of them will make some contribution to the subject, and while perhaps they cannot be accepted, they will bear study. I venture to suppose that in a newspaper office like yours there are a good many such discussions. . . ."

"That is what our daily editorial conferences are; and, over a period of years, the give-and-take grows uncommonly like a Platonic dialogue. I think perhaps that is where I first began to comprehend the Platonic method of dialectic."

"By that method the subject is explored, various opinions are given their weight, and the participants feel that they have spent their energies to good purpose, even though no definite conclusion emerges."

"Do you suppose that method existed in Athens before Plato?"

"I should think it likely. The prime of Athens came a little before Plato, in the period of the three great tragic dramatists, yes, and I include Aristophanes too. I think a culture is in its finest flower before it begins to analyse itself; and the Periclean Age and the dramatists were spontaneous, unselfconscious."

"The analytical spirit gets going in Euripides, the last of the three; and also rather more of the discussion method, the dramatist putting forth this or that point of view, not as anything final, but only so that it may 'have its say.' "

"How many people saw those plays?"

"In Athens about twenty thousand, though the citizenry itself was much more, probably one hundred and fifty thousand. Imagine them sitting there from dawn to dark on a March day of the Greater Dionysia watching three tragedies followed by a farcical satyr play, by each of three competing poets, and one of those trilogies would have been the *Oresteia* of Aeschylus. Where in our modern world is an audience that could take such a 'helping'? "

"Print has had a damaging effect," said Whitehead. "Before the mind had the assistance of the page it was given much harder work to do. When you remember that Athenian prisoners of the Syracusan expedition were given their liberty because they could recite choric odes from Euripides, obviously it was not mere snippets of the text which they had memorized."

"Do you ever find the sight of library stacks disconcerting? What if one knew everything in those volumes: would he be any better off—or worse off? Or the question comes, Can excessive reading actually enfeeble one's thinking apparatus?"

"I read very slowly," said Whitehead. "Sometimes I see myself referred to as 'a well-read man.' As a matter of fact, I have not read a great quantity of books; but I think about what I read, and it sticks."

(Remembering the size of his library in the house at Canton, again in the apartment at Radnor Hall, and even here in the Hotel Ambassador, books overflowing from study to dining-room, to limit the case even to those present-and-voting, his remark about not having read a great quantity of books was to be taken relatively.)

"What do you think of this modern emphasis on *speed* of reading?"

"Speed is not for me. On the other hand, some of my reading is 'skippy.' Last night, for example, I was rereading that book in your lap on the Jesuits, but finding, at the beginnings of successive chapters that he was still on the same aspect of a subject whose point I had already grasped, I did not hesitate to skip."

We were next discussing the kind of book about which one must do something, if there is to be any benefit from the reading. The *Meditations* of Marcus Aurelius can be read through in a matter of hours, but to incorporate those precepts into thought and action may be a life's work. Then I asked:

"Living and working as you have and do in academic communities, does it ever strike you that acquisitive scholarship can be overdone?"

"The universities," said he, "are like any other necessary implement—like a gun. We must have them, the work of civilization could scarcely be carried on without them; but while they are very valuable, they can also be very dangerous. The reason Harvard has kept its place at the top as a capital of thought is the graduate schools, where knowledge is wedded to action."

"An idea which has been occupying me of late I would like to put up for criticism. It is that in nineteenth-century America the influence of religious thinking was still very powerful; that at the turn of the nineteenth into the twentieth, the rise of science and then the first world war so impaired that influence that leadership passed to the educationists, say after 1920; but that now numerous signs seem to indicate that in another generation or so, the germinating power in American civilization may be the artists—using that term in its broadest sense—the creators."

"Your dates confuse me a little," said he. "I would have said that you have already had two very happy periods of flourishing in this country; one in New England during the first half of the nineteenth century, when you really enjoyed one of the world's great ages, though it is not yet as famous as it deserves to be; and the other in the late eighteenth century, with the framing of your American Constitution. I am not suggesting that these framers were acting entirely on original initiative; some of their ideas were a hundred years old—going back to Locke, for example—or much older; but they were unique in laying down, not details of procedure but general principles for the conduct of a great democratic state. I know of only two instances when a work of such magnitude was accomplished consciously. The other was done according to principles which would not have satisfied either your or my ideals of liberty, and yet it certainly saved civilization and bequeathed a point of view, even to the Middle Ages, which enabled the monastic foundations to transmit the ancient heritage; I mean when Augustus Caesar appealed from the narrow patricians and the unreliable plebs to the solid middle class, first of Rome and Italy and later of the empire. Nobody could admire the English governmental system more heartily than I do; but equally nobody could say at exactly what point the idea of a limited monarchy came in. The growth was unconscious. It was not an idea which originated with any person or at any specific time.

[168]

But the Augustan Principate and your Federal Constitution were the results of conscious effort. The English system, too, is very difficult to copy, and it has been copied successfully only by people of English stocks setting up colonial societies, in places like Australia, Africa, or North America."

"You are evidently using 'artist' in the sense of creators of great states."

"And you are using the word 'creative' in a sense which I give to the word 'novelty,' " resumed Whitehead. "A hundred thousand years ago—or sometime—nobody knows when—there came a turn in the development of man which brought about a very rapid advance. It was man's capacity for origination, his capacity for novelty, his curiosity, his liking for investigation. My fear for humanity is that they may lose it. One of the few places where it is still free is here in the United States. I don't say there aren't ways in which you could improve. I think there are regions where you would do well to reduce your rate of murders—but even allowing for Chicago at its worst, in the 1920's, before your authorities stepped in and put a stop to it, life in general, your life, my life, is less subject to interference and less in danger here than any place else on earth. It is only in certain happy ages and lands that conditions are favourable to the development of talent Greece in the fifth and fourth centuries B.C. was one; Rome in the first century A.D. was another; and even then the range of talent elicited by the temporarily favourable conditions is a limited one, not nearly the whole range of potential talents or of gifted individuals receives the needed encouragement. And when those fortunate times do come, we don't know how to keep them going."

"How short-lived the Elizabethan drama was," I remarked; "in full bloom between 1590 and 1612, then by the 1620's it had begun to thin out."

"I was thinking of that very period," said he. "Art flourishes when there is a sense of adventure, a sense of nothing having been done before, of complete freedom to experiment; but when caution comes in you get repetition, and repetition is the death of art. Here in America you had a good period up to about 1860; then the idea came in that nothing was any good unless it came from Europe."

"Yes, men like Emerson and Thoreau can be seen pushing it away from them; but after the middle of the century it does descend like a blight."

"The two world wars," said he, "have destroyed Europe and liberated America."

"Unless we are thwarted by our loss of racial homogeneity?"

"On the contrary, you have gained by that loss. I know of no other situation in history similar to yours, in having assembled the vivid and adventurous spirits of numerous races in an environment favourable to the creation of a great culture, except in the Mediterranean Basin of the fifth and fourth centuries B.C. (its most brilliant period), when Greeks and Phoenicians and Italians and heaven knows who else were bobbing about in rowboats, mixing races and founding new societies. It will be strange if you don't profit by your situation."

"I am not quite sure I understand what you mean by 'repetition is the death of art.'"

"Then take architecture. I was brought up in a part of England where everybody landed that *did* land, from Caesar on through the missionaries, the Danes, the Normans, and the rest. My father's church was one example, and Canterbury Cathedral was another. (I can see it now, the spot when Thomas à Becket was murdered, and the armour of the Black Prince in the south aisle of the chancel.)—I have read and don't hold at all with T. S. Eliot in his view of what went on in Canterbury Cathedral. Mind you, I don't pretend to know a great deal about it, but I feel sure it wasn't like *that*.—All the successive ages are embedded in those buildings; walls of the early churches, then the heavy Norman arches, then the lighter and more fanciful Gothic of the middle period, and finally the too-fanciful late Gothic; but no repetition; only the very slightest reliance on what went before, always some novel departure."

"A while back," I said, "you were speaking of the death of truth which results when men attempt to codify it into some dogma or institution which they hope will conserve it for posterity. Even Plato, in his old age at least, seems unwilling to let his ideal society take its chances (possibly, it is true, because he had seen the disaster to Athens); but isn't the difficulty with all such attempts that the sum of existence is larger than any system, however large?"

"The desire for a pattern of existence," said he, "is a natural and very common wish that our experience should have some meaning, some order, that it should make sense. The hypotheses of science are the same. The pattern may not represent anything more than our conception of our lives, as we would like to believe them to be, or our hypothesis of a scientific process, but it steadies us. If we are speaking of naïveté, it is the scientists who are naïve. For years they have been welcoming hypotheses which destroy their previous assumptions, and welcoming them as a condition of advance; whereas the theologians—and I consider Christian theology to be one of the great disasters of the human race—if they admitted that their assumptions had been upset, would consider it a major defeat for themselves (when all the while their position has been shaken and so altered that the tenets of today would, in certain intellectual levels, be hardly recognizable as those of the same or similar people seventy years ago). But much the same is true in science, and whether the scientists realize it or not, their 'advance' has been upset."

"Kirsopp Lake [1] once remarked in my presence that his father, a physician, being asked late in life what had done the

---

[1] Kirsopp Lake, theologian. Born Southampton, England, 1872. Lincoln College, Oxford. Professor of early Christian lit. Harvard 1914–1919, Winn professor of ecclesiastical history 1919–1932, professor of history 1932–1938.

most in his lifetime to relieve human suffering, answered, 'Anaesthesia and the decay of Christian theology.' That was in 1922. Both you and he put the accent on 'theology.' "

"We needn't go into the question of whether Christ was entirely an authentic historic personage, or one of those figures on whom are laid the needs and sayings and aspirations of a period," answered Whitehead. "We begin rather, I think, with an agricultural middle class in Palestine, very sound, remarkably well educated for its time and place (from the reading of the scriptures in the synagogues like our King James Bible in the churches) and with a remarkably high standard of morality; and then you have the other set, in Jerusalem, what I may call 'the faculty.' Two powerful popular preachers arose at about the same time, John the Baptist and Jesus. Both were intensely disliked by the faculty in Jerusalem because their preaching spread and popularized a new and purer morality. So one was executed by Herod, a native ruler, and the other by a Roman procurator; he didn't, it is true, do it himself, but he allowed it to be done. Now there was nothing really new in this popular preaching, most of the ideas were already present in the older prophets of the nobler strain—Isaiah, Amos, Jeremiah—but it was put with a new force and immediacy.

"I have said before, probably to you, that the trouble starts with the interpreters of Christianity. The disciples were admirably solid people. And there was at first a hope that the powerful Greek notions which were abroad in the world at that time—ideas of liberty, democracy, the horror of brutality, and so on—would be blended with the best of Jewish thought— not all of which, of course, was equally good; but the gracious and merciful insights were there by flashes. But then the disaster starts. You get it in all of the following interpreters of Christianity from Augustine, even in Francis of Assisi; the gentleness and mercy of one side of Christianity, but based logically on the most appalling system of concepts. The old ferocious God is back, the Oriental despot, the Pharaoh, the

Hitler; with everything to enforce obedience, from infant damnation to eternal punishment. In Augustine you get admirable ideas, he is full of light; then you enquire into the ultimate bases of the doctrines and you find this abyss of horror. Their hearts were right but their heads were wrong. And there was no appeal from their heads. In Saint Francis, for example, it is hardly credible that the two worlds, that of grace and mercy, and that of eternal damnation, could exist in one and the same breast. This theological disaster is what I mean when I speak of the mischief which follows from banishing novelty, from trying to formularize your truth, from setting up to declare: 'This is all there is to be known on the subject, and discussion is closed.'

"I may have spoken to you before about the static civilization of China. A time came when things ceased to change. If you want to know why, read Confucius. And if you want to understand Confucius, read John Dewey. And if you want to understand John Dewey, read Confucius. Confucius wanted to get rid of the silly ideas. The simple facts ought to suffice for you; don't waste time asking questions about the ultimacies *under* those facts. (Mind you, I greatly admire what John Dewey has made possible in the development of your western universities; I am speaking here about the consequences of the doctrines of pragmatism.) Thus, the Chinese discovered the magnetic needle. Iron placed in certain positions would cause a pointer to aim north. 'Now that,' Confucius would say, 'ought to be enough for you. The fact suffices.' But when the magnetic compass is brought westward into Europe, what happens? Immediately the silly questions begin to be asked: 'Why? What makes the needle point north?' And straightway all sorts of fruitful consequences ensue; as that, mathematics, which had been well-nigh useless for two thousand years, is pressed into the service . . . and so on. Now these are just the 'superfluous' questions which pragmatism would ignore. Of course"
—he smiled as he said it—"if you say in print that the individual

[173]

should be listened to and that these 'silly questions' ought to be asked, you will instantly be pestered with letters from three thousand idiots whose questions *are* silly!"

"That is true," said I, "for I *have* said it in print and *have* been pestered with letters from three thousand idiots."

"But the point is," he resumed, "that the 'silly question' is the first intimation of some totally novel development. Suppose we admitted this principle in the sphere of morals. What is morality in any given time or place? It is what the majority then and there happen to like, and immorality is what they dislike. But the 'silly question' as applied to morals would open the way to a discovery of the few ultimacies behind *all* systems of morals, a region in which very little has as yet been done."

XXIII

September 10, 1941

EARLY in the summer I had told Professor Whitehead that I had been keeping his conversations in my Note Books since 1933. He knew that I had occasionally used parts of them transcribed almost verbatim in the editorial columns of the *Globe*, for when I did, a copy was always sent him. The immediate reason for speaking of it was that North, Margot, and Eric, his son, daughter-in-law, and grandson, were in England, and two of them, North and Margot, in London under repeated bombings. Beyond this personal anxiety was his concern for England, for Europe, and the future of civilization. He suffered from the war with a peculiar intensity, for, more than most, he understood what was at stake for the future of mankind.

There had been no thought of publication. My idea was to offer him some novel diversion, however brief, from this daily strain, which had clearly begun to tell. Copies of these conversations in typescript had begun to be made in midsummer and sent to him as fast as finished. This had progressed to about the first hundred pages, for the years from 1933 to 1937, and was to continue through the autumn until they were brought up to date.

It was now Wednesday, September 10, 1941, and I went to Cambridge to see him late in the forenoon. In the College Yard the elms were yellowing somewhat earlier than usual, although it was still a sultry summer day.

The apartment at the Hotel Ambassador, being five floors up, was cool and airy; the Venetian blinds keeping out the glare. It was Whitehead's day to be spent in bed, so I was received in that chamber, a cheerful room, bright with sunshine, its walls tinted a light blue. He sat propped on pillows, a reading table by his side, looking cool and comfortable.

He had been reading the typescripts of the Dialogues, was satisfied that they were in substance what was said, and asked:

"How can you remember so accurately?"

I told him what my previous experience had been; shorthand reporter as a youth, and thirty years' practice of recording the conversation of others.

He turned pages of the typescript, pausing here and there.

"Your prospects of getting these published," he said, "aren't for the present very bright. I come of a long-lived family. When my grandfather died, at the age of eighty-seven, his old friend Sir Moses Montefiore sighed, 'Poor Whitehead, cut off in the prime of life!'"

"If I would swap you for a book about you," I told him, "I would be a poor hand at a bargain."

"You have suppressed your own remarks more than I wish you had."

"My purpose in writing was to remember yours."

He suggested that in future, if I went on recording the conversations, the remarks of the other speakers be reported more fully. We understood each other without more words; but what was understood was this: the ideas advanced by the other speakers were necessary to the flow of the thought, even though

[175]

they might not be particularly important in themselves. Dialogues are interchange and I divined that he did not care to be represented as indulging in monologues or monopolizing a conversation, neither of which he ever did. Being dialogues, they proceed on the principle which he has already noted in the *Dialogues* of Plato, various speakers setting forth different points of view but without any attempt at dogmatic finality.

"About our discussions of Hellenism and Hebraism," I said apologetically, "you may think I brought that subject up too often. My only excuse is, if it *is* an excuse, I had been studying for years the relationship of those two main forces in Western civilization, and you are one of the few persons who would be of any value to me. You have read the books and done the thinking. Perhaps our repeated discussions have had this advantage—like 'sonata form' in music, the theme keeps returning with enriched development."

"The Jews," said he, "as a race, are probably the most able of any in existence. Now when a gifted person is charming and uses his exceptional ability generously, he is a paragon and people adore him; but in the same way, if a person with unusual ability is disagreeable, his ability makes him just so much the more disagreeable, and thus the disagreeable individuals in that race are the more conspicuous."

"They are not one bit more disagreeable than the Anglo-Saxons," said Mrs. Whitehead. "Having been brought up in Brittany, then taken to England, I came fresh to both, and I know."

"There is a type of well-to-do Englishman," he said, "who has been well established as to property and family for two or three generations, the product of a rather narrow training, and with very limited sympathies, whose reputation for being a disagreeable person is world-wide."

"He is even a figure in literature," said I.

"Yes, and even in the literature of his own country," said Mrs. Whitehead.

"On the other hand," said the professor, "you get a type of rather impecunious second or third sons of well-to-do families who are cut off from inheritance by our law of primogeniture, and they go out to the colonies, behave pretty well, are much respected and use their talents constructively."

I returned to the question of America and the artist in the present century, which I rather thought had been misdirected in our previous conversation.

"I didn't mean to have you think," said he, "that the artist isn't an immensely important figure in America today. As a matter of fact, you are in a situation here now much like that of the Mediterranean world, centring in the Aegean, say, roughly, between 1000 B.C. and 100 A.D. There was remarkable ease of water transportation, assisted by a lot of convenient islands; it promoted the movement of ideas and the mixing of gifted races. A 'pure' race is likely to be stupid—the Lacedaemonians —but mix the native Attic stock with Dorian invaders or the Ionians with Asiatics, and the results are brilliant. I think the one place where I have been that is most like ancient Athens is the University of Chicago. You see, I am looking for your American equivalent of the Aegean, and I believe it is the Midwest."

"Geographically, the Midwest may be our Aegean," said I, "but our trireme is the motor-car."

"Great events," said he, "points of new departure in human history, are seldom if ever the product of a single cause; they come when two or three causes coalesce. Add to your motor-car the collapse of Europe. (It is no longer considered necessary for your scholars to go to Berlin or London to find out what is happening; in fact, it is impossible.) Then to those two, namely, the collapse of Europe and the motor-car, add a third factor, the blending here of strains from several superior races, the gifted individuals of which are already beginning to appear. And we mustn't forget the means of rapid communication and transport, airplane and wireless, which have unified life on this planet, while placing America at the top of modern civilization."

Returning to the artist's place in our national development, he said, "In the arts, too, you get a great departure when naïve people, because they are keenly interested in the important things, treat an old subject in some novel aspect. The Midwesterners have the great advantage of being naïve. In New York, for example, your type tends to be blasé; they have heard everything, and consider that the simple subjects are hackneyed. So they are. But great art is a dealing with simple subjects freshly. What could be more hackneyed than Shakespeare's plots? True, he set them here or there in time or place, but his characters are all Englishmen of Elizabeth's time viewing these old and simple problems in the light of contemporary life. Why, the plot of *Hamlet* was an old story three thousand years before Shakespeare took it up. But the naïve people view everything freshly, and so they take old things and make them new."

"You remember Goethe, late in the eighteenth century when people were beginning to flock to America, making someone return from America to Europe and say, 'Here, or nowhere, is America'?"

"The situation is reversed; Europe has collapsed; civilization is in your hands, and now," said Whitehead, " 'here, or nowhere, is America.' "

He spoke of the part the Catholics may have in our future.

"The United States looks to be about the only promising field they have left. England, in the seventeenth century; France, in the eighteenth; Germany and Italy in Fascist hands, Spain in revolt, Mexico Communist, South America not very profitable. I wonder how influential American bishops are in Rome? Marxism is now considered to be their chiefest enemy, the stressing of the economic motive. Over the centuries see how they have yielded inch by inch. From 1000 A.D. to 1500 A.D. the pope was, I suppose, the most powerful individual in Europe. Then he was defied by the Tudor monarchs in England. Since then the papacy has lost the support of the Bourbons, the Hohenzollerns and the Hapsburgs; and the Church takes second place to the national state. But the Catholic clergy accommodate themselves to changed externals."

Before I left we were discussing methods of composition and whether the typewriting machine would permanently worsen the writing of English prose.

"People compose," said he, "in one or the other of two ways. I first observed this when collaborating on a book with Bertrand Russell. He loved words, and words actually satisfied his craving for expression. He admitted this. But people compose either in words directly, the words satisfying their ideas of things, or they compose in concepts and then try to find words into which those concepts can be translated. I may add that my own method is the second."

XXIV

November 19, 1941

THANKSGIVING Eve I dined with the Whiteheads in Cambridge. As the evening went on we discussed whether there was much help in the Bible for people like us during the present world tumult. He said there was no longer much of anything in it for him. I mentioned the Beatitudes, some of the sayings of Jesus, and the saga of Elijah on Mount Carmel.

"That is a great saga," said he, "but no more."

"The two who have never failed me," I said, "are Beethoven and Plato."

"Plato is the great one," he answered quietly.

I asked what he was reading.

"In my curious overwrought state," said he, a little wearily, "it is hard to tell. I have to try now one thing, now another."

"It is hit or miss," said she.

We were speaking of the Protestant clergy, and he remarked that a group of Congregational parsons who once came to him struck him as very able people, "liberal, open-minded, equipped to cope with situations. I thought they were, as a group, superior to the Harvard faculty."

It was an inquiry among us three:

Who prop, thou ask'st, in these bad days, my mind?

He had given up the Bible. I said the beauty of nature gives me occasional moments of peace, the crystalline green of a curling breaker which flashes the instant before it foams; it will be equally beautiful a hundred-thousand years hence; it is good, it is true, it asks nothing of me. I am merely permitted to partake of its quality of eternity.

"Some of my utmost sustainment," said he, "I have got out of English poets; not the eighteenth-century people, certainly not Pope, though I like the Churchyard man, what is his name? Gray—but the nineteenth- and seventeenth-century men. My experiences since the first world war, however"—he spoke wearily—"have been such that I find it hard now to read poetry. If you have had the feelings they try to depict, and have really felt deeply, the poetry doesn't verbalize them."

XXV

December 10, 1941

IT was two days after the undeclared attack by the Japanese on our fleet at Pearl Harbour. After dinner at the Faculty Club with Louis Lyons, who had just returned from Washington with a budget of not-very-cheerful news (he is curator of the Nieman Foundation at Harvard), I telephoned to ask the Whiteheads if I could come and call for half an hour.

By good luck no one else was there. Since our minds had been full of nothing else but Pearl Harbour for the past two days, there was a tacit agreement to keep off that subject.

Mr. Whitehead sat with an envelope containing the whole sheaf of my typescripts thus far. He wore his spectacles and dipped into the pages for some correction here and there.

"It is very unusual," he said, "to get authentic records of conversation from the past."

"None occur to me at the moment," I replied, "except Boswell's *Johnson*, and Eckermann's with Goethe, and Eckermann's are seldom general conversation so much as monologues by Goethe, valuable though they are."

"The novelists," said he, "don't help us much here, for they must always be getting on with their story; although occasionally a mediocre novelist like Anthony Trollope does bring back exactly the kind of talk I heard amongst my father's friends when I was a small boy, the provincial clergy with an occasional dean and archbishop."

"Later than that," said she. "It was still going on when I arrived at your house. I remember it well."

"The letters of authors seldom give it to you," said he, "for they always know, whether they admit it or not, that their letters will be printed. What posterity really want to know is what people talked about when they got together, and there's very little of it. I should think these pages of yours might be more valuable a hundred years from now than they are now."

"Before they can be printed," said Mrs. Whitehead, smiling, "there will have to be a few 'demises,' including our own. We talk with you completely off guard."

"I know that, and therefore nobody has seen them except my sister, who typed them. She has said that they make an "Introduction to Whitehead"—that abstract ideas which the average reader might find it difficult to get from your published works, here come out in casual conversation, quite easy to grasp. Most of the matter, it seems to me, is new. I don't remember much, if any, of it in your books."

"No, it is not in any of them. . . . I was trying to think of the name of that Roman banker to whom Cicero wrote letters,

Atticus. There you have a semblance of conversation from the ancient world—at least the topics in which educated men were interested; and you get some of it in Plato, though of course not even the educated man of Athens was up to Plato all, or even most, of the time."

"Occasionally, though, you do get a bit in Plato that must have come straight out of life. I am thinking," said I, "of that comic anecdote in the *Laches* about a naval battle where a marine, fighting with a scythe-spear, stuck it into the rigging of the other vessel and couldn't pull it out again; and so as the two vessels wore past each other he ran along his own ship hanging to the end of the scythe handle till he had to let go. The crews of both ships knocked off fighting to laugh and applaud the act. His scythe-spear was waving in the air on the other vessel. It was evidently a yarn that went all over Athens."

"You get those homely touches in the earlier *Dialogues*," said Whitehead, pleasantly reminiscent, and cited one or two more, but he resumed:

"Writing only brings out comparatively superficial experiences. Man has had it a relatively short time—shall we say about four thousand years?—first in the form of chipping pieces of stone for the decrees and boasts of monarchs; then on papyrus. For only about three thousand years, or less, have men written down their thoughts; let us say from Homer's time. Now for ages before that you had immense quantities of human experience accumulating in men's bodies. The body itself was, and still is, an immense experience; the sheer harmony of its properly functioning organs gives us a flood of unconscious enjoyment. It is quite inarticulate, and doesn't need to be articulate. But in bulk, and perhaps in significance, it far outweighs the scope of the written word. That, by comparison, is mostly trivial."

"Even with the very greatest masters of the written word," I remarked, "Dante, Goethe, Aeschylus . . . one is left aware of how pale the statement is in comparison with the experience itself; Goethe can only suggest the misery and horror of the Gretchen tragedy; Dante's *Inferno* can be only a shadow of what he imagined; or the murder of Agamemnon, and the agony which came before it and after. What perhaps the written word *can* do is recall to us our own experiences, or give us intimations of experiences which we are likely to have. But since you say the written word is comparatively superficial, what is it that does come first as conscious experience, after these floods of sheer bodily self-enjoyment?"

"The moral values, I should say," he replied, after a longish pause for reflection. "Even dogs have them, in the form of simple-minded affection and loyalty."

"Even that 'subtle-soul'd psychologist,' William James," said I, "was immensely interested in the behaviour of dogs and touched by their affection. He sometimes used them as illustrations when he was lecturing."

"Dogs do better than cats," observed Mrs. Whitehead. "Have you noticed how people divide in their likings, the one sort for cats, the other for dogs? Cats are selfish and self-centred," she added, leaving the inference to be drawn, but he supplied it, smiling:

"If a dog jumps up into your lap, it is because he is fond of you; but if a cat does the same thing, it is because your lap is warmer."

"Are you ever aware of human beings having a predominance of 'cat qualities' or of 'dog qualities'—canine personalities as distinct from feline personalities? Among the felines I would class the person who 'doesn't like people.' Precisely what does that phrase signify?" I asked.

"Self-centredness," suggested Mrs. Whitehead, "and a nature that broods over 'never having had its due.' One, I should think, produces the other."

"After the moral values developing in early men (since we are speculating on origins), what," I asked, "would you say came next?"

"The aesthetic," said Whitehead. "When a nightingale sits up all night singing to his wife, and singing very well, too, you can't make me believe that aesthetic values of a very high order are not present."

"Tell him about our poor nightingale in Surrey," prompted Mrs. Whitehead. As he looked a little at a loss for the episode, she supplied the setting:

"We had a cottage in Surrey in the early spring, and, believe it or not, on the first of May, after the nightingales had arrived, there was a fall of snow. The poor dear caught cold, but went right on singing; and he never did get back to proper pitch all that summer."

"Yes," said Whitehead, smiling, "we had the experience of hearing a nightingale sing out of tune."

"I would rather hear a performance with heart in it," said I, "than an impeccable technique."

"And mind you," said Whitehead, "the same holds for personalities; they make their effect more by what they are than by anything they say. Even when you are using words effectively, they gain a great deal from the physical presence of the speaker; warmth, accent, emphasis, are emanations from body and spirit."

"Of course the very best writing is an attempt to convey in printed words some of those overtones which are sounded by the voice and emanated from the physical personality."

"Yes," said he, "and occasionally with surprising success. That is a property of the very best writing."

"In what you have just said, you 'countenance' me in a perception toward strangers of which I have been aware for years," said I. "It is not necessarily an intuitive perception of beauty or goodness, although it often takes that form; rather, it seems to be an unconscious emanation from the face and body and spirit of a total stranger which one's wireless somehow picks up and signals that, in one sort or another, there is interest and vitality in that person."

"There is nothing surprising in it to me," said Mrs. White-head. "We have just been reading Mrs. Margaret Deland's autobiography (it's there on the little stand at your elbow) and —did you know her?"

"No. I wasn't so fortunate. She was one of my mother's favourite contemporary authors. Didn't she and her husband stand a little aside from social Boston?"

"That is what I meant," said she, ". . . their taking into their home unmarried mothers, to save them from suicide and degradation and steady them by letting them reorganize their lives around the love for the child until they would get on their feet. *There* you have that sense of the interest and worth of a stranger even under a cloud." And she went on to speak of an experience she had had rescuing a beautiful girl, ". . . with that hectic glow of the consumptive. I drove to eleven places in London before I found one that would take her in. First, a Church of England home. 'We don't take second offenders' . . . and so on till we came to—what do you suppose?"

"The Salvation Army?"

"Right. We were received as long-awaited friends and taken in as if we were week-end guests. I asked how much it would cost to maintain her there. 'Nothing,' was the answer. 'If you can afford to pay, of course we shall expect you to do so, but only so that we can take in someone else.' The girl stayed there fifteen months of her own choice and was quite happy."

"What finally became of her?"

"She married a greengrocer, but being consumptive, she died young."

"How good a rating would you give the Salvation Army as Christians?" I asked Whitehead.

"Excellent," said he; "they take their Christianity simply."

"As simply as Francis of Assisi?"

"Oh, much more simply than he. They aren't nearly as encumbered with a bad theology."

"You *do* consider the theology a bad one, then?" I baited him.

"The trouble," said he, "comes from intellectualizing upon a religion. Jesus was not very intellectual; what he had was a profound insight. Humanity in the Eastern mediterranean between 500 B.C. and 200 A.D. began to write down their intimate thoughts and a great age resulted. I am speaking of course of the exceptionally gifted men who wrote down their thoughts. Paul comes as quite a drop from Jesus, and although his followers included many estimable persons, their idea of God, to my mind, is the idea of the devil."

"How about Buddhism?"

"It is a religion of escapism. You retire into yourself and let externals go as they will. There is no determined resistance to evil. Buddhism is not associated with an advancing civilization."

XXVI

April 5, 1942

SPRING at last, one of the first mild evenings, with a vague stir of exhilaration in the air, robin song, the brilliant yellow of the forsythia and pink of the flowering almond blossoming in the College Yard. Having dined at the Faculty Club, I telephoned Mrs. Whitehead, asking if I might call.

"Come ahead!" said she. "You'll meet nobody but Grace DeFriez."

The Ambassador is only five minutes' walk from the club. Over the elmtops in the west the sky still glowed a burning umber. I had not seen the Whiteheads since February, such is the heartless pace of this city in winter. She was looking tired, but bright as ever. His study door was shut and we sat a little while conversing in the living-room, where she had a vase of English violets on her chair-side table, which diffused their fragrance in the room. She spoke about women she knew who could dismiss all thoughts of the war:

"They 'mustn't be depressed; happiness is necessary to their health.' . . . They 'must have complete new outfits, or they might look shabby.' How do such minds work? They're beyond me. Theoretically I envy such insensitivity; actually, I would rather die than be so obtuse to events around me."

"Since you've confessed, so will I. I have one of those theoretical envies: he is a real-estate dealer, quite a fine fellow— the world as it is exactly suits him and he is exactly suited to it. I doubt if he ever wanted anything but what he has: a big house, a tennis-court, wife, family, good income. In low moments I say to myself, 'Why couldn't you have been like him?' "

"But you don't mean it for an instant."

"Of course not, How is Alfred weathering the season?"

"Working too hard, some days better than others, but nothing serious."

She rose, opened the study door, and said quietly:

"Lucien is here."

His voice within made a cordial exclamation.

I went in. He was sitting in one of the big armchairs with a leg-rest, reading a large typescript under a study lamp.

"This tells," said he rising, "how to bring about a world order in three hundred years, if enough people could understand what he is talking about."

I remarked that most of such blueprints assume that the world's entire population is of the same mentality as a college professor.

"Yes," said he, "and that would take a good deal *more* than three hundred years, besides being of doubtful desirability."

The doorbell rang. He answered. It was Grace DeFriez.

"We are going to have a good time," said he delightedly.

Someone quoted a nursery rhyme and a question arose of their antiquity.

"I believe some of them go back to Egypt," said he. "They get new trimmings as they come down the ages, but essentially they are the same."

"Children are your true die-hard conservatives; they pass along the oral folk-lore—including naughty words—undeviatingly from crop to crop," said I. "And some of the words are sharply regional. There is one I used to hear as a boy in the Midwest which I never heard east of the Alleghenies, until a Montana boy who was visiting me used it: 'helleshen,' or 'hellishin.' It's probably some local variant of 'hellish.' "

"My children," said Grace, "bring home the same stories and jokes I used to hear and repeat when I was their age. I hadn't thought of them for years."

"The one place where my Americanism breaks down," said Whitehead, "is on the jokes in *The New Yorker*. I can generally see the humour of the pictures, but the captions are often too much for me."

"Oh, you needn't feel sensitive about that," said Grace. "My children often have to explain the jokes to me. It makes me realize how out of date I must be."

"And you needn't feel sensitive about *that*, either," I offered comfort, "for a good many of the jokes are sharply regional—New Yorky."

Mrs. Whitehead said, "I can understand the jokes about the fat women—"

"Helen Hokinson's?"

"Yes. But I don't think fat women are funny. I feel sorry for them, poor things."

"You are like Sir Richard Livingstone's son, Rupert, a kindly boy, who used to see *The New Yorker* on some reading table in Oxford. He said, 'I laugh at the jokes, but I have a feeling that I oughtn't.' "

"My feeling is," said Mrs. Whitehead, "that such excess flesh must be a glandular affliction and shouldn't be laughed at."

"Then I can relieve your conscience. Come in to Huyler's on Tremont Street any afternoon at three o'clock and I will show you scores of women mowing away sweet cakes with sugar frosting filled with whipped cream."

"Oouff!" says she, with a grimace. "Don't expect me!"

By some transition—as to whether weight, like hanging and wiving, goes by destiny—we came to the question of free will. Mrs. Whitehead thought we have very little; occasional margins of deflection, although within those limits we might exercise considerable control.

"I think," said Whitehead, "that although in the final act we are so conditioned by unconscious previous thought that it looks automatic, as a matter of fact we have been determining that act by an enormous amount of rejection and selection. It all depends on what ideas are entertained and how we entertain them; some may be dismissed at once as horrible and repugnant, others dwelt upon as pleasant. After this rejection and selection has gone on for a sufficiently long period, the final act *is* conditioned, but we have had a large share in doing it."

"May I follow the process a little farther upstream?" I proposed. "Behind what is selected or rejected haven't we the economic position, which may determine whether one has easy access to superior standards; then the inherited disposition, which may be congenial to certain types of choice and hostile to others?"

"Yes," he assented, "the area of choice seems to exist between those antecedent determinants and the final, seemingly automatic act. But you can catch yourself entertaining habitually certain types of ideas and setting others aside; and that, I think, is where our personal destinies are largely decided."

"If you two could have got out to see the film of Shaw's *Major Barbara* I would have haled you there," said I. "Grace saw it and we have already discussed it at length. The point is that Shaw has rewritten that feeble last scene, at the armament factory, and now seems to be saying, 'These forces of nature are in themselves neither good nor bad; all depends on how they are used; and the unique function of man is to learn how to use them properly, though the moral values we lend them are entirely of our own devising; if they promote comfort and harmony, we term them "good"; if the reverse, "evil." The great mystery remains, how did any life come into being on this planet capable of conceiving such values at all?'"

"Whoever would have dreamed," said Whitehead, "when this earth was a mere molten mass, of any such forms of life as have appeared? The method of nature seems to be by the production of novelty—some totally unexpected turn of origination. By and by the earth cooled, and the seas appeared; aeons later, plant life and animals."

"And what hideously fantastic animals!" said Mrs. Whitehead.

"And finally, man," he resumed, "after perhaps a million years. And who that watches the heavens can doubt that forms of life just as amazing exist on other planets? The nebulae, too, have their life cycles; come into being, are obliterated, and pass into some other form. Where do the moral ideas first appear? Actually, they appear *before* man; animals have them; birds know when they have done wrong."

"Dogs," said Mrs. Whitehead, "are far more moral than most human beings; they are more self-effacing and more self-sacrificing. Watch a dog try to help someone he loves; the beast puts us to shame."

"I think that our power of conscious origination is where free will comes in," said Whitehead. "We are continually choosing between the good and the less good, whether aware of it or not. Even children do so before they can hardly speak. When one of our boys was little (he wasn't punished, for he did nothing to be punished for) he evidently had a code of his own which he sometimes violated. The only way we would know it was that he would crawl under the bed. When we saw his little shoes sticking out from under the bed, we always knew he was guilty, though we never knew of what, nor asked, for he couldn't have told us. He wouldn't come out unless dragged by the heels. That done, all was expiated. Being dragged out by the heels he evidently considered a full atonement."

Grace said she wished she knew some way to get dragged out from under the bed by the heels, it would simplify so many complicated problems of ethics.

"And mind you," Whitehead continued, "children must have such ideas long before they can talk. This child called himself 'Goo,' and one day I heard him passing under the open window of my study murmuring to himself, 'Goo can walk now. Goo can talk now.' "

"Something similar happened when Ivins was little," said Grace. "He was a heavy baby, not light on his feet like Polly, but a little ice wagon. One day he suddenly discovered that he could stand. He was terribly excited and cried, '*tan! tan!*' He kept tumbling down, but getting up on his legs again. I suppose they see larger persons doing these wonderful things and, long before they can talk, resolve to do them too."

"An enormous part of our mature experience, also," said Whitehead, "cannot be expressed in words."

"Dr. McFee Campbell, the professor of psychiatry in the Harvard Medical School, said something similar a few evenings ago," said I, "—that words are clumsy, or quite inadequate to express certain experiences or emotions."

"That is what poetry at its best does," said Whitehead, "—comes somewhere near capturing in a net of words one of those powerful, evanescent moments, of happiness or pain. After all, a word is only a sound, and the relationship between that sound and an experience is very artificial and arbitrary. Look up the poet's words in the dictionary, and you will find that the meanings there given do not total the poet's; he has *added* to their meaning by emotional overtones, so that in some cases you follow the accretions of meaning which successive poets have added to words. But always in the poetry itself is a fragrance of experience which the poet alone has been able to capture, though we recognize it as also our own."

"Don't we all have some such moments of intense being," I

asked, "when we are peculiarly and uniquely alive? And there they remain, eternal springs, into which we can lower our buckets time after time, and years later, without exhausting them."

"Yes. But it is not *the* experience," corrected Mrs. Whitehead. "It is a *memory* of the moment when we lived so intensely. You see that mirror on the inner wall? Bernardine gave it me. It came from Florence, and I have never happened to see another. It is a 'black' mirror. If it were white, the persons and scenes reflected in it would be mere fresh aspects of their daylight selves; but seen in this curious black medium, they look disembodied; they are 'memories.' My black mirror is the world of memory. And what the poets are able to do with words to save these intense moments of ecstasy or pain from oblivion is a black mirror."

"When first I came to see you," said Grace, "when you lived down by the river, that mirror was the first object that I noticed in your living-room."

"It is different every hour of the day," said Whitehead, "and, being hung where it is, it reflects the sunsets. The effect is extraordinary; again, as Evelyn says, they look like the *memory* of a sunset—or of a very abstruse idea that escaped one. Whenever I hear, as sometimes I do, one of my colleagues say that there are no ideas which cannot be expressed clearly in simple language, I think, 'Then your ideas must be very superficial.' "

"You once said to me," I reminded him, "that certain writers, philosophers among them, think in words; but that you think in concepts, then try to find words to express them. Now what happens between the concept and the word? How do you translate the one into the other?"

"God knows!" said he, fervently. "Sometimes the sentence comes, and sometimes it doesn't."

"He tears up a good many sheets of written paper," supplied his wife in parenthesis.

"Do you visualize your thought, even abstract ideas?" I asked.

"I don't know. Do you?"

"First let me qualify my remark. I don't handle such high voltage of abstraction as you, and yet, having worked at it for a quarter of a century, I know how hard it is to translate even fairly simple abstractions into simple language."

"You handle difficult enough abstractions," said he reassuringly. "I have read your articles."

"Then I can answer. When concentration is at its most intense, the abstract idea seems to be a kind of disembodied substance floating in space; but directly underneath it is some totally irrelevant visual scene—generally from my childhood, say a meadow in summer sunshine."

"That is most singular. No. I don't think I visualize like that."

"Please explain to me," said Grace to the philosopher, "what you mean by concepts."

"I will tell you," said he, his eyes beginning to twinkle. "There opposite me sits Lucien Price. I have a concept of him; of his personality, of his appearance, of the kind of person I think he is, all very definite to me. But when I try to put him into words, what have I? Well, I can say, 'He is a valued friend. I am always glad to see him. His personal appearance is of such a sort. . . .' But I could say exactly the same of Lawrence Lowell."

The two women laughed much harder than I did.

"Alfred," said Grace, "this conversation has reached a climax. You will scarcely do better than that."

"Do you grasp the concept?" said he.

"Perfectly! But I don't think Lucien does. He looks dazed. Do you grasp it?" she appealed to me.

"I'm not sure that I want to."

"Have some ginger-ale," says she, "that will revive you."

After the fortissimo passage ending with Mr. Lowell, Whitehead resumed on a quiet note:

H

"Some of the finest moral intuitions come to quite humble people. The visiting of lofty ideas doesn't depend on formal schooling. Think of those Galilean peasants."

"Our Mary, who has done our housework for nearly twenty years," said Mrs. Whitehead, "has a little girl named Margaret. One Easter she asked about the story of Jesus and the Crucifixion; wanted it explained. So Mary sat down with her and went through it. 'And Jesus died on the Cross?' asked the child. 'Yes,' said her mother. 'And his mother was standing by all that time?' 'Yes.' 'But why didn't his mother die for him?' Mary was quite taken aback."

The question then arose why and how a noble or original idea, after having been promulgated, is debased almost beyond recognition. Inventions are turned from production to destruction; Christianity is made a pretext for persecution; the classics of symphonic music are hawked about night-clubs in garbled versions which are almost obscene. In its original form, does such an idea have to come to an exceptionally lofty nature; and is it necessarily debased by exposure to the commonalty? Whitehead took it up:

"Intuition may be an angel," said he, "but intellect can play the devil. Of course you must have intellect to manage the ideas that come through intuition; but the mischief enters when the ideas begin to be certified and classified and organized into rigid formulas. Christianity is a fearful example. The Jews had originally a barbaric morality which was gradually undergoing humanization at the hands of their finer spirits, although it was also from time to time rebarbarized by the coarser. I don't remember that the Buddhistic religion was ever guilty of such fearfully immoral ideas as the Hebrew theology in its earlier form or the Christian in its later: that mankind were to be either saved or damned, and damned to eternal torment. Rather, the Buddhist held that we are, all of us, so imperfect that we must keep returning lifetime after lifetime for purification through experience until we are worthy to lose our identity in the all. But the Jews, looking around them, saw always an Oriental despot, and so, looking over the world at large, thought there must be a despot over all, and the consequence was they conceived one of the most immoral Gods ever imagined."

"Fancy Jehovah telling Abraham to sacrifice his son!" said Mrs. Whitehead.

" 'An honest God is the noblest work of man,' " I quoted Samuel Butler.

"It is true," said Grace, "Jehovah did things which any one of us would have hesitated to do."

" 'Hesitated?' " said Mrs. Whitehead. "You mean horrified."

"Do you remember that remark of Thomas Hardy about the 'jealous God' in *Tess of the D'Urbervilles?*" I asked.

"No," said Whitehead. "What is it?"

"I remember it," said Mrs. Whitehead. "Quote it him."

" 'But although to visit the sins of the fathers upon the children may be a morality good enough for divinities, it is scorned by average human nature.' "

"How amiable the Grecian gods appear by comparison," said Mrs. Whitehead. "They may have had their crimes and follies, and have been no better than they should have been, but their offences were more urbane."

"Yes," I said. "Even if they, too, went to the devil in the end, they had a good time going. The point is, the Greeks always reserved the right to laugh at their gods."

"The total absence of humour from the Bible," remarked Whitehead, "is one of the most singular things in all literature."

"Goethe notices it in the Prologue to *Faust*. Mephistopheles is made to twit God with his lack of humour," I said,

My pathos would but move Your Grace to laughter,
Had not you long since laughter quite abjured.

"The absence of humour from the writings of the ancient Jews may be explained," said Whitehead, "by the fact of their always having been a depressed people. They were always being invaded, and overrun, and deported hither and yon. The Greeks, on the other hand, no matter what happened to them, or whether they really were on top or not, always regarded themselves as being on top."

We began comparing the *Iliad*, in which the gods laugh, with the Bible. The authors of the Bible conceived their function to be that of edification—if you didn't like it, you *ought* to; the authors (or author) of the *Iliad* considered themselves artists. If they failed to interest you, it was not your fault, but theirs.

"But has the *Iliad* had the effect of good that the Bible has had?" objected Grace. "I read the Bible stories at the right age and later their shine never came off."

"The *Iliad*," said Whitehead, "is probably the origin of our idea of the gentleman. But the gentleman is not a complete answer."

As the evening wore on we fell to discussing the relative merits of maple syrup and suet pudding.

"Maple syrup? That gluey substance?" said Mrs. Whitehead. "I abhor it."

"She walks out on the choicest article New England can produce!" I appealed to my fellow-Yankee.

"Go slow," says Grace. "I'm not too strong for maple syrup myself."

"If you really want to take me on my weak side," confessed Mrs. Whitehead, "try me with suet pudding!"

"Suet pudding!" exclaimed Grace. "*That* awful preparation?"

"It's not awful. It's quite heavenly. On that side I'm quite, quite unregenerate."

"So here we are," said Whitehead, "after having discussed the loftiest abstractions, down to suet pudding. The historic cycle is complete; it is the decay of a civilization, into suet pudding!"

XXVII

May 5, 1943

AN evening at the Whiteheads' with Edward Weeks. It had been planned for months, yet this was the first time it had been practicable for all of us. Since Whitehead's work has been appearing in the *Atlantic Monthly* for many years, both when Ellery Sedgwick was editor and since the editorship has been assumed by Mr. Weeks, they were well acquainted.

After having dined, we walked up Prescott Street to the Hotel Ambassador in the twilight of one of the few mild evenings in this painfully belated spring.

He had asked whether anybody else would be there except the Whiteheads. I didn't know, but hoped not. They were alone, to the great satisfaction of us both; lamps lighted, shades and blackout curtains drawn, and the living-room brightened with big bowls and vases of spring flowers.

Mrs. Whitehead had had a severe sprain to her ankle, almost a fracture. It was a surprise to find her walking on it.

"It hurts," said she, "but I have to do it. . . ."

Conversational preliminaries were then of the briefest. In the May *Atlantic* had appeared a leading article by President Conant of Harvard, "*Wanted: American Radicals.*" It proposed a third choice between the two old alignments, a radicalism that should be indigenous, Jeffersonian, with a good word for Andrew Jackson, Emersonian in the temper of his "American Scholar," with Walt Whitman for its poet; and respectful but aloof to Marx, Engels, and Lenin. It was addressed to planning for the post-war world: foreign policy, internal problems such as ownership or control of the tools of production, decentralization, attack on a stratified society, and an attempt to redefine culture in democratic and American terms.

"I say," Whitehead appealed to the editor of the magazine, "what response are you getting to Mr. Conant's article?"

"It is still a little early to judge."

"I should think you would get fifty letters in each morning's mail, denouncing him for writing and you for publishing it."

"What do *you* think of it?"

"His idea of having a redistribution of wealth every generation is challenging. I don't say it is new. But as presented by him it lacks practicality. You could do it by taxation, but that would merely come to the government's getting it. A certain amount of surplus wealth in the hands of private individuals is favourable to all sorts of experimentation."

"What is going to become of the English landed aristocracy?"

"It has already happened," Whitehead replied calmly. "They are ruined. The government takes their land, allows them to remain in the houses as custodians, but the land is turned over into cultivation, and trees are grown not as ornaments but as a crop. Old trees are being cut down for war purposes and small pines planted."

"My England!" sighed Mrs. Whitehead. "I am glad I shall never see it again."

"After the war," he continued, "I doubt if we shall ever again have as big a foreign trade, and that means we must do more in agriculture."

Mr. Weeks, who has just returned from a transcontinental tour, spoke of the sweeping industrialization of the West, from Texas on up the Pacific Coast to Puget Sound, at the expense of the inland agricultural states. The report was given in some detail and listened to intently, since it is all too recent to have been described very conclusively in print. This led to certain questions about the conduct of the magazine, due to curtailment of the paper supply, which he answered briefly but explicitly. He said that American publishers have been warned by English ones not to create a powerful competitor in the form of the government, with unlimited access to the paper pool and power to commandeer printeries.

There was a year in the 1920's, money still being flush, when it was told me at the Old Corner Book Store that in this country alone twenty thousand new books were published. I mentioned this, naming the year.

"You are wrong about that," Weeks corrected me. "About nine thousand were new. For the rest, they counted reprints."

"Even at nine thousand," (which was my point) "quantities of them must have been worthless."

"You look straight at a man who has published twelve books," said Whitehead, looking back at me, "and say that many of them can't have been worth printing!"

The conversation turned to whether men of exceptional intellect are successes as statesmen.

"They rarely get a chance to try," said Whitehead. "The kind of man who is wanted to run a state, and the kind of man who mostly does run it, is the one who, while he may not be exceptional intellectually, has a good nose for what needs to be done."

"Can we think of any exceptions?"

"Disraeli!" exclaimed Whitehead and Weeks in the same breath. "Thomas Jefferson would be another of my candidates," added Weeks, after a moment of reflection.

"The men who founded your republic," Whitehead continued, "had an uncommonly clear grasp of the general ideas that they wanted to put in here, then left the working out of the details to later interpreters, which has been, on the whole, remarkably successful. I know of only three times in the Western world when statesmen consciously took control of historic destinies: Periclean Athens, Rome under Augustus, and the founding of your American republic."

This raised an inquiry as to what extent statesmen in power at great historical crises can be alive to the magnitude of the destinies involved. Augustus—the ancient world was in the gravest peril when he took over Rome, yet could he remotely have envisaged what was at stake for the future of Europe and the West?

"No," said Whitehead. "Being a Roman, he wanted to save

the Roman Empire. In so doing, it resulted that the Roman Empire became the bottleneck through which the culture of the ancient world passed into Northern Europe and to the Western Hemisphere. And now, after five hundred years, the civilization of the Renaissance is crumbling. In great historical events you can seldom assign a single cause. Several causes coalesce. The Russians got sick of their fearfully wasteful czarist government; the Hapsburg monarchy was ready to fall; France was decaying far faster than we supposed; and Germany had that unstable monarch, Wilhelm II. Bismarck did his work too well. He would be horrified if he could see the lengths to which it has been carried. The collapse of the five-hundred-year-old Renaissance civilization was not caused by any one of these; and all of these are only a few of the causes. Add to these the industrial revolution and the new scientific techniques. The question was, would this machinery fall into the hands of the bad people or of the good people? At the start of the industrial revolution, a hundred years ago, the machinery fell, I should say, on the whole into the hands of fairly good people; they exploited the poor, but at least they used it for production. But in our time, these new technologies have fallen, temporarily let us hope and believe, into the hands of the bad people; predatory gangsters. All of these causes were cumulatively present; the separate events were results. I don't say that Europe is done for for ever; it will recover in time of course; but it is collapsed for a generation, if not longer. Three of the modern states with good societies which I hope will survive are Denmark, Norway and Sweden."

He went on to speak of the element of chance in history—how a British expeditionary force bound for China was diverted to Calcutta just in time to help quell the Sepoy Rebellion, and concluded humorously:

"Divine Providence seemed to be on our side."

"But Divine Providence plays no favourites," said Weeks laughingly, and cited that extraordinary succession of seeming coincidences on the Hudson River which revealed the plot of Benedict Arnold.

" 'As luck would have it,' " quoted Mrs. Whitehead, from Samuel Butler's *Erewhon*, " 'Providence was on my side.' "

But what *is* "coincidence," the question was resumed. Sometimes it appears beneficent; again, as with the Athenians before Syracuse, it looks maleficent, and in such a sequence as positively to suggest foreordination. What are we to suppose? Do the causes lie deeper than mere brute accidents?

"The causes, I am inclined to think," said Whitehead, "are there all along, and the events which we see, and which look like freaks of chance, are only the last steps in long lines of causation."

A tray was brought in. The little cakes were in a silver basket which, as an inscription on it read, had been presented to Mr. Whitehead's father, the vicar, in 1858.

As conversation was allowed to drift for a few minutes, there was space to enjoy the pictorial element. The three sat in shaded lamplight; Weeks, as usual, looking slim, trim and vigorous, though more than usually alert; Mrs. Whitehead stretched at her ease, the lamp beams falling more directly on her face, which gains expressiveness with age. An embroidered shawl was thrown over her knees, and beside her was a bowl of garden flowers. Occasionally she or Weeks smoked a cigarette. Whitehead's eyes retain their blue brilliancy undimmed, his complexion is still ruddy, his voice clear, strong, and melodious. As he speaks, he turns from one to another of us; his speech is deliberate, perfectly articulated, everything weighed, the qualifying clauses duly entered, the language precise and almost mathematically exact. The youth of his face is astonishing. This is often remarked by others. It is the illumination of thought within which gives him this glow and glisten. Also, it is communicated; one's own perceptions are heightened.

The discussion was resumed by Whitehead's saying:

"Americans care more for equality than they do for liberty.

You have it in a sense in which we do not, but you are much harder than we on the people who don't make good. Over here it is assumed that if a man doesn't make good it must of course be his own fault. There is much more fellow-feeling in England between the upper classes and the labouring people. With us, classes are more solidified, but while our class-lines run horizontally, our lines of friendship are vertical."

This called forth a remark that, especially since the present war has so shuffled our population, it is noticeable how people try to ease the situation for one another.

"The kindness of the American people," said Whitehead, in his gentlest tones, "is, so far as I know, something unique in the history of the world, and it is the justification of your existence. Your immigrants, before the 1880's when your immigration began to be commercialized by the steamship companies, came, in the main, because they liked the American idea. In fact, one cause of the collapse of Europe may be that so many of the abler people left Europe and came over here. Your German 'forty-eighters' are one of your best population strains."

"We didn't fare so badly, as it turned out, with most of those who came after the 1880's—" observed Weeks, rising to light Mrs. Whitehead's cigarette—"little as some of those who brought them over here may have intended the result. It is probable that their cheap labour affected the living standards of our workers for a generation, but their children went to our public schools and learned a lively sense of their civil rights."

"England, too, got some of the German forty-eighters," said Mrs. Whitehead. "You will find them among the wealthy manufacturers in places like Birmingham. And they have this peculiarity, that among them is, so far as I know, the only anti-Semitism in England."

"Anti-Semitism was very rare," assented Mr. Whitehead. "In my home village in Kent my father's old friend Sir Moses Montefiore was a Jew and no one ever gave it a thought."

"I fell in love with this place when I came here to live," said Mrs. Whitehead, "and where I love I'm not critical. But I do notice a hardness toward shop assistants by customers. It would be just as easy to be kinder when they haven't what one wants. In your streetcars the young and the old are treated royally. Grey hair never has to stand. But in between I have seen women standing who ought to have been seated—one, who looked as if she was about to have a child—that very day. . . . On the other hand, this is the sort of thing that can happen: one summer at a cottage in a Vermont village our plumbing went out. I was told the plumber was a very peculiar, independent man, and maybe he would fix it, and maybe he wouldn't. Anyhow, we sent for him. He didn't come. Late in the afternoon, while Alfred and North were off somewhere, and I was sitting on the porch, a man came in, dressed as we all are up there, in a sweater. I said my husband would be back shortly and asked if he wouldn't come up and wait. We chatted. He was interesting and well-read. By and by I asked him if he would have tea. He said he would. So I brought it. We had tea and I was growing more and more interested in what he had to say, when finally he said, 'Well, I guess I had better have a look at your plumbing.' "

"Had you no inkling who he was?"

"I suppose I might have had; but I hadn't."

"One thing we lack, though, and that is a visible, tangible past," said Weeks. "We try to invent it; we get it out of books, but it is always an effort. And this pastlessness is emphasized by our mobility. We not only never die in the house where we were born, but we move out of it before we are out of knee breeches, and when we go back to visit our birthplace, the house has been demolished and on its site stands a filling station. In the New Jersey town where I was brought up, and where the suburbs of New York were already reaching into that countryside, there was only one 'Great House.' We children of the town were never invited there to tea, though we were allowed to visit its gardens, but it stood for something in our life of the imagination."

"Our sense of the past in England," said Whitehead, "is so all-pervasive that it is quite unconscious with us. Everywhere we turn, the past is before us, in buildings, monuments, history, legend—five hundred years of it, a thousand years of it. And it enters, of course, into all that we think and do."

"How was this 'pastlessness' in the town where you grew up?" Weeks turned to me.

"We had less past than you. A building in the Western Reserve of Ohio that had stood seventy-five years was 'old.' But what we lacked in past we made up in equality."

"That would mean," asked Professor Whitehead, "that anyone who got rich went away?"

"No one went away rich. It was necessary to go away in order to get rich. Among those who stayed, there were a few shadowy class-lines, but at bottom everybody was felt to be about as good as anybody else, if he paid his debts."

"You have omitted one class-line of the American small town a generation ago," said Weeks.

"What is that?"

"It was not respectable to get drunk."

"That is true. The orgies of the 1920's had blurred my memory of it."

"Do you think there is any possibility of a re-enactment of Prohibition?" Mrs. Whitehead appealed to Mr. Weeks.

"The waves of that Prohibition movement are beating against the *Atlantic* office more heavily month by month. I hope there is no danger of a repetition. But arguments come in that are deaf and blind to every lesson of experience. How about liquor smuggling in England," he inquired of Whitehead, "when you lived on that Kentish coast? Was there an incentive to bringing it in, or was there nothing to bring in that couldn't be had just as easily at home?"

"On the marshes near the sea," said Whitehead, "stood a very old church. All I know about it is that a hundred and forty years ago, say in Napoleon's time, a great deal of very superior brandy and wine used to come up those marshes and was stored in the vaults of that church, with the approbation of the vicar. And more than once, when word was brought, during service, that officers were coming up the road, the whole congregation adjourned to get that liquor out of the way— assisted by the vicar! That is evidence," he concluded, beaming upon us, "of how intimately the Established Church shares the life of the nation."

XXVIII

June 3, 1943

EDWARD WEEKS and I play a return engagement with the Whiteheads. It was a day of summer heat which, coming suddenly after the cold, backward spring, took the gimp out of everybody. At 53 Chestnut Street, the house of Weeks was in curl-papers; they were to leave for their summer at Beverly Farms next morning.

Beacon Hill in June can look quite bridal. Flowers blooming in the little areas between iron fences and red-brick house walls; wisteria and ivy climbing house-fronts; fresh foliage and grass plots in dooryards and Louisburg Square. No sooner does the town turn beautiful than we go away and leave it.

There was a quick shift of scene from Boston to Cambridge. In order to reach the Whiteheads' at the appointed time, we took a taxicab. Their blackout curtains were drawn, but all the windows of all the rooms being open, a light breeze drafted through refreshingly. Some June garden had filled the vases of this living-room with irises, peonies, and yellow lilies.

No preliminaries.

"Your June number of the *Atlantic*," said Whitehead to Weeks, "is brilliant."

"Luck," said he, modestly, "but one is very thankful for it. Just the right things came in at the right moment."

(Among the right things were "Bring Back the Liberal Arts" by F. K. Rand, "The Unimagined America" by Archibald MacLeish, "Western Star" by Stephen Vincent Benét, and "The Hoover Frame of Mind" by Rebecca West.)

It appeared that Mr. Weeks had been in Washington, "where I had an hour's talk with Wavell, or rather, was talked to by him for an hour."

"How did he seem?"

"It was about Tobruk, Crete, and India; none of it too cheerful. He seemed worn and tired, not discouraged, but pretty well used up." (Weeks was softening this. It had come into the newspaper office that the impression Wavell made in Washington was of a man all but exhausted.) "What he told was interesting. He had taken over that command in Africa when it looked anything but hopeful; and they were as surprised as anybody at how fast and how far they were able to go."

The discussion swung to the situation in India. They said that Roosevelt was careful not to intrude on British colonial affairs.

"I admire him for that," said Mrs. Whitehead. "God knows we've made mistakes enough; but they must be corrected by ourselves. Are you for Roosevelt? . . ." She hesitated and made as if to draw back.

"Very much so," said Weeks. "I'm a Democrat."

"Good! One never knows which way people are going to jump on that question. We grow used to feeling our ground first. There ought to be some emblem we could wear so as to recognize one another," said she.

"A campaign button on our lapels," suggested Mr. Weeks. "But that might prove more awkward than none."

I remarked that it had sometimes brought good luck for people to be politically incommunicado, especially in touchy times.

"Indeed yes!" said Whitehead, smiling. "It was a piece of especially good luck for us that our first two kings of the Hanoverian dynasty couldn't speak English. When finally we got a third who could, he involved us in that trouble with you people, from which we have not yet fully recovered, and, to make matters worse, George III was an exemplary family man, well liked by the people: 'Farmer George,' good husband, kind father, that sort of thing: he had all the domestic virtues which gave fatal weight to his appalling political ineptitude."

"Even the Nonconformists," added Mrs. Whitehead, "respected him."

"Haven't you said," I asked him, "that the Hanoverian dynasty was only tolerated on good behaviour?"

"They were brought over by a group of Whig nobles," said Whitehead. "These nobles were the 'committee.' Had the first two Georges proved meddlesome, they could have been sent home. It was George III, in my opinion, who caused us to be on the wrong side when the French Revolution came along. Otherwise, I think we might have enacted the reforms of the 1830's in 1789. Had we done so, we should have got on much better with the French, and we would have gone into the Industrial Age of the next century without those dreadful urban slums."

As the conversation veered to the art of letters, Weeks asked Whitehead what shape he thought literature might take when this war ends.

Replying, Whitehead spoke of the tendency toward satire after a war, instancing Lytton Strachey after the last war, but said that such men, however amusing, are sterile and the ensuing crop is likely to be thin.

"Do you think," asked Mr. Weeks, "that we shall be repossessed by the Freudians in literature?"

"They are an example of what I mean by the naïve acceptance of a part of the truth as the whole truth," said Whitehead. "The ideas of Freud were popularized by people who only imperfectly understood them, who were incapable of the great effort required to grasp them in their relationship to larger truths, and who therefore assigned to them a prominence out of all proportion to their true importance."

"Add to that," said Weeks, "their popularity with a post-war generation which wanted to be told exactly what these incomplete interpretations of Freud seemed to say."

"You once remarked" (my question had been long pending) "that between the time when experience enters into us and when it is uttered forth again in language or in action there is a gap about which we know nothing. Have you gone any farther with it?"

"Last week during commencement," Whitehead replied, "a brain specialist was here. He said that our bodily experience is transmitted to the brain through the spinal column, and especially to that part of the brain at the back of our heads. I had often observed people with big bulges at the back of their skulls and thought, 'Isn't it a pity that they couldn't have had those bulges at the front of their skulls where it would have done them some good,' but it appears that I was quite mistaken. This surgeon informs me that a man can have quite a lot of his brain removed from here or here" (he pointed to his left and right temples) "and get on quite as well as ever; but if any serious disconnection takes place at the back of the neck, the man is an idiot. Philosophers have known for centuries that our senses are no reliable testimony to the existence of the outside world. That has been known not only since the seventeenth- and eighteenth-century men, but as far back as the Greeks. There was absolutely no reason to infer the existence of external reality from any evidence brought in to us by our senses. It is all subjective. The outer world may not be there at all. And yet, as a matter of fact, the only human beings who do not assume the existence of that outer world as a reality are in the lunatic asylums. But all the while, our knowledge of it is brought to us up our spinal columns through our bodily experience, the pleasurable functioning of our organs. For our bodies *are* a part of that external world, just as much as this chair in which my body is at present sitting. So I wouldn't advise you to let anything serious happen to the back of your neck. The front of your head; yes, you can be as careless with that as you like, and still get on fairly well; but if the back of your neck gets dislocated, then you are really in a bad way."

This led to some gaiety at the expense of masseurs. When the discussion sobered down again, we came to that passage in *Adventures of Ideas* (page 355) where a striking sentence seems to bear upon this mystery of what happens between the time when external experience impinges on body, spinal column, and brain, and the time when it is uttered forth again. That sentence is:

The process is itself the actuality.

This was quoted to him with the remark, "People have told me that once it gets into their heads, it won't come out. I think I know what it means; at least, I know what it means to me. But would you tell us what it means to you?"

"It took a long while, centuries in fact, for philosophers to get beyond the idea of static matter," said he. "Certain substances, like water or fire, could be seen to be changing rapidly; others, like rock, looked immutable. We know now that a piece of granite is a raging mass of activity, that it is changing at a terrific rate; but until we did know it, a rock seemed to possess little or no life, though it looked immensely permanent. But, since there was obviously quite a little mind about, the older philosophers brought it in from the outside. There seemed to be divisions between one part of the universe and another. But in the light of what we now know, there is no dividing line between the infinitely vast and the infinitely small. The element of time affects it too. Our human bodies change from day to day; certain external appearances of them are the same, but change is constant and sometimes visible. The constellations do not appear to change at all, though we know that they do, as we know that the nebulae have come into their present form but are also passing into another. Whether the change occurs in a minute or in billions of years, is merely a matter of human measurement; the fact of change is not affected by our using, as human beings, the only standards of measurement we have, which are necessarily affected by the limitations of our own lives. We exist here under certain conditions of space and time within which we have to function, and these conditions, unless watched, colour our judgments. . . . This little table by my side"—he tapped it with his fingers—"is in process of change. If you were to shut it up somewhere for ten thousand years and then went back to look at it, the change might be so pronounced that you would hardly know it had been a table; yet the process which would produce that so visible change is going on in it right now, although for all practical human purposes it is the same table you saw the last time you were here and the same one I have seen around for forty years. Change is constant, whether we measure it by minutes or millennia; we ourselves are a part of it; we have been brought into existence in a certain quarter of the universe in consequence of its processes, and there is no reason to suppose that other types of existence, unimaginable to us, have not been produced elsewhere in the universe. Those other lives could scarcely strike us as much more different from us than we now know ourselves to be different from our ancestors. Some of our more immediate ancestors would be quite congenial to us; but as they grow increasingly remote, your ancestors would be creatures which I doubt if you would like at all."

(He had been telling us in simple terms that our judgments are sharply conditioned by time and space, but that the actualities are outside of both, and that change is the process and is itself the actuality.)

"To what extent," I asked, "did mathematics let you into these secrets?"

"Mathematics," said he, "is essentially a study of types of order. In its earlier forms it had to do with number and quantity. That is its historical origin; the idea of mathematical logic is comparatively modern. But while mathematics is a convenience in relating certain types of order to our comprehensions, it does not, as used to be supposed, give us any account of their actuality. You have probably studied the Euclidean geometry, but I doubt if it diminished for you any of the mystery of life."

"I did study the Euclidean geometry, but, not being good at mathematics, it rather increased the mystery of life," I confessed.

"Euclid's geometry was once supposed to be an exact description of the external world. The only world of which it is an accurate description is the world of Euclidean geometry. When it began to be challenged in the eighteenth century, the ascertained deviations from it were at first considered, even by their discoverers themselves, to be errors."

"You once remarked that at the time when the discovery of the magnetic needle found its way into Europe, 'mathematics had been almost useless for a thousand years.' How useless?"

"Archimedes, when the Roman soldier stabbed him, knew as much mathematics as was known at any time until, say, the fourteenth century, when its advance was resumed."

"And we have no control over the process by which the arts or sciences advance or retrograde in one age or another?"

"Take it in our own time," he replied to the question out of his own experience. "I was in Cambridge in the 1880's, first as an undergraduate, later as one of the staff. If was from two hundred to two hundred and fifty years since mathematics had had its fresh impetus from men like Descartes and Sir Isaac Newton; there were certain borderlands where affairs in that science were considered indefinable, but in the main, mathematical physics looked sound and solid. . . . By the turn of the century, nothing, absolutely nothing was left that had not been challenged, if not shaken; not a single major concept.

This, I consider to have been one of the supreme facts of my experience."

"Could the same be said of religion and ethics?" I asked.

"Yes, with this difference, that philosophy and science welcomed these new hypotheses which upset their old ones, and thus profited by them; whereas, religion resisted the new ideas and has suffered in consequence."

"Can this rate of change be expected to continue?" asked Weeks.

"The consequences of these new ideas in science will continue to affect our lives profoundly, especially their techniques. We talk about the changes wrought on society by the 'Industrial Revolution' of, roughly, a century ago; beginning, say, about 1790, and coming on up into the nineteenth century. They are as nothing when compared to the scientific revolution which has been going on for the past fifty years; say, since 1890. But new techniques are easier to grasp and less important in their results than new discoveries; they are also illusory, for they give people an impression that advance is still going on when, as a matter of fact, its impetus may have already spent itself."

"In view of some of the uses that are being made of the new techniques," said Weeks, "we could perhaps afford to pause a little, until man catches up with them sociologically."

"It was in the nature of things, I suppose," said Whitehead, "that these new techniques should fall into the hands of bad people. . . . And then, too, the techniques in their turn assisted to fresh discoveries. But after one such experience in a lifetime of the impermanence of the most solid-seeming ideas, one is chary of overconfidence, and in the last words I have written (at the end of that essay which concludes the volume on my philosophy) I have said: 'The exactness is a fake.' "

"That looks bad for the editor of a magazine," observed Weeks. "How much exactness can be in *our* pages?"

"It looks worse for a daily newspaper," I added with corresponding candour.

"You can append notes at the bottoms of your leading articles," suggested Whitehead, by way of letting us down easily, "explaining that this is what looks true today but that tomorrow it may be something quite different."

"That is about the frame of mind in which my 'leading articles' *are* written. Nietzsche has remarked that nobody knows what news is important until a hundred years afterward."

"The life of an idea," Whitehead dealt with this, "varies widely. Some live two hundred years, others two thousand. Some last no longer than a year or two; and others have to wait centuries before they are taken up and put into effect. Here again, the element of time is capricious. But no period, I think, has ever seen such a complete overturn in the established modes of thought as this past half-century. There is one philosopher who would not have been surprised. In reading Plato today we have occasionally to say, 'Poor fellow, he didn't know this . . . or that'; but in the main he had anticipated most of these possibilities. Fewer allowances, on the whole, need be made for him than for anyone else. Aristotle now . . . Aristotle would have been horrified; for he divided and classified into separate genera and species. But Plato holds. I find myself more engrossed by his later work, embodying metaphysical ideas—like the *Theaetetus*—than in the earlier ones, where he is more concerned with sociology, some of which, to our notions, don't come off too well."

We joined in comparing this with what often happens from long study of some great artist—how we gradually find our preferences gravitating to his later works, as to the last quartets and pianoforte sonatas of Beethoven. . . .

"The works of Plato I return to again and again," said Whitehead, "are the ones which come after the *Republic*. His method is to announce his subject, then present it rapidly in numerous aspects, few of which had occurred to anybody else, and which arouse eager activity in the reader's mind. Those ideas are thrown out more or less at random: this done, he begins to relate them to the lives of those people living in his own time who would be most nearly able to grasp them; then, as he goes on, he 'commonizes' them until they seem to have been brought within the comprehension of the multitude; but, mind you, in so doing much of the virtue of the ideas will have evaporated."

"You once showed me a passage in the *Timaeus* which exactly conforms to your description of this process."

"When ideas are commonized, they tend to lose their force. That which relates them to the specific forms of life in any given period is necessarily ephemeral. Something of this ephemerality is also in the ideas themselves even in their purest and most powerful form. I have tried to allow for that fact when dealing with the ideas of philosophers in other periods; obviously their thinking, however abstract, was coloured to some extent by the land and time in which they lived, by the historical forces at work, by the intellectual climate, and all the peculiar conditions governing life when they thought and wrote. This point seems to have been missed by all, or most, of the people who have written about my work, and it invalidates much of what they have had to say. I have made my point clear, both in speech and writing; but if it isn't grasped, it isn't. One cannot go on repeating. There is an instance of what I mean in those last two lectures, at the end of the volume I mentioned. Plato's God is a God of this world. Augustine combined Plato's God with St. Paul's and made a fearful job of it. Since then our concept of this world has enlarged to that of the universe. I have envisioned a union of Plato's God with a God of the universe."

The clang of the big clock-bell in the tower of Memorial Hall striking the hour was a startling reminder of time in the midst of this contemplation of eternity. In through the open windows drifted the mild air of the sultry June evening. Mrs. Whitehead and I went out into the kitchenette to bring the tray of biscuits, whisky, and water. Their own drinks were temperate: for her, plain water without ice; for him, plain water with ice.

While we were breaking out ice cubes a burst of laughter sounded from the living-room.

"We're missing it," said I.

We hustled back.

"He was speaking," said Weeks, "of the modern gap between statesmanship and specialized learning, and I reminded him that the *Atlantic* had published his paper on that subject."

"And I reminded him," said Whitehead, blandly, "that he had cut the first four pages."

"Yes, and you were very wrong to do it," said she, standing over him, and shaking an accusatory forefinger. "We have regretted ever since that we gave our consent."

They had him at their mercy. He pulled the silk shawl over his head in mock terror. There was laughter and the episode was accepted as comedy.

"I considered those opening pages essential to my discussion," resumed Whitehead. "They distinguished between the arts and the sciences, between literature and history, and between a static and an active social system. I am magnanimous; I forgive you, even if you did suppress my thought, for I cannot print those ideas elsewhere now."

"They are printed in full," said I, "in '75-1, Proceedings of the American Academy of Arts and Sciences,' where you delivered the lecture, for I begged a dozen copies from the secretary to send to friends."

"Have you any left?"

"Yes."

"Could you let me have one?"

"You shall have it tomorrow."

There was another quarter of an hour before we had to go, during which the conversation came back from universals to particulars, such as the impending coal strike, and how far anyone would get if he tried to publish an impartial account of the issues. We left shortly after ten o'clock.

In the taxicab, Weeks explained why he had cut the opening pages: "It showed that it had been delivered as a lecture, and people prefer to read what appears to come to them as freshly written."

Next day I reread the opening pages of the lecture as published by the academy. It seemed to me that Whitehead had said in the opening three columns of that pamphlet more than most men can say in thirty.

XXIX

June 10, 1943

THERE had been another wartime commencement, and the College Yard, where I crossed it, was being cleared of scaffolding timber, which had been put up for the out-of-door ceremonies. The grass plot looked trodden into hard ground. Academic Cambridge, like any other academic town out of term-time seemed suddenly deserted.

It was a loury evening with rain in brew and a rising wind. The Whiteheads were alone and seemed more than usually at their ease. In no time at all we were out beyond the harbour jetties and into the conversational open water. It was about the gap between written and spoken language, between literature and vernacular.

"It is quite unlikely," said Whitehead, "that Cicero spoke to his friends in the language of his letters, to say nothing of his orations."

"A slave population complicates it, too," Mrs. Whitehead added. "No matter how vivid or picturesque the vernacular may be, if it is used by a servile class it is avoided by the educated."

I said that the gap seemed particularly wide in English.

"Not so wide as you might think," said he. "The London poorer classes, for example, have an extraordinary appreciation for Shakespeare. His language doesn't put them off at all; their sense of humour is about the same as his; they think the same things are funny. All this is not surprising for they were the sort of people for whom the plays were originally written. There is a school of technology in the East End for which I used to be on the visiting committee, and I saw a good deal of it. One evening a teacher was going over a page of literature in a textbook with his class, and asked the meaning of an unusual seventeenth-century word. One of the young men answered correctly. He was asked how he happened to know. 'I saw a play of Shakespeare's (he named the one) 'at the Old Vic last Thursday night, and that word was used in it in the same sense as here.' "

"The English sense of humour as it expresses itself in common vernacular," said Mrs. Whitehead, "is likely to be coarse; it is also very funny. It is not like French slang, which generally has a nasty innuendo behind it; the English slang is good, honest coarseness that hits you in the face."

"If I may say a good word for American slang," said I, "it is that, besides being fresh and vigorous, it is almost always sweet and clean, pure animal high spirits."

"That is true," he assented, "and very much to your people's credit."

"Slang is the bane of my writing life. Being in a newspaper office I hear it spoken continually, and for a newspaper-reading public complicated ideas need to be in seemingly simple language, but with the literary language to fall back upon at need. For this, slang looks like a short cut but isn't; it is a dead end, a blind alley."

"As a lit'ry gent," Mrs. Whitehead twitted me, "the vigour of a growing language makes you uncomfortable."

"Perhaps. But it also makes me uncomfortable to watch the

subjunctive and auxiliary verbs fade out of our commonly spoken language."

"I'll tell you what," said she suddenly, "as between your speech and ours, American and English, it is a difference in 'style.' If we have style in ours, even in the vernacular, it is because we can't help ourselves; we are unaware of it; but I think idiom and vocabulary, for the time being at least, are spread thinner over here. I often sense a paucity of words even with my friends here who have had most access to them, and if I do hear 'style' in speech, it has had to be acquired (however meritoriously) and that means it had to come out of books."

"A striking instance of that came under my notice in one of our Massachusetts small towns," I said. "He was a fourteen-year-old English boy brought over here to live. Parent for parent and class for class he was no different from the American boy scouts he played with; in fact, they had had, if anything, rather better advantages; and yet every time that English lad opened his mouth he shamed me with his beautiful speech, a natural English idiom. It was nothing he was aware of. He was speaking the only way he knew."

"You Americans have one great advantage which would scarcely have occurred to you," said Whitehead. "I mean Americans of the old English stock. It isn't generally realized, but English literature from the time of Charles II on up to the end of the eighteenth century was so much influenced by French that it lost its distinctive character. That is one reason it is so dull. Restoration comedy, for example, is more French than English."

"Brilliant though it is, it often smells to high heaven."

"The eighteenth-century poets, too," he continued, "are starched and go in the stiff brocades of imitation-French. Now you people in America escaped that. You were off over here maturing whatever it was that you were going to say, and although some of your great figures, like Jefferson and Franklin, were in France during the revolutionary ferment, which the

French felt from you and you from them, so that it is commonly *supposed* that the influence of France on America was considerable, nevertheless it was really much less serious than the influence of France on English thought. Coleridge, Wordsworth, and the later English Romantic poets, Byron, Shelley, Keats, were the reaction against it. On the other hand, when it comes to your use of the language itself, as distinguished from the thoughts you express with it, your situation is, it is true, enormously complicated by your influx of stocks other than English."

"That burden falls on our public-school teachers, and here in Boston, at least, they are meeting it valiantly. Down in Newspaper Row one hears Italian, Greek, Jewish, and heaven knows what other races, of little newsboys crying their wares in correct Bostonese, down to broad *a*'s and softened terminal *r*'s."

"The same need has produced the 'English' courses in your colleges. In the public school, Sherborne, in the west of England, where I was sent as a boy of fifteen, my father, the vicar, having tutored me until then, we never heard of such a thing, nor at Cambridge either until nearly a generation later. The training was Greek, Latin and mathematics. Ancient history came along in the course of Latin and Greek; English history we read because it interested us, and it might surprise you to know how actively we discussed the ancient civilization and how apposite the lessons of the Aegean islands and its adjacent mainlands seemed to us English boys of our own island in its relation to the larger seas and continents. Russia, in those days, was 'Persia' to our 'Greece.' English literature we read for pleasure, especially the poets. Two of Shakespeare's plays were 'taught' us—I can't remember which ones, but I *can* remember that I never cared to read those two plays again, although I read and reread the rest of Shakespeare with delight. Of the modern languages, German we took seriously; but the two subjects which were beneath our serious consideration at school were French and physics." He paused and said, smiling mischievously, "Of science just as little was taught as possible."

"Why not French?" I asked.

"What?" exclaimed Mrs. Whitehead. "Take a 'Froggy Frenchman' seriously in those days? Remember, I was brought up in France and spoke only French until I went to England when I was a girl of seventeen. I spoke English, only no one could understand me."

"The first evening we spent together," volunteered Mr. Whitehead in reminiscence, "I spent showing her pictures, because I couldn't understand what she said."

"Yes, but," said she, "I soon realized that I would not 'do' as I was, and however hard I may have worked to learn English, I worked harder to drop my French accent. One of our Cambridge friends, a delightful man, Theodore Beck, being out in the East somewhere met a Trinity man who had known me and said, 'Have you heard that Whitehead is married?' 'No. Who is she? What is she like?' 'Whitehead has made a great mistake,' said our friend to Beck. 'He has married out of his tripos (out of his subject).' "

"What puzzled me about the two of you for a long time, before I knew you, was that although you had lived, more or less perforce, on the cream of things, in the sense of mental interchange, in Cambridge and later in London, you weren't in the least 'choosy.' Although it never occurred to me in those days that I could come to your Sunday evenings, I was told that anybody over here might come who liked, and that you did get them in droves."

"Sixty to an evening," said she, with pride. "But they came out into the kitchen and helped me."

"I had known professorial families who had come here from other universities and had had, for a while, rather a hard time learning to feel at home in Cambridge. When you people came, it seemed to be a general love feast."

"Tell me," said she, "did we seem very 'foreign' at first?"

"At first, yes. I can remember when the change took place; it was between '34 and '35."

"What made the difference?"

"I loved you both."

She said that explanation sufficed.

"How long have we known each other?" asked Whitehead.

"Eleven years."

"Friendship abolishes time. I feel as though I had known you forty years."

"There is an English novelist whom I used to read and re-read, the reason being that his pages were my only access at that time to the world where you moved as a matter of course, a world where people understood ideas and handled them easily. I mean George Meredith."

"It is true, we did enjoy the society of Trinity and King's, the two colleges where we most naturally knew people," said he, "and by 'society' I do not mean, of course, a silly sense of elevation, but association with people of congenial minds. But in neither Cambridge did we ever pick and choose." He named over several of his colleagues, among whom my ear noted the name of Jebb.

"Jebb? He edited my Sophocles," I exclaimed. "Jebb was always at my elbow in a Greek text when I was here in college, and I often wondered what he was like; but this is the first time I ever picked up his tracks."

"He was a delightful fellow and had a charming wife. She was not exactly learned but you wouldn't have wanted her to be. Her husband had rather a fiery temper which was carried off by the charm of Mrs. Jebb."

"*Lady* Jebb," Mrs. Whitehead corrected him. "Don't rob her ghost. She loved the title."

"The place I came into collision with him," continued Whitehead, "was at elections of Fellows for Trinity, about which he felt very strongly. Each time we came out from such an election, Sir Richard was generally not on speaking terms with

[221]

some one of his colleagues. I would have to say to my wife, 'I say, pet, do ask the Jebbs to dinner. Sir Richard isn't speaking to me at present.' One of his performances which I remember best and enjoyed most was the time he rode into the river on his bicycle."

"Lady Jebb was very kind to me when I arrived in Cambridge as a bride. 'My dear,' said she, 'have as many brothers as you like, but no cousins.' It was good advice and I followed it."

"To me," I said, "as an undergraduate, the editor of my Sophocles was an Olympian."

"Even to his temper!" agreed Mrs. Whitehead demurely.

"He also gave me one of my 'English' courses, about which you were speaking a moment ago. For I, like you, learned about English from Greek."

"Mind you!" Whitehead warned me—"those 'English courses' in American colleges are very necessary. If the ancient Greek and Latin classics aren't taught, then English must be, as best we can. Only I hope they won't make it too dull. Teachers, unless they are born to it, aren't the best persons to make young people love good literature."

"Can you tell me," asked Mrs. Whitehead suddenly, "why men make so much better teachers than women? As a whole, I mean. When a woman teacher *is* good (and I was one and wasn't) she is splendid, but an exception. With men, there is something about it which comes to them naturally (if at all), and they love doing it."

"Confining our remarks to persons not present," (I glanced at the teacher on my right) "it seems to 'take' men in the form of a desire to impart. Richard Wagner had it, knew that he had it, and said in a letter to Mathilde Wesendonck that that was how it took him. One sees the same thing in quite humble people, and it can be very touching: it is compounded of a genuine love of human beings, and a desire to help them . . ."

"Plus the pleasure of holding forth?" asked Mrs. Whitehead.

"Suppose we appeal to the member of the profession present. What can you say for them?"

"Only," said he, eyeing us blandly, "that being one myself, I consider them admirable people."

"The desire to dominate comes into it," his wife stuck to her guns.

"A distinction needs to be made, I think," said he, "between the desire for domination and a love of effective action. The world is always full—and never more so than now—of people who want to dominate"—he shook his clenched fist in the air and set his jaw grimly—"*for the sake of dominating*. But the beneficent people, people like the professional classes and men of creative imagination, want effective activity. You, for instance, when you write your articles, aren't moved by a desire to dominate . . ."

"Even if I were, the illusion of dominating would be impossible to maintain."

"I admit there is a very slender dividing line between the two," said Whitehead, "but it is the division that is important. On one side is sheer love of domination, on the other is the pleasure of effectuating some beneficent activity. . . . Take Wagner's operas, which you love. I don't believe they do you a bit of harm. To you, they are a world of poetic imagination; but to a good many Germans of today I am sure they mean, '*We looted you once, and we shall do it again!*' "

Again the italic was Whitehead's, both in look and in tone.

"Was there ever," I asked, "such a wholesale repudiation of moral principle by supposedly responsible people, as in modern Germany?"

"There have always been people animated by an unscrupulous will to dominate," said he, "among all nations. They were uppermost for longer or shorter periods. What is new about this situation in Germany is its extent and duration. It has been going on longer, with greater intensity, and with wider and more devastating effect."

"You mentioned Meredith, a moment ago," said Mrs. Whitehead. "How could he ever have put two such utterly irreconcilable natures into one woman as he put into Diana? The two could never have lived together in the same skin; they would have burst it!"

This led to a comparison of English and Russian novelists.

"The novel on the grand scale," said Whitehead, "seems to have been done best by the Russians—Tolstoy, Dostoevsky, Turgenev. Except in such hands, where the whole range of society is presented—the family, the political, military, and economic systems, and the clash of personalities and ideas—the novel is concerned largely with the prevailing social habits of a given place and time. This tends to restrict it to secondary range as an art-form, not quite up to those tremendous universal themes of the great Greek tragedies. But, have you noticed that there are a good many second-rate works of art which survive and have a long life—which they may not deserve as well as their betters—because they embody some continuingly popular subject? It is true, a widely popular subject is likely to be a good one, but for purposes of survival the work must appeal to a good many people."

"How our world would like to know whether the thirty-three Greek tragedies which we have are the best of the three hundred and nineteen known to have been written by the three great tragic poets," I said. "Gilbert Murray thinks that the ones which survived probably *are* the best. But if we are to speak of the novel as sociology, the work of fiction which I would read if I wanted a picture of middle-class England in the mid-nineteenth century is by a woman, and the title of it is *Middlemarch*."

"I'll tell you another novelist," said he, "who, I think, comes as close to it, if not closer to the reality, and that is Anthony Trollope."

"Only of you, dear, and your clerical family," said his wife, making him a comic grimace, and in her very sweetest tones.

"I don't deny," she added wickedly, "that the picture is a likeness."

"How about dialogue?" I asked. "How much of it in print or on the stage is a plausible likeness of the way people actually talk?"

"Hallo!" exclaimed Mrs. Whitehead. "Here we are, back at our question of the gap between written and spoken language."

"It is 'sonata form'— the return of themes. . . . Dialogue, as actually spoken, seldom goes into print effectively unless something has been done to it—often quite a little. It must sound the way people talk, but if you try setting down their talk verbatim, you may find that it doesn't seem as lifelike as it ought."

"Art," said Whitehead, coming to our rescue, "is the imposing of a pattern on experience, and our aesthetic enjoyment is recognition of the pattern. The mistake is to think of words as entities. They depend for their force, and also for their meaning, on emotional associations and historical overtones, and derive much of their effect from the impact of the whole passage in which they occur. Taken out of their context, they are falsified. I have suffered a good deal from writers who have quoted this or that sentence of mine, either out of its context or in juxtaposition to some incongruous matter which quite distorted my meaning, or destroyed it altogether."

"Is it something which professional philosophers would be likely to do?"

"I have a poor opinion of philosophers, as a class," said he. "The few first-rate philosophic minds need to be understood in relation to the times in which they lived and thought, and this is precisely what is not done. A philosopher of imposing stature doesn't think in a vacuum. Even his most abstract ideas are, to some extent, conditioned by what is or is not known in the time when he lives. What are the social habits around him, what are the emotional responses, what do people consider important, what are the leading ideas in religion and statesmanship? Descartes, for example, was comparatively a simple man. I think he forgot the seventeenth century."

"So did those who lectured on Descartes here when I was an undergraduate, and it was the same when they came to Spinoza and Leibniz."

"Aristotle better illustrates my point," said Whitehead. "He founded modern science. His divisions of observed phenomena, which he supposed to be whole truths, have been ascertained to be no more than half-truths, if that. Aristotle's divisions into species and genera are true in the sense that we know a dog is different from a baboon, and that both are different from a man; but you and I and the dog and the baboon are all descended from minute particles of animate matter which originated somewhere at the edges of the sea and land millions or billions of years ago. And yet if we are to have science, what Aristotle did was exactly the right thing to do. In science you must have order, and for that you must isolate certain types of order for observation. But again, with science as with philosophy, the subject cannot be understood without studying it in relation to the life which surrounds it. We might just as well have had the Industrial Age in the time of Archimedes; everything necessary was known; the only things lacking were tea and coffee. That fact so affected the habits of people that the Industrial Age had to wait centuries until people in Scotland watched their kettles boil and so invented the steam-engine.

"There is one philosopher," he continued, "who provides his own environing sociological interpretation, and that is the greatest mind ever produced by Western man, Plato. He writes in the dialogue form, several persons are speaking, you get their various points of view, are given a notion of what sort of characters they are and by what surrounding social habits and political institutions their thinking has been affected—the city state, its industry, its economic system, its family life, and traditional customs. I said a while ago that words could not safely be treated as entities or ideas detached from their contexts. They acquire their true meanings from the momentum of the passage, as the beauty of a star is not only in its colour and brightness but also gains from the grandeur of its surrounding immensities."

This was going to require some time to sink in, and, since we were engaged in a conversation, not reading a book which one can lay down or reread for a paragraph, I said, in order to give myself twenty measures' rest:

"For the past year I have been spending evenings with the last quartets and piano sonatas of Beethoven, which are some of the most abstruse music ever written. I don't pretend that I understand them except in parts, but they, too, like the beauty of a star, gain from the grandeur of their surrounding immensities of thought. They plunge one for hours at a time into a world of abstract values, like higher mathematics, and I actually think they have made me better able to comprehend some of the higher mathematics of abstract thought which I hear from you. Music is of course highly mathematical and it is also abstract. It is peculiar, too, in having at one and the same time an emotional and an intellectual content. I do not presume to define music, but I do think that music is a mathematics of aesthetic."

"I would accept that definition," said he, "for I think we take in quite as much through our sense of hearing as by our sense of sight, perhaps more. Mind you, I don't mean to compare our dependency on the two senses, for we are more dependent on sight, since we have mobility. But I think we respond more to a solemn sound, to music, or to a great bell. It establishes the emotion almost instantaneously, and we think about it only later. Organ music much more easily conveys a devotional attitude than visual objects. Your national anthem, which I hear frequently over the radio, does not, fortunately, lend itself to being shouted by mobs in unison, but it admirably serves its purpose and, hearing it, I am more moved than I am by the sight of your flag. I say nothing," he smiled as he spoke, "about the relative merits of your national flag *as* a flag. The point I am making is that, with the sense of sight, the idea communicates the emotion, whereas, with sound, the emotion communicates the idea, which is more direct and therefore more powerful."

"Mr. Judd, the manager of the Boston Symphony Orchestra, and I were at a performance of Ibsen's *John Gabriel Borkman*," I remarked. "In the second act, someone plays Saint-Saëns's *Danse Macabre* behind the scenes. The play is powerful, but when the music stopped, we looked at each other and smiled. The music, though toned down so as not to blur the dialogue, had smashed the scene. It had done just what you said—spoken to the emotions directly."

"Ninety per cent of our lives," he replied, "is governed by emotion. Our brains merely register and act upon what is telegraphed to them by our bodily experience. Intellect is to emotion as our clothes are to our bodies: we could not very well have civilized life without clothes, but we would be in a poor way if we had only clothes without bodies."

The clock of Memorial Hall had struck nine. Mrs. Whitehead brought the tray of hot chocolate. In the time remaining we talked of a period in history which had looked very fortunate, one in which all three of us had, at varying lengths, lived.

"One of the happiest times that I know of in the history of mankind," said he, "was the thirty years, roughly, from 1880 to 1910. I am not suggesting that there were not a great many things which needed changing; but we intended to change them and had set about doing so. For people like us, moderately comfortable, the conditions were ideal—not too much money, engrossing work to be done, and a sense of purpose and progress in the world."

"We were working, too," said Mrs. Whitehead, "for ends which were often against the interests of our class."

"My wife, between the ages of twenty and twenty-five, had a

difficult time," said he. "She had her living to earn in London."

"I was young and unprotected and had to go alone to and from my work. My clothes exposed me to pestering, because they were not the right kind for a working girl, but I had to wear them, for they were the only ones I had."

"For myself," he continued, "I may say that all my life I have had perfect conditions. And in those years between 1880 and 1910, we often used to speak of what a wonderful world to live in our children would have."

XXX

June 19, 1943

AT the previous luncheon of the Saturday Club in May, Whitehead had been absent. He sent word that the edict forbidding the use of gasoline for going to social gatherings applied, so far as he was concerned, to taxicabs, and since the Cambridge subway was out of the question for him, he must stay away. The regret was general. I remarked:

"We ought to be ingenious enough to get him here. The Checker Taxi Company has horse-drawn cabs on the street."

"You and Alfred Kidder are appointed a committee to see what can be done," said the chairman.

This commission led me to the South End where, in the stable of the Checker Taxi Company, the nineteenth century is still going full blast. Here were ostlers, grooms, and at least thirty good horses, and vehicles that are now museum pieces: hansom cabs, victorias, landaus, broughams, barouches, surreys, traps, flys, and a tallyho. The very stable-smell itself was a museum piece; how it brought back the good old days! A one-horse brougham was chosen, very smart, upholstered with Morocco; bevelled plate-glass windows, speaking-tube, and side lanterns. It was forty years old, had belonged to some wealthy family whose name I forget, and used to be sent over the road to Washington every winter.

★   ★   ★

(The Saturday Club will arrive at its centenary in 1955. "Mr. Emerson very often left his study in Concord on a Saturday to go to the Athenaeum Library, call on friends, or see his publishers on business. He was likely to stop in at the original 'Corner Book Store' on the corner of Washington and School Streets." Six years before it was started Emerson was talking over with his friends a plan for a club where lonely scholars, poets, and naturalists, like those of Concord, might find congenial company when they came to the city. Two clubs actually resulted, and nearly at the same time. One, the Magazine Club, gave birth in 1857 to *The Atlantic Monthly*. The Saturday gradually displaced or absorbed it. Among the early members were Emerson, Hawthorne, Longfellow, Lowell, Holmes, Motley, Dana, Whittier, Prescott, Agassiz, and Parkman. Its luncheons were, and are, on the last Saturday of each month from September to June, with some skirmishing each June to meet the Harvard commencements. In those brave days of the nineteenth century they sat from three o'clock till nine, at the Parker House, in a large front room where long windows looked out on the bronze statue of Dr. Franklin—what a prized member he would have made!—in the green grounds of the City Hall. It now meets at the Union Club on Park Street, almost within a baseball's throw of those two original landmarks, the Athenaeum and the Old Corner Book Store, now moved to Bromfield Street. These facts and quotations are from the first of two plump volumes of its annals, *The Early Years of the Saturday Club*, by Edward Waldo Emerson.)

★   ★   ★

Luncheon was at one-thirty. The cab was ordered to be at the Hotel Ambassador in Cambridge at twelve-thirty. It was there on the tick, a brougham but not the one ordered. Later, it appeared why. This one was a little seedy, the handle was off the door on its port side, it was upholstered in royal purple, and though it had various odours, including the horsy one, I could smell no traces of funeral wreaths about it. So we got in.

It was no motor-car. The seats, though cushioned, were hardish; knee-room was none too generous, hard rubber tyres on wooden wheels do not much mitigate the jolts of paving blocks (and all this used to be considered luxury); but the windows were open, it was a radiant June day with a fresh breeze and blazing sunshine. The shortest route to Park Street was down Cambridge through the factory district and over the Longfellow Bridge.

Our equipage attracted attention. William Hill, the cab driver, wore a high black silk hat, not as new as it had been once, and a blue coat, ditto, with brass buttons. Pedestrians seemed surprised. They first thought it was an advertising stunt, I think, and were looking for the sign. Since there was no sign, their next idea was that it might be a pair of undergraduates on a spree, and peered in to see who was riding. The occupants did not fit that theory. Everybody grinned and some laughed outright. As the cab rolled down through the factory district, the little boys playing in the streets, untroubled by inhibitions, shouted jeering remarks; and occasionally a passing taxicab driver would lean out and deliver a wisecrack to our cabby, "Step on it, Grandpa!"

All this was not much more than a subconscious accompaniment to the subject under discussion.

"We are," said Whitehead, "in the dissolution of that historical period which I date, roughly, from about 1450 A.D.; which, in turn, began with the break-up of the Middle Ages. I doubt if anyone in the thirteenth century realized what was already happening."

"Is it ever generally possible," I asked, "for people to grasp the fact of a major social break-up until it is upon them?"

"My own father will illustrate that," he replied. "He was born in 1827 and lived until 1898, a span of seventy-one years. He had watched, and taken as a matter of course, the first Industrial Revolution, the one which began late in the eighteenth century—the steam-engine, the factory system, and so on; but he never even faintly surmised the second and greater revolution by technology. He was a vicar, and the world in which he lived looked safe and solid. Yet it was almost at its end in the year of his death. . . . England's being the first to industrialize affected our history in a way curiously inverse. Instead of liberalizing us, at the period of the French Revolution, it made our government conservative and we resisted the advanced ideas of the eighteenth century instead of welcoming them."

I said that in epochs of rapid change a great deal, *too* much, depended on the sort of personalities that were brought uppermost into positions of power.

"It is a great pity that Erasmus was not a stronger character," said Whitehead. "His ideas were the right ones, and could have provided a much happier solution for the development of Christendom than the one which came. But he lacked the force; and the matter fell into the hands of Luther and Calvin, who made a fearful botch of it. The view of Erasmus was that of the sensible and enlightened people, and if it could have been effectuated by an able leader there never need have been an Ignatius Loyola, and a Council of Trent. Calvin and Luther made the egregious blunder of throwing away the whole aesthetic appeal of the Church, which was one of its best elements. You know how bleak the Protestant services are, little for the emotions, little or no appeal to beauty."

"You might be interested to know that our friend Livingstone, after having read a recent biography of Luther, wrote me that Luther seemed to him 'like a fouler-mouthed Hitler.' "

"Livingstone," said Whitehead, "is a man whose perceptions in such matters as these I would trust farther than anyone's.

What was wanted in that period of transition was someone to generalize the old conceptions and give them a liberal turn or a symbolical interpretation which could have made them acceptable to the forward-looking people. This was what was done for the old Greek religion of the Olympians in the fifth century B.C. by the great tragic poets, Aeschylus, Sophocles, and Euripides, and later by the philosophers, Plato principally. They were able to take the old gods, Zeus, Apollo, Pallas Athene and the rest, soften down the barbarities of the old theology, criticize it, turn the primitive myths into symbolism, and by carrying the people along with them—big, popular audiences at the public performances of their dramas—build a bridge from what they had formerly believed in but no longer could, to ideas which could gain acceptance by civilized men."

"Myth," I remarked, "is said to be the form in which people communicate their most deeply felt truths before they have arrived at the stage of general ideas, and those Attic dramatists, using mythical plots, had the enormous advantage of appealing at once to the emotions and to the intellect, both to the average citizens and to the educated, with the result that the two groups could feel and act more in harmony."

"Any system of thought based on this earth of ours," said Whitehead, "is extremely limited in its conceptions—either theology or philosophy—and most of them have been. We know now that our earth is an insignificant planet swinging round a second-rate sun in no very important part of the universe. The response to that knowledge of first-rate people talking together as you and I are talking—assumed," he said smiling, "that we *are* first-rate people—should be immeasurably larger than it is. I see no reason to suppose that the air about us and the heavenly spaces over us may not be peopled by intelligences, or entities, or forms of life, as unintelligible to us as we are to the insects. In the scale of size, the difference between the insects and us is as nothing to that between us and the heavenly bodies; and—who knows?—perhaps the

[233]   I*

nebulae are sentient entities and what we can see of them are their bodies. That is no more inconceivable than that there may be insects who have acute minds, though," he smiled again, "their outlook would be narrower than ours. My point is, that we are part of an infinite series and since the series *is* infinite, we had better take account of that fact, and admit into our thinking these infinite possibilities."

"As a young man you had the advantage of hearing and sharing what was talked over in the common-room of Trinity—"

"Add King's," said Whitehead.

"King's and Trinity then; this went on all through your twenties and thirties; those men were indubitably first-rate, there were many scientists among them as well as humanists. All this was in the 1880's and 1890's, on the eve of these tremendous social and technological changes which have burst upon us. It would seem as though they would have guessed that something was up, if anybody could. How much inkling do you think they had?"

"On the scientific side, certainly a good deal. I went up to Cambridge in 1880. For a boy of nineteen I was a good mathematician. My teacher was a pupil of Clerk Maxwell, who had died only a year or so before, and he, too, was eminent. The Newtonian conceptions were still in full force. Clerk Maxwell had worked at reconciling them with the then new discoveries in electricity; but in mathematical physics the work looked to be about done. The attempt was to explain away by mathematical interpretation some remaining discrepancies between what was understood and what wasn't—and in the attempt to do this, everything was upset. The people of Trinity between, say, 1885 and 1895, some of them men of genius, knew in general what was coming in the way of scientific advance, but what they could not, of course, foresee was what the social consequences of the new techniques would be. There is not a single concept of the Newtonian physics which was taught as a whole truth, that has not now been displaced. The

Newtonian ideas are still useful, as useful as they ever were, but they are no longer true in the sense in which I was taught that they were true. This experience has profoundly affected my thinking. To have supposed you had certitude once, and certitude about the solidest-*looking* thing in the universe, and then to have had it blow up on your hands into inconceivable infinities has affected everything else in the universe for me."

The cab had crossed the Longfellow Bridge and was heading up Cambridge Street instead of Charles.

"Which way do you suppose he is going?" asked Whitehead, peering out.

"These are the steep streets up the back side of Beacon Hill. He can't be going up any of these. I suppose he and his boss talked over the route and chose the one easiest on the horse," said I.

"The horse wanders about a good deal from side to side," said Whitehead. "He doesn't seem used to a carriage. I wonder if he could have been a saddle horse. His idea of making things easier for himself seems to be trying to turn into every side street."

(This was a shrewd guess. At the end of the trip, William Hill admitted to me that he had owned the horse only since last Monday.)

He drove up through Scollay Square, along Tremont Street past the Granary and King's Chapel Burial Ground to Park Street corner, thus avoiding any hill until the last hundred yards of the way, the first slant of Park Street up to the State-house. A horse-drawn vehicle halting at the Union Club again attracted a good deal of attention, the more so as it was headed into the alleyway between the club and the Ticknor mansion and had stopped plumb across the sidewalk. A motor-car blocked the inner end of the alley. The cabman asked me to get the people inside to move it.

He had done well. We entered the club at 1.25 P.M. I gave the cabman's message to the clerk at the desk. He looked as though he had been accosted in Choctaw. I repeated it: "Professor Whitehead has come to the luncheon of the Saturday Club in a brougham. The driver says he cannot hold the cab on the hill and wants to drive into your alleyway which is blocked by a car." The clerk looked just as blank. I said: "Come on out. I'll show you."

He came. He laughed immoderately but moved the car and the cabman drove in, on level pavement, in shade for the horse, and out of traffic. (End of the first half, and our side ahead.)

William Phillips, under-secretary of state from 1933 to 1936, and ambassador to Italy from 1936 to 1941, is a member of the club and was present. He had quite recently come back from his mission to India as personal representative of the President with the rank of ambassador, and after luncheon talked about it by request for perhaps half an hour, then invited questions. Excepting some characterizations of Linlithgow, the viceroy, Auchinleck, the commander-in-chief, and Field-Marshal Wavell, he was careful to say little that could not have been given at a press interview; but he made it evident that the United States is very unpleasantly involved in that quarter, and that the British Government's repressive acts are giving the lie in Asia to our pretensions as liberators.

In the discussion which followed he was questioned by Whitehead, Professor Harlow Shapley, the astronomer of Harvard, Bliss Perry, Jerome Hunsaker, the aeronautical engineer and head of that department at the Massachusetts Institute of Technology, and Cameron Forbes, who, having been governor-general of the Philippines and ambassador to Japan, conversed on the terms of one who has had experience of his own as a diplomatist in Asia.

The room was cool and pleasant even though outside the afternoon was oppressively hot. It is long, high-ceiled, and has rather an ornate early nineteenth-century chimney-piece at one end, for the building was originally the town house of

Lawrence Lowell's parents and he once remarked that this room had been his mother's bedchamber. One looks out over the treetops of the Common, which are just now luxuriantly foliaged and richly green from the rainy spring. Above them was a sky of June blue, whitened by the strong sunlight, and full of silvery clouds in full flight before a south-west wind.

Before we left, Edward Forbes, the secretary of the club, asked me to have a look at "the book." There was only a moment, for the cab had been ordered for three-fifteen and it was now nearly three-thirty, but in that moment I saw the signatures of Francis Parkman, William James, and that of his and his brother Cameron's grandfather, R. W. Emerson.

Edward Pickman and Alfred Kidder went out to have a look at the cab. Remembering their college years, they said the episode would not have been complete if they hadn't, and that in order to live up to the tradition, the cabman ought to have been slightly drunk. He was not; but they were gratified to observe that he had been no teetotaller.

It being Saturday afternoon, and fine weather, the world and his wife and their little boy were in town, afoot, on the sidewalks, and most of them on Tremont Street, where we had a household errand to do at S. S. Pierce's: three heavy pasteboard cartons, already ordered by telephone, to be picked up, for gasoline rationing prevents them from delivering groceries in Cambridge. When the cab drew up at the curb in front of the store, the shoppers, mostly women, were hard put to it to mind their manners. At first glance they would look astonished, then amused, then bewildered, and then try not to laugh. They could see at a glance, of course, that we were ethically jumping the gun on gas rationing, but they weren't prepared to take the whole nineteenth-century regalia quite so literally.

"I think," said Whitehead, when the provisions were stacked, two cartons beside the cabman's knees and one beside him on the seat, "I think that if we leaned out of the windows and bowed, we would be received with cheers."

[237]

It wasn't so far off that, as things were. Sailors in Navy uniform turned their heads after us and grinned, boys in Army uniform stopped dead in their tracks to gawp; shoppers, with arms full of bundles, stopped and stared, obviously trying to figure us out. At stops for traffic lights, some of the bystanders' conjectures were audible. We could have had plenty of repartee from the sidewalks if we had wanted it.

What was more memorable than all this, however, was the splendour of the June day. Excepting the Granary and King's Chapel Burial Grounds, you don't see much greenery driving back as we did. It was the same way we came—through Scollay Square and out Cambridge Street across the Longfellow Bridge; but everywhere there *was* a tree or a wisp of grass-plot, it was fresh, luxuriant green, and the treetops were all bending and blowing in the sou'wester. In its June dress, under the blue June sky, the city for once looked beautiful.

We were jolting over the pavement-blocks of Cambridge Street. Whitehead was speaking of the varying general characteristics as between English and American women.

"American women," said he, "are conventionalized by the prevailing sameness of their education. The theory is that, being brought up with boys, playing with boys and boys' games, going to school with them, and often to college, too, they would gain in individuality. As a matter of fact, it is not as successful as you would expect it to be. I suppose the most successful women, *as women*, were in the eighteenth century. (I am speaking, of course, of those in the more fortunate classes.) There they seem to have wider scope for their innate and characteristic abilities. My wife is one of that type. She grew up in what was practically an eighteenth-century family, aristocrats; the aristocratic influence was modified by her having been obliged, as a young woman inadequately prepared, to earn her own living, and she did it! But if you want to know what the eighteenth-century woman was like, spend an evening with my wife."

"Having spent several of them," said I, "the same idea had already occurred to me."

"Mind you," he resumed, "I don't say that your American women aren't tremendously vital and effective. In many ways they are more liberated than our English women. But, taken as a class, among the more active ones, the kind that carry on public work besides running their own households and families and running them well, I think our English women have a wider scope. . . . I tell you what," he summarized abruptly, "if I were to be born a woman, I would want to be born in America and live here the first thirty years of my life, and after that, in England. In that way I think a woman would get the best of both worlds."

"Is your family's friendship with your servants, which I have noticed to be a deep and genuine thing, an individual affair, or typical?"

"Much more typical than individual," said he, "and I can tell you why. The employer and employee relationship, with us, is much more kept out of it—singular though that may seem— by our class system, with its vestiges of feudalism. Friendships between persons of different classes are much more possible because, knowing that it is a mere matter of luck which class you are born in, we don't look down on people for not having risen."

"In this country, until quite recently," I assented, "the assumption was that if people hadn't gotten on in the world, it *was* their own fault, and, especially in the Midwest where I was reared, until within this present generation, there was something in it. That is one of the great gaps between the previous generation and this: we did have, or thought we had, security; this present crop has never known it, and hasn't it to look forward to."

"Servants have always been my friends," said Whitehead. "As a child of six I used to trot around with our gardener as he went about his work, and he taught me the names of flowers and plants; again, as a child, I used to spend months at a time at the house of my maternal grandmother, overlooking the Green Park in London, and her housemaid, Jane Wychelow, read Dickens aloud to me: *Pickwick Papers* and *David Copperfield*. She made them tremendously alive. My mother's family, while socially somewhat better placed, hadn't the intellectual distinction of my father's, and they were very contentious people. When they fell out with one another, as they frequently did, they always took their case to Jane Wychelow and *she* patched it up. Jane was the cement which held the family together."

"There in the middle of London, with Dickens being read aloud by your grandmother's housemaid, did his characters," I asked, "strike you as whimsical caricatures?"

"No. Dickens's characters *are* the poorer classes of London. They aren't caricatures at all. That idea arises naturally enough among readers who do not know the Londoners, but to us, the delight of Dickens is that he is describing real people, the like of whom we have known. Their whimsey is most characteristic. I know of no place which produces it like London."

"We were speaking a few evenings ago about novelists who did and did not bring it off. Thackeray?"

"He sees too much of one class and not enough of the other. His attempts are ambitious but not quite brought off. Trollope's characters are much more real. I recognize them exactly, for I have lived among just such people."

"A moment ago when we were speaking of servants, I was going to say that in the Midwest when I was a boy, if you didn't make a friend of the 'hired girl,' as the servant was called, and have her at the family table, you just didn't have one!"

"The sense of human equality," Whitehead took it up again, "is affected by prevailing ideas of opportunity. Human abilities are infinitely varied; some are successfully elicited in a given environment, others are not elicited at all. The possible combinations of human abilities are as infinite a series as the possible environments which would be favourable for drawing them out, but it is largely a matter of luck whether the two fit. To assume, as it is so often assumed, that genuine ability consists in forms of aptitude which happen to be wanted in a given time and place, and forms, too, which lead to economic advancement, is totally an error. The faculties which respond to such opportunity are a very small range in the human scale."

"You have spoken more than once of the element of luck, even in the most determined lives," said I. "How about your own?"

"There were two vacancies at Cambridge, when I was a young man, that were most lucky for me. One was a Fellowship, the other was a lectureship. Had it not been for the second, I would probably have taken a teaching position in a Public School and never have gone much farther."

"Some people strike me," I suggested, "as carrying inside themselves the magnetism which creates their opportunity. It looks like luck, but I do not believe it is. Perhaps you were one of them."

"No. I never created my own opportunities," said he positively. "I have done fairly well, but there has been an element of luck in it."

"You have had a good deal of administrative work to do, at Trinity and later at London University—what amounted to living, simultaneously with your life of thought, a life of action. . . . Before I put my main question, let me ask an incidental one: What is your opinion of the University of London?"

For reply he described in some detail what its functions are and what some of his duties in its committee work had been, concluding, with a smile, "Being a part of it, I think we did a damned good job!"

"Which brings me to my second question: as between your life as scholar, and your life as executive, which developed you more?"

"I learned my profession out of books, of course; but the administrative work developed me quite as much; in fact, I should be inclined to say, more. But for the continual meeting and dealing and talking with people, I might have stuck in the ruts of an academic scholar. I am a great believer in conversation. Outside of the book-knowledge which is necessary to our professional training, I think I have got most of my development from the good conversation to which I have always had the luck to have access."

"At Trinity, yes; and later in London. But suppose yourself to have spent those years in a newspaper office. . . ."

"You, too," said he, "have had an immense advantage from your office conversations."

"The talk at the *Globe*, it is true, is much better than most academic people would suppose. In fact, if I were to confess, I would have to say that it is of a much higher voltage than I can get from a good many academic enclaves. They don't encounter as many kinds of life as we do. In a sense, too, newspaper men lead a life of action. It is no mere speculative existence, for even after we come in off the street as reporters, and write as I do, we must at least be able to say something in print about urgent questions and say it responsibly enough so that we will not get a brickbat through our office window next morning."

"I would call that 'a life of action,'" said Whitehead, "as well as a life of thought. And my own, now I come to think of it, goes back to my days as a schoolboy. I was a leader in games, and, though you might not guess it now, a good football player and a passable cricketer. Sherborne was a school of about four hundred boys, ninety of whom lived in the dormitory. As head boy of the school and captain of the playing teams, I had to keep order in the dormitory. So all my life I have had the discipline of having to run things. . . . I say, we must be nearly back." He had been glancing out of the cab window, where sidewalk pedestrians, now more numerous again as we rolled into the residential streets of Cambridge, eyed the outfit with astonishment, and then remembered themselves, perhaps, in time to smother a laugh.

The return trip was made in forty-five minutes. William Hill had got us there and got us back without incident, unless you consider the trip to have been one continuous incident. Upstairs in the apartment Edward Pickman was waiting to carry them off to Dudley Farms in Bedford and Mrs. Whitehead was smartly gowned, hatted, and gloved for the journey. She asked how our cab ride had gone.

"We went and came," said Whitehead, "in an atmosphere of considerable public attention."

"You mean 'derision,' " said she.

"Well," he conceded, "I would say 'smiles.' "

"The trip was much less uncomfortable and went much more quickly than I had expected," I remarked.

Whitehead didn't take up the question of comfort; as to the other he said genially:

"I have had a delightful afternoon, but I don't associate it with *speed*!"

XXXI

July 27, 1943

AFTER a busy and hot day in the city, it was a refreshment to go over to Cambridge and dine with the Whiteheads at six-thirty. No one else was there. A breeze had sprung up and was drawing pleasantly through their open windows five stories up and overlooking lawns and trees.

There had been joking about the dinner. Mrs. Whitehead had said:

"I'm not sure we can give you enough to eat. We ourselves dine on five butterflies and find it quite sufficient." I told her three butterflies would be enough for me in warm weather.

Professor Whitehead was in his study, so we went in there. Being dressed in white and without his coat (I was invited to shed mine, and did) he looked cool and uncommonly fit. Mussolini had just fallen, and I remembered that two summers before in this very room, Whitehead had said to me, "Machiavelli has written the rules of a short-term success, say from fifteen to twenty years." Also that there was an old Roman who had been legate of Upper Germany under the Emperor Domitian, and who though ill and racked by pain, clung to life "so that I can survive that brigand for one day at least." I said it was some satisfaction to have seen Mussolini go down.

"It is *good*!" said Whitehead.

" 'Brigand' for him!" said she. "He is a foul scorpion!"

I asked Mr. Whitehead if he was writing anything.

"No," said he, "but I have been reading what you have been writing."

At first I could not think what he meant, for I have written little daily journalism since April; then it occurred to me that the *Atlantic* for August, which was just out, contained my "Eye of the Hurricane."

There had been a conference between several headmasters of New England preparatory schools and members of the *Globe* editorial staff on the plight of liberal education in wartime as it affected boys below the conscription age of eighteen. The danger was of their education being abandoned, if not entirely to the military sciences, certainly to science at the expense of the humanities. There was no knowing how long the war would last, and if several successive crops of adolescents were denied their only access to general education and to those civilian habits of mind on which our society had depended for the transmission of its liberal traditions, our war might be a Mississippi steamboat race, stoking the furnaces with cargo and cabin furnishings to end with a victory won by a hulk empty of everything but its industrial boilers and military engines.

"You raise all of the right questions," said Whitehead, "but I could not agree with all of your conclusions. If in America, unlike England and some of the European continental countries, you undertake to give a good education not to a few but to all your people, the form it takes will need to be modified. I would be inclined to require universal education up to, say, the age of sixteen; then, between sixteen and nineteen, infuse it with the elements of practicality. After that there would need to be the widest possible access to opportunity for further study, both in institutions and outside of them, as by university extension lecturers, so that people could satisfy their curiosity about all sorts of subjects and find their special aptitudes. Their reading, too, would be enlivened by personal association with the lecturers. I would make some of this advanced education compulsory, and keep up the process of education to the age of ninety." This last he said smilingly; but all the same, he meant it. "Mind you," he resumed, "I doubt if these great universities with their high concentrations of specialized learning and societies of scholars so shut off from the daily lives of average people are altogether a good thing."

"The same idea has occurred to me, and repeatedly," said I. "My own phrase for it is that they grow intellectually dandified."

"There are numerous groups of professional people in this, in any city, whose instruction would be quite as valuable to the public as that of university lecturers," (we had been called to dinner and were walking out to the table) "and one of these groups are the newspaper men. They ought to lecture more than they do."

"One of the puzzles to me," (I had decided to come out with it) "is that after three centuries of Harvard's pumping supposedly and often really educated men into the city of Boston, more hasn't come of it. Oughtn't the city to have done much better than it has?"

"It *has* done well, uncommonly well," he replied with

emphasis. "Will you name me an American city which has done better? Your professional people maintain, on the whole, a very high standard, especially the medical profession. What do you expect of it?"

"A steady blaze of genius, I suppose, is all that would satisfy me; and also, perhaps I know too much of the city's seamy side."

We sat at a beautiful little Duncan Phyfe mahogany table set for three, the late-afternoon yellow of sunshine filtering in from the west through the slightly tilted shutters of the Venetian blinds, which, a few minutes later, the sun having set behind the tower of Memorial Hall, Mrs. Whitehead raised, letting in the still strong and clear but paler light of the afterglow, which fell full upon the philosopher's serene face. The "five butterflies" for dinner was certainly understatement, for we dined, I thought, sumptuously (though Mrs. Whitehead said "simply"), with glasses of a chilled sauterne beside our plates. She explained how the fowl, the salad, and the apple pie had been done; the "sumptuousness" came from skilful touches in the cookery. She told me what they were, adding:

"Cookery is one of those tasks which are insupportable unless done for people one loves. But for that, I myself would be willing to live on bread and cheese and would vastly prefer to."

"People are unlikely to get good food, no matter how many cooks they have, or how much they pay for them," said Whitehead, "unless the cooks love the people for whom they cook."

I said the two best cooks I had ever known, one a Yorkshire woman, the other Irish, did come exactly in that classification, in addition to which they were both devout, one a Protestant, the other Catholic.

"Cooking," replied Whitehead demurely, "is one of those arts which most requires to be done by persons of religious nature."

"And a good cook," added his wife, "cooks to the glory of God."

[246]

We lingered at the table in the fading afterglow. By now the breeze which drew in at the large window was deliciously cool and refreshing. In that tranquil light it was one of those summer evenings which seem like a pleasant eternity.

We shifted scene to the living-room. Whitehead was saying that his leaving Cambridge at fifty and going up to London was one of the determinants in his development: "It plunged me into the *practicalities* of education. At Cambridge I had had experience in political work and organization, but the actualities of life in London were much broader." He told many of the things he had to do and how they carried him amongst all classes. "Our polytechnical schools," said he, "are a specimen of the kind of thing I meant when earlier in the evening we were discussing universal education. I know the system of popular education in London has been criticized as inadequate, but from close association with it, I think it is admirable. It gives all sorts of people access to studies useful to them in practical life and also in the arts; and you find people of all classes and all ages haunting them."

"As showing their 'classlessness,'" said Mrs. Whitehead, "a young man we knew, who was enormously wealthy, and had had the best instruction in painting on the Continent that money could buy, found on coming home the best instruction he had found anywhere was in one of these London polytechnics."

"I am hearing, again, a partial explanation of something which has puzzled me about you two ever since I have known you. Pickled in donnish society though you have been pretty much all your lives, you are the least donnish of dons."

"In what way do you notice it?" asked Mrs. Whitehead.

"Understanding of common life. Restrict the case to your sympathy with the working class: that is something which experience had taught me not to take for granted with the average college professor, at Harvard or anywhere else. Here and there a specialist? Yes, in sociology perhaps. They have limbered up somewhat in the past few years, possibly because their own security has been affected."

"One of the great fallacies of American thinking," said Whitehead, "is that human worth is constituted by a particular set of aptitudes which lead to economic advancement. This is not true at all. Two-thirds of the people who can make money are mediocre; and at least one-half of them are morally at a low level. As a whole, they are vastly inferior to other types who are not animated by the economic motives; I mean the artists, and teachers, and professional people who do work which they love for its own sake and earn about enough to get along on. This habitual elevation of the type of ability that leads to economic advancement is one of the worst mistakes in your American thinking and needs to be unceasingly corrected by people who speak to the public, as you do."

Some of it, I said, was a hangover from our pioneering days when the subduing of this continent did take courage and ability.

"Yes," said Mrs. Whitehead, "but even there, a fine distinction must be drawn. The swollen fortunes were seldom made by the pioneers; they were made by the men who came after."

"The mischief of elevating the type that has aptitude for economic advancement," said Whitehead, "is that it denies the superior forms of aptitude which exist in quite humble people. Who shall say that to live kindly and graciously and meet one's problems bravely from day to day is not a great art, or that those who can do it are not great artists? Aesthetics are understood in too restricted a sense. People who can live beautifully in humble environments have a most advanced understanding of aesthetics—compared with which the ability to paint pictures on canvas," (he did so in dumb show) "delightful as that may be, is a rudimentary form."

"You confirm me in a glow I often feel when meeting my neighbours on the village street, the carpenter, the postman, the lobster fisherman—their goodness and geniality warm me to my marrow, and I smile inwardly, thinking, 'Life comes before literature.' "

"Fifty thousand years ago," said Whitehead, "or five hundred thousand—I don't know how long—when man, perhaps suddenly, took a turn of development which produced his faculty of enjoyment, he produced something whose possibilities are infinite. A human being—you, Evelyn, I—has certain capacities for enjoyment developed, partly because inherent, partly by training. There is a good deal of luck in it. You, for example, besides your enjoyment of literature have the faculty and training for the enjoyment of music. Some have the faculty for enjoying mathematics, but it is latent, and has to be brought out by study. We aren't *born* with the faculty of enjoying mathematics. Others, though born with the latent faculty of enjoying music, either as listeners or as performers, aren't *born* as either performers or highly intelligent listeners; both must be developed. The range of our faculties for enjoyment is enormous and has been explored hardly beyond a fringe. Even the insects must have it, though I don't know enough about them to surmise what their forms of enjoyment are. . . . Now the singular part is that man, in his social systems, has so far given so little scope to the development of our faculties of enjoyment. There have been various fortunate periods. Turbulent as the Italian cities in the Renaissance were, they did occasionally have rulers with acute perceptions for various and new forms of human enjoyment, and the rulers of certain small German principalities in the late eighteenth and early nineteenth centuries, too, were successful in fostering certain forms, principally music and the theatre. Small states, I think, do it better than large ones. The small German states were able to produce excellent provincial opera throughout the nineteenth century, while the French Government, though it maintained an excellent theatre, tended to rigidity of classicism. There was little experiment, and ideas always require adventure."

"That 'time lag' between the individual and his social system throws me back upon your remark of last year about the relationship between man's infinite possibilities, and the limitations of finite form. States concern themselves with the organization of material existence, which is a very finite thing. You may remember how once, when you lived out in the Blue Hills, we talked about the fact that there has never been, except incidentally, a Culture State, only Power States with a little creativity on the side; and you remarked that you doubted whether the state was best competent to foster the creative arts."

"When big states attempt it," said he, "they tend to formularize men's faculties of enjoyment and creativity. That tends towards rigidity. I doubt if state supervision would be good for the arts in America. The vitality of thought is in adventure. That is what I have been saying all my life, and I have said little else. Ideas won't keep. Something must be done about them. The idea must constantly be seen in some new aspect. Some element of novelty must be brought into it freshly from time to time; and when that stops, it does. The meaning of life is adventure."

"It is an adventure to be born," said Mrs. Whitehead, gravely, "and a very dangerous one."

She spoke standing. Behind her was the wall tinted its peculiar shade just off black; she wore a black gown with white embroidery at the throat; her hair is white, and there in the tranquil summer twilight her aspect was that of a striking portrait canvas by some eminent painter. The glimpse was only instantaneous, the moment of pause required to deliver her remark, then she turned away to go into the dining-room.

"How about the adventurers," I asked, "whose adventures are, for all their good will, mistaken and mischievous?"

"They are damned fools," said Whitehead emphatically. "That is where learning comes in. Adventurers must use their reason and must know the past, so as not to go on repeating the mistakes of history. One of my anxieties about this war has been lest a rigid system be imposed on mankind and that fragile quality, his capacity for novel ideas, for novel aspects of old ideas, be frozen and he go on century after century, growing duller, more formularized until he and his society reach the static level of the insects. Asia has known something of this sort. Good things no doubt were being said in China a thousand years ago, but for at least two thousand years, each century was a little less interesting than the century before; and when people want to tell me what civilization owes to India they have to start back at about 500 B.C. You may have wondered at my coolness, not to John Dewey personally, whom I respect as a man and certain aspects of whose work I admire, but to his thought. The reason is that the emphasis of his thought is on security. But the vitality of man's mind is in adventure. The Egyptians in 500 B.C. obviously had an enormous history behind them, yet there was no adventure in it. Contrast with it the little they have bequeathed to Western man with the much in aesthetics and morals that we have inherited from the Greeks and the Hebrews."

"I was doing so as you spoke. That old Egyptian priest in Plato's story was unconsciously recognizing some contrast of the sort when he told Solon, 'You Hellenes are never anything but boys. . . . In mind you are all young.'—The boy is adventurous."

"My hope is," replied Whitehead, "that out of this war, America will take the leadership of humanity. America, as I see it, is the only hope. There is adventure here, and a welcome for novelty. You could do for the future of humanity what Greece and Judaea did for the modern world as against Asia and Europe. The Jews had certain moral ideas but these would not have come to much without the Greeks."

"What would you say was the contribution of the Greeks?"

"The aesthetic view of life."

"I noticed a moment ago when you used those two words,

'aesthetics' and 'morals,' in connection with Hellas and Israel, that 'aesthetics' came first."

"Properly so," said he.

"Beauty is 'a wider and more fundamental notion than truth'?"

"Yes. Apart from beauty, truth is neither good nor bad."

"That was how the Puritans tumbled overboard," said Mrs. Whitehead, who had returned during the discussion. "They cast out beauty. They began well, by believing they were made in the image of God. They ended by making God in their own image."

"And how fast such cream can curdle: it is less than a century from the Plymouth Colony and William Bradford to Cotton Mather."

"The idea," said Whitehead, "was losing its vitality. It had ceased to adventure. The inheritors of it inherit the idea without inheriting the fervour. Their progenitors would have gone to the stake for it, and some of them did. Perhaps there was no longer any stake for its inheritors to go to; they knew how strongly their forebears believed, felt that they ought to feel the old fervour and tried to or pretended to, and so gave the impression of being hypocrites."

"Your own parents," Mrs. Whitehead reminded him, "didn't believe as strongly as they thought they did."

"They *thought* they still believed strongly," he took it up, "and *their* parents had been strong believers; but by the time mine came along, the idea had cooled off to a point where, today, the attitude of my parents might have been regarded as hypocritical. Mind you, I don't say it was. They were quite sincere. Only, the attitude had changed, and they represented their religion to us chiefly as a means of keeping order—order in the family and order in society. But that is something quite different from religious conviction."

"One sees a similar change in the Cathedral of Strassburg," I remarked. "Nobody had prepared me for it and it was a great surprise. The nave and aisles are late Gothic, light and graceful in its elegant logical perfection; the older parts at the chancel end are Romanesque, from an age of strong belief, and their effect is so powerful that they dim the force of the nave, beautiful though it is."

"Architecture," said Whitehead, "is a good illustration of the life cycle in adventures of ideas. It happens that it is one of the art-forms in which I am most interested. Let me take English Gothic. You start with early Norman, Romanesque, and go on century by century through, roughly, the four successive styles to the fifteenth century when it comes to an end. What was happening in those four successive centuries was that the new aspects of the idea were being discovered and developed; successive elements of novelty were being introduced and explored —the abundant fenestration, the height of the piers, beauty of tracery, and the like—until there seemed nothing more to be done. The possibilities of novel aspect had been used up, the Gothic idea comes to a full stop, and you get a complete break. They go back to the architecture of Greece and Rome, adapt it to the changed world of the Renaissance, and you get, instead of a Gothic abbey, St. Paul's. But the classic style of ancient architecture brought into the modern world has, I think, this peculiarity: although it does lend itself admirably to a host of purposes and can generally, in the hands of a good craftsman, be made to look well, it lacks that . . . that final something . . . What shall I call it? . . ."

"Transcendence," suggested Mrs. Whitehead.

"Yes," he accepted the word, "that final 'transcendence.' I mean that it doesn't produce the building which I would take a four-hour railway journey to see. A new material, as well as a new way of looking at the idea, may give it the happy turn," he resumed, "as when your early New England settlers brought the English house to these shores but had to build it of wood. It was the same style but with fresh and delightful modifications. With your stone houses I doubt if you have done so well. . . ."

"We hardly got round to them until the 1840's and 1850's, 'Gothic revival'; and you know how short a time that lasted. . . ."

"I don't think they are considered very successful."

"It was an attempt to return to the Gothic style without the Gothic tradition."

"The greatness of Lawrence Lowell included this perception of the difficulty in keeping an idea vital," Whitehead suddenly opened his own idea into a novel aspect, "and this form of his greatness is not yet generally appreciated. He had seen that what is wanted is a certain period of systematized instruction for young men, then that they be allowed to explore for themselves, with or without professional guidance, various areas of learning or achievement. To this he saw the need of adding the oldest form of entertainment and instruction known to the human race; namely, conversation. If you will notice, his foundation of the Junior Fellows is on these principles. They are chosen as nearly as possible for merit from all over this continent and their pursuits are as varied as the arts and sciences. They have had a certain amount of systematized training and some achievement to their credit. Their association is so organized that they meet to dine and spend an evening together at least once a week in conversation with one another and with a wide variety of notable guests drawn from all the professions. There is no 'departmentalism.' The men studying literature are at elbows with men studying biology or mathematics. In the Harvard faculty itself I notice a good deal of departmentalism. You would think the men in one department had nothing to learn from their colleagues in another, or else that"—his eyes twinkled roguishly—"they were protecting themselves from contamination. I consider it a monstrous presumption that university lecturers should think themselves competent to go on talking year after year to young men, students, while holding themselves aloof from the opportunity of learning from eager youth, which is one of the most valuable things on earth. . . ."

"Lecturers," observed Mrs. Whitehead, "are licensed to brag!"

"When you use the expression, 'eager youth' as 'one of the most valuable things on earth,' will you explain more explicitly what you mean by it?"

"I mean—" he hesitated, pondering his definition—"the glow of a young man . . . (I'm afraid I shall have to use a portentous expression, but it isn't portentously meant) . . . I mean the glow of a young man who has just discovered some great work of literature. It isn't the book which he has discovered which is so important: it is his glow over it. There you have the sense of adventure, of newness, the old idea seen freshly in some new aspect. It is this which university instructors should be on the watch for, and should respect wherever it appears, instead of being a trifle irritated at over-eager young men."

"Coming as I did from the Midwest, I had the feeling that in New England enthusiasm was bad form. Harvey Cushing, who came from out there, had noticed it and said that, for himself, the resistance of inert mind and matter to any innovation, surgical or other, was so heavy that a man who had (as he had) anything new and difficult to accomplish must have great enthusiasm as a flywheel to carry the saw of his idea through knots in the log."

"Coming from England to New England, as we did," said Mrs. Whitehead, "we experienced not a drop in temperature, as you did coming from the Midwest, but a rise. After the social climate of England, that of New England seemed a blast from a furnace."

"New England's intellect," I said "(a good many strangers have noticed it) often makes a better first impression than New England's heart."

"Had it occurred to you," asked Mrs. Whitehead, "that New Englanders may be timid?"

"No. It hadn't. But they often are, the best of them. And if I hadn't liked them, why did I stay? I admire the people, and the scenery, and the mellowed culture, and the libraries, and the orchestra, and I can hardly remember having heard good conversation among young men until I came here."

"There is a club in Cambridge," said Whitehead, "to which I had access as a young man. Tennyson and his friend Hallam, the one who died young, were among its founders. They called themselves 'the Apostles.' The members are undergraduates and when you have graduated you 'take wings' and become an 'Angel.' The new members are chosen entirely by undergraduates and on the ground that they are likely to prove interesting. At each meeting—they were on Saturday nights—some member presents a paper setting forth ideas for discussion. This takes about twenty minutes. The members have previously drawn lots for the order of their speaking after the initial presentation of ideas. Each one is expected, when his turn comes, to stand on the hearth and say whatever is in his mind. The understanding is that nothing of what is said here shall ever be repeated outside as having come from any member. In fact, no one is supposed to know who the members are, though, as a matter of fact, they are sometimes guessed. Quite a number of distinguished men have come through the 'Apostles,' and once a year they have a dinner in London which the 'Angels' attend. The chairman, who sits at the head of the table, is an 'Angel,' and the latest-chosen 'Apostle,' who sits at the other end of the table, is vice-chairman. Members of Cambridge colleges are not permitted to enter another college after ten o'clock, but we used to congregate just before ten o'clock, our number being restricted to twelve, and our conversations went on into the small hours. The quality of it held up surprisingly well—at least until the war."

Twilight had deepened into dusk and dusk to darkness. The room was so cool and pleasant with the night breeze coming in at windows that we had continued sitting in the darkness, which seemed, if anything, to promote conversation. We continued speaking from the restful shadows.

"Mr. Lowell's foundation of the Junior Fellows," said Mrs. Whitehead, "received mention by the newspapers of course, but not in anything like the proportion that its importance to the future deserved. What *is* 'news'? If Mrs. Lowell had run away with the chauffeur, or if Mr. Lowell had been carrying on an affair with the housemaid, the newspapers would not have so restricted their space as they did about the Junior Fellows."

"You are asking," said I, "who is to blame. It depends on whom you ask. If you ask me, I think the necessity of a newspaper's paying its way as an article of commerce is at the bottom of it. What is needed is a Hippocratic Oath for journalists. What would a university be like, if it had to live by its fees?"

"It wouldn't exist," said Whitehead.

"In southern England," Mrs. Whitehead took it up, "there used to be very little music. The people there were supposed to be congenitally unmusical. Of late, since the B.B.C. has been broadcasting only good music, they have grown very fond of music, have started groups of village musicians, and want only the best music themselves. In England each owner of a radio set has to pay a small tax: that supports the B.B.C. and no advertisements are allowed on the air. The damnable heresy is that people don't want the best. On that plea they are given whatever debased matter may be expected to sell and the tendency of this is steadily downward."

"Having combated that damnable heresy inside a newspaper office for more than half a lifetime and proved that it *is* a heresy—not without, it is only fair to say, some collaboration from its management and its owners—I am still astonished when I see decent-looking people in the public vehicles reading small type under the most blatantly vulgar headlines. They don't look like people who would care for that kind of thing."

Mrs. Whitehead suggested, "They may finally succumb and learn to like the poison after they have been sufficiently tainted. . . ."

K

"On the credit side," said Whitehead, "I notice that a large part of what is written for the serious columns of your newspapers is to set before the readers their responsibility for maintaining the social system. The aspects of this are various, but that in the end is what it all comes to: the readers are being reminded that the preservation of a social system depends on them. Now responsibility for a social system is the groundwork of civilization. Without a society in which life and property are to some extent secure, existence can continue only at the lowest levels—you cannot have a good life for those you love, nor can you devote your energies to activity on the higher level. Consequently, a sense of responsibility for the continuance of a social system is basic to any morality. Now this form of responsibility is almost entirely absent from Christianity. Jesus hardly mentions it, except for one or two remarks."

"And one of these," said Mrs. Whitehead, " 'Render unto Caesar,' was evasive."

"There were historical reasons for this lack, I grant you," he continued. "The Hebrews had no independent state to govern, and a man cannot be blamed for failing to consider what there was in his period no occasion for considering. He said what an able thinker might be expected to say. His historical situation did not elicit a code of ethics concerned with responsibility for a social system; but the absence of such responsibility has been a characteristic of the Jews for centuries. That is one reason for their unpopularity. You may say that the way they have been treated in many of the countries of their sojourn has not permitted such participation, and I quite agree. But that absence has involved Christianity in an almost perpetual self-contradiction. It held that the externals of life are not worth caring about and at the same time insisted on types of moral conduct which cannot be observed—without perishing—unless the externals of life are sufficiently well organized. A society run on strictly Christian principles could not survive at all."

"That kept appearing," I remarked, "in the social criticism

of the nineteenth century, especially among the Russians, like Tolstoy and Kropotkin; Christian anarchist, and philosophical anarchist. But in the other European (and American) nineteenth-century social critics, one keeps encountering this sense of puzzled exasperation: 'You call yourselves Christians and your society Christendom; then why don't you . . .?' What has appeared now, which hadn't then, is that the comparative social stability of the century from 1815 to 1914 had deluded even many of the ablest thinkers into regarding a stable social system as an assured thing."

"It was not until the unification of the modern world by scientific techniques," he replied, "that people realized that social stability would have to be one of the prerequisites of ethical behaviour. This has been forced on us by the types of men in control of the state machinery in certain countries, who have obliged us to fight them in order to be able to maintain any of the social decencies."

"Yet the moment we have admitted that," I raised the question, "what sort of morality do we want a stable social system to maintain? A few evenings ago I was startled by hearing an author, a man I very much respect, refer to someone, in a book or a public speech, as 'extolling all the bourgeois virtues.' Now I have heard the bourgeois criticized sharply enough and know some of the grounds for that criticism. But couldn't our world do with a few bourgeois virtues?"

"One of their virtues," said Whitehead, "is paying their debts. And a robust virtue it is. You can't have a stable society without it."

The clock in Memorial Hall had struck ten. Knowing that I had a train to catch, Mrs. Whitehead considerately rose and switched on a light. We had been sitting in the darkness for nearly an hour past.

Mr. Whitehead went out with me to the elevator. "I always feel," said he, "that I have two duties to perform with a parting guest: one, to see that he doesn't forget anything that is his; the other, to see that he doesn't take anything that is mine."

XXXII

January 13, 1944

THE first volume of Santayana's autobiography, *Persons and Places*, had just appeared. At the Whiteheads', where I was spending the evening, it prompted a discussion of irony.

"Not long ago," I reminded Whitehead, "you defined irony. I have remembered the words, but am not sure that I understand what you mean. You said, 'Irony is a depressive frame of mind.' "

"The connection in which I said it has escaped me," said Whitehead, "so I had better start afresh." He considered awhile, puckering his nose and knitting his fingers, elbows on the arms of his chair. "Irony, I would say," he brought out presently, "signifies the state of mind of people or of an age which has lost faith. They conceal their loss, or even flaunt it by laughter. You seldom get irony except from people who have been somehow more or less cleaned out."

"Lytton Strachey?"

"His name was just about to be on my lips," said Whitehead.

"He was a delightful person," said Mrs. Whitehead, "but a great sufferer."

"Bodily or mentally?"

"Not so much bodily, though he was always frail and often ailing. (He was the son of an elderly father.) But more, mentally. His personal appearance was ridiculous and he knew it. That portrait of him by Augustus John, which is often mistaken for a caricature, is not, but on the contrary, an excellent likeness. And his voice was high and squeaky. He suffered from being so unlike other people."

'Strachey's irony," said Whitehead, "was that of an intellectual set who have abrogated their responsibility for a social system. We in England were treated to a stiff dose of this after the previous war by what I may for convenience term 'the Bloomsbury set.' I grant you that some of them were able people. . . . But confining ourselves to the decent ones," he continued, "there were two whom I knew well as young men and often think of as together, however different they may have been. One was Logan Pearsall Smith and the other was Strachey. Both were men of learning and cultivation but there was this great difference between them, at least as I saw them: Pearsall Smith was determined to write and to write well—and he did; but Strachey wrote because he had to. It was in him and had to come out. And yet the paradox of it is that while Pearsall Smith had no followers, for he lacked the originality of the other man, Strachey, who did have followers, was the cause of their doing a great deal of harm."

"And also," added she, "some of them were plain rotten. . . ."

"Strachey came at the end of what had been a robust age," continued Whitehead. "I grant you he was able and witty, but he was immediately imitated by a host of writers who lacked both his wit and his ability, and they did a great deal of harm. How would you define Santayana's irony?"

"Denigrating and destructive," replied his wife promptly. She told of meeting him repeatedly at the rooms of an Oxford undergraduate who was a close relative of his who admired Santayana and was always having him in for tea. "Santayana was for ever treating the young man ironically. The youth was no heavy intellectual, but I saw what was going on and thought it shabby. It is the irony of one who, lacking faith himself, tries to destroy it in the young—which *I* think devilish!"

"We Americans are often spoken of as incorrigibly naïve," I replied, "but after reading this volume of Santayana's autobiography, admiring its superb prose and flashes of insight, and laughing at his digs at us, I found myself doubting whether all of us are so dense as not to know when we are being sneered at from behind a veil of irony."

"Your people would take that good-humouredly, as they take a joke on themselves," said Mrs. Whitehead, "but let no one suppose that you wouldn't understand what was going on. You have a contemporary novelist of your own in our midst who sneers at you that way; it is taken good-naturedly, but he doesn't fool anybody. And his sneers come from unbelief, beginning as sneers generally do, from unbelief in himself."

"That suggests a puzzle in Santayana. He writes lyric prose about Catholicism; but is it possible, knowing all that he knows—I mean everything from ancient folk-lore to modern psychology—that he can still number himself among the true believers?"

"Catholicism," said Whitehead, "lends itself to being beautifully written *about*! It is very old, it is hugely diversified, picturesque, has its poetical and aesthetic aspects, and can be made very entertaining. A man wouldn't need to be much of a believer to do that, and I dare say that a non-practising Catholic like Santayana, who, as a writer, is a great artist, has done so charmingly. . . . When it comes to his philosophy, however, I confess to a different feeling. The interest of philosophy depends on the sincerity of the philosopher. He has looked at the universe in a certain way, has seen phenomena under some fresh aspect; he is full of his vision and anxious to communicate it. His value to other men is in what he has seen. Now most philosophers do intensely mean what they say, and all of the great ones do. With Santayana's philosophy, I have the feeling that he is merely playing with ideas, all is cool, detached, and almost indifferent. He just misses greatness and I believe it is because he is lacking in sincerity."

"What would you say about Socratic irony? Would that fall within the terms of your original definition?" I asked. "Or the dramatic irony of the Greek tragic poets? I mean the shuddery spectacle Sophocles makes of Oedipus unwittingly condemning himself out of his own mouth, uttering speeches which mean one thing to him and the exact opposite to the awestruck spectators. Or the tragic irony which Aeschylus gives us in the *Agamemnon*—such scenes as the king walking into his palace on that purple carpet, which his queen has persuaded him to do as a symbol that she will have success in murdering him. Greek tragedy is drenched with such irony."

"That," said Mrs. Whitehead, "is irony of situation."

"With the Greeks, certainly," said he, "in the fifth century B.C., which is of course the period of the great dramatists, you certainly do not have decadence. It is doubtful whether anywhere or at any time men have lived so vividly or more widened the scope of human faculties. But what you do get in that century is a questioning of the older religious forms. They had ceased to believe that the gods were supernatural personages, as their ancestors had believed, but they saw that the gods could still serve useful purposes as symbols. Then, with regard to the irony of Socrates—whether you take him as an historical figure, or a little under the aspect of his literary character in the *Dialogues* of Plato—there had been, of course, lively sceptical criticism of the traditional religion—by the Sophists and that lot—but you also had in that society something similar to what we have much more commonly in ours of today: namely, that in one and the same period and region, you may get, as we in London had in Bloomsbury, an intellectual movement that was distinctly decadent, while just around the corner from it might be the beginning of a fresh and vigorous life of the mind and of society; so that you can seldom say that an age is all of a piece. In every age of decay there may be a half a dozen seeds of the future, as in the decline of the Roman Empire you have the rise of Christianity, only—out of these half-dozen seeds, there is no telling at the time which will die out and which will live to take over what is left of the affairs of Rome. This makes a reason the more for tolerance since there is no knowing out of which seed the future will sprout. There is an admirable letter by the

Emperor Trajan[1] on this subject, about the Christians, who were considered a nuisance. Trajan says that rather than persecute them it is better, if you can, to pacify them and keep them quiet."

The question arose whether myth is the form in which primitive peoples express their general ideas before they possess a language of abstractions, with the result that later, the myths are perceived to have been abstract ideas. I had raised this question before, but I raised it again, thinking that something different might come out, and it did.

"The myth," said Whitehead confidently, "comes *before* general ideas exist. When it first arises, I think there is no thought of personalizing any abstract conception at all. Rather, the myth-makers see certain personalities clashing, with specific results, or see one force arising in the universe around them, to be opposed, or aided by another force, and these processes are personalized. Later, these myths are rethought by more philosophical minds and are seen to contain the germs of abstract ideas; just as, a moment ago, we were saying that when the Greeks ceased to believe in their gods as superhuman beings, they saw that they still contained aspects of symbolic truth."

"Some biographer of Shelley," said I, "Clutton-Brock, I believe, said that Shelley is one of the few myth-makers who have survived into the modern world."

"Shelley is a very great poet," said Whitehead, "and I used

1 "The method you have pursued, my dear Pliny, in the proceedings against those who were denounced to you as Christians, is extremely proper; as it is not possible to lay down any fixed plan by which to act in all cases of this nature. But I would not have you officiously enter into any enquiries concerning them. If indeed they should be brought before you, and the crime is proved, they must be punished; with the restriction, however, that where the party denies himself to be a Christian, and shall make it evident that he is not, by invoking our gods, let him (notwithstanding any former suspicion) be pardoned upon his repentance. Informations without the accuser's name subscribed ought not to be received in prosecutions of any sort, as it is introducing a very dangerous precedent, and by no means agreeable to the equity of my government."—Book X, *Letters*, Gaius Plinius Caecilius Secundus (Pliny the Younger). Mommsen suggests as date for Book X 108 or 109 A.D.

to read him a great deal at one time, when I read poetry. I do not read it now."

"The reason I raise the question is this: most great literatures have had a folk mythology behind them. We Americans seem to have none—at least in this sense, that most of our past on this continent takes place in the full glare of historical record."

"You Americans are creating your myths now," said Whitehead.

This led to a lively discussion of what some of our myths are.

"One of them is democracy," replied Mrs. Whitehead wickedly.

"The political concepts on which your American society is founded," said Whitehead, "are a kind of myth, and yours have a long history. Starting in fairly modern times (I mean, leaving out their Graeco-Roman and Hellenic-Hebraic origins) they stem from Locke in the English seventeenth century, come on down to the great Frenchmen of the eighteenth century, but are never given practical effectuation until they come to the founders of your republic. The purport of that political myth is to improve and safeguard the lot of the common man. In your nineteenth century, however, that myth in America undergoes a serious reversal. The right of the common man to a good life is interpreted as the right of a few exceptional individuals, say one in a thousand—or less—to exploit the resources of a new continent in such a way as to make themselves inordinately rich. When I say 'exceptional' I do not wish to be understood as meaning that they are superior. In every other relationship of life besides the making of money they may be, and quite often are, inferior. But as the nineteenth century proceeded on this continent, they were the ones who ran away with your political myth, and with them it degenerated into the false and vulgar idea that anybody in America could get rich if he were willing to set his mind to it. In this present century you are having to rescue the original conceptions of your political myth

K*

from those few individuals controlling corporate wealth who falsified it."

"You set me wondering," I said, "how the future will rank the Victorian Age."

"Socially," said Whitehead, "it was stuffy, and stuffiness marred a good deal of its literature, since literature is sharply conditioned by the social forms amidst which it arises. The eighteenth-century people, in England and France at any rate, were much more lively and vivid than the nineteenth—though when you say that you must always remember that you are speaking only of the fortunate few at the top of society. Where the nineteenth century excels is in its concern for the common people. That is new. The concern was clumsy and fumbling for a start, did not by any means reach all of them, but it was genuine and it sets the nineteenth century off from every one that has preceded it. And when this present world conflict dies down, that is the side of our modern age which, if it can be saved, will be most worth saving."

"Culturally how do you think the Victorian Age will be ranked?"

"It will be ranked among the world's few great ages, but as the least of them."

"Can you give me an idea of where and how?"

"Yes. Somewhat like that period of the Roman Empire after Tacitus, when life is fairly safe and sound, but not very brilliant; an age of silver, not of gold."

"What dates are you taking as the Victorian Age?" asked Mrs. Whitehead.

"Nineteenth century would be a better term, he replied," "and I should begin the nineteenth century in 1830, ending it of course at 1914. In 1830 most of the men who made the greatness of that century were still in college."

"Tell me," asked Mrs. Whitehead abruptly, "what English poet or poets of the nineteenth century do you still read, if any? . . . Shelley?"

As her question was addressed to me, I confessed to quite a list of them, including Tennyson.

"What poems?"

"*The Holy Grail* at Christmas, *The Passing of Arthur* at New Year, and *In Memoriam* at frequent intervals."

"*In Memoriam*," said she, "doesn't come off. To have been successful it would need to have been the outpouring of a soul in torment, and it wasn't."

Knowing that her husband thought considerably better of it than that and has discussed it as one of "those great serious poems in English literature," the case was carried to him.

"Tennyson," said he, "was a great poet with a mediocre subject. His subject was Victorian England."

"I give you the nineteenth-century English novelists," said she. "Some are good; others less good; but didn't that century do well in science? There's Darwin . . ."

Whitehead didn't take this up, and I thought I knew why; because in science the nineteenth century, certainly until toward its close, would have made a poor showing in comparison with the seventeenth, "The Century of Genius," as he has called it in *Science and the Modern World*. At that point I tried to get Goethe and Beethoven in, only to be reminded that our nineteenth century was deemed to have begun in 1830, whereas Goethe died in 1832 and Beethoven in 1827.

"But while this concern for common people distinguishes our period and is one of its admirable traits," Whitehead resumed, "there is the question whether more widely diffused opportunity will not depress talent and genius to less exalted levels. The eighteenth century had its means of identifying talent and fostering it, inadequate though the means often were. How will exceptional ability—I don't mean ordinary talents, but really exceptional powers—be identified in a completely democratic society?"

"There I disagree with you," said Mrs. Whitehead decidedly, emphasizing her conviction by rolling up her ball of yarn more and more vigorously. "The levelling will release talents where they were never released before, and *raise* standards by diffusing opportunity. I will give you an example of how this process is already at work. From the nineteenth century only the best novels have survived; they were published among more having less merit or none; but when a good one appeared in the nineteenth century it was an event. Today, while the number of novels, bad, good, indifferent, which are being turned out, is much greater, the publication of a good novel isn't so much of an event, for there are quite a good many of them."

"As one who doesn't read enough contemporary novels to have any right to an opinion," I said, "it strikes me that Tolstoy, Dostoevsky, Turgenev, Tchekov and Gorki, who wrote novels under the czarist autocracy, at least haven't been surpassed by any writers known to us since the Revolution of 1917."

"But would you call Soviet Russia a democracy," asked Mrs. Whitehead.

"We English and Americans," answered Whitehead, "are singularly unimaginative in our interpretations of the term 'democracy'; we seem unable to admit under our definition any form of society which does not conform closely to our own. See the way their armies fight in this war. The whole Russian people is evidently unified in the determination to free their soil of the Germans. No question arises but that that shall be done. Their unity for defence is complete, because they are defending a social system which they feel to be their own. I believe that the two great powers which will emerge from this war will be Russia and America, and the principles which animate them will be antithetical: that of Russia will be cohesion; that of America will be individualism."

"Do you see anywhere in contemporary political thought any new idea as daring as the discoveries in science and the resulting inventions have been in the past fifty years?"

"There is Marx, of course; though I cannot speak of him with any confidence."

"Lenin put him to work."

"Yes, and it is a singular fact that the prophet of proletarian revolt found the first practical effectuation of his ideas in a society predominantly agrarian."

"Only," offered Mrs. Whitehead as correction, "because it was rottenest and ready to fall."

"I wonder," said Whitehead, "if Lenin didn't die at about the right time. Hadn't he accomplished his work, and wasn't a man of a less theoretical and more practical talent the man wanted?"

"How do you think Trotsky would have done?"

Whitehead said he doubted if Trotsky would have been of much use as head of a socialist fatherland, or to speak more explicitly, Soviet Russia. I remarked that "when Trotsky was being deported from Russia by Stalin, he said, as I remember, that Stalin was intellectually a fearful come-down after Lenin, and that Russia would be ruled not by a great thinker but by a man with the political mentality of a ward boss."

"His peculiar abilities," said Whitehead, smiling blandly, "seem to be finding useful scope at present."

"You remind me—and I shall remind you—of what you said to Constable at the Saturday Club when it was being discussed whether Churchill's boots could, if necessary, be filled by Anthony Eden, Churchill having just had pneumonia. Constable, who had known Eden, said, 'He is not a brilliant man, but he is a thoroughly decent fellow,' and you said . . ."

"What did he say?" asked Mrs. Whitehead mischievously.

"He said, 'Churchill is a better prime minister flat on his back in bed with pneumonia than any other man in England up in his boots. Eden may be a decent fellow but this is no time for decency!'"

(It had set the table in a gale of laughter.)

The tray of chocolate came in next, it being now about ten o'clock. The chocolate was, if possible, better than ever, or else we were all hungrier than usual, and meanwhile the conversation had shifted somehow to school discipline.

"As head boy at Sherborne," said Whitehead, "I once had to thrash a boy. He was guilty of stealing money. The headmaster said, 'Either you must thrash him in the presence of the school or I must expel him.' That left no choice, I had to go ahead with it. The masters, of course, were not present; it was done only in the presence of the boys."

"How did you feel about it?"

"I didn't like it; but I had to do it, and in those days, the late 1870's, flogging was still an accepted part of the discipline. The headmaster, who was an exceptionally kind-hearted man, occasionally had to do it himself, and after having thrashed a boy, we could see him bury his head in his arms and weep. You could have heard a pin drop!"

"Were you ever thrashed by your parents when you were a child?"

"No. When I needed to be punished they would give me a dose of medicine and tell me they were sorry I wasn't feeling well."

"My parents thrashed *me*," said Mrs. Whitehead rebelliously, "and it didn't do a bit of good. It was the Breton rearing, which was stern. As children we were brought up on the mediaeval folk tales which were still rife in the countryside, and I remember, once when something went wrong with me, being told—like the wounded knight in the tourney, who said, 'I thirst'—being told, I say, in the words of the king, '*Bois ton sang, Beaumanoir, et tu n'auras plus soif.*' "

We were peering through an album of old photographs, looking for two of the cricket teams at Sherborne when Whitehead was a youth in his teens. They were taken in front of what seemed to be an ancient Gothic gateway. I said it looked very old.

"The school," said Whitehead, "celebrated its twelve-hundredth anniversary in 1941, and is supposed to go back to

King Alfred. One of its buildings was an abbey and the little room I occupied in my last year was supposed to have been the abbot's."

"Can you pick him out of that group of young men?" asked Mrs. Whitehead.

There were two group photographs in the same spot from two successive years; and he was more easily identifiable in the second, or elder, group than in the younger.

"A singular thing about our schooling there," said Whitehead, "and it was by no means confined to Sherborne, but was characteristic of all English schooling of that time—we studied the literature and history of the Greeks, but took from it only those aspects which seemed to resemble our English life and affairs. Thus, Athens was a naval power, and England had a navy, and, the larger aspects of modern naval power not yet having been grasped, we thought of it as being mainly applied to the coasts of Europe, as the Athenian naval power was applied to the coasts and islands of the eastern Mediterranean. Mind you, nobody realized that this was going on. We were merely taking from the ancient world what seemed applicable to ourselves. And similarly, when it came to Rome, although we read the great authors of the late republican period and in the time of Augustus, the part of Roman history which seemed analogous to our own were those later centuries after the literature has lost its greatest names—I should say Tacitus was the last—say the three centuries following the year 70 A.D. when it was a question of Rome's maintaining its ascendancy by wise statesmanship, and able civil administration. . . . As between the Greek and Roman authors of their respective great ages, namely the fifth century in Greece and the Augustan Age in Rome, I find the Greek immeasurably superior to the Roman. The ideas are immensely more original and vital. In fact, the only Roman author whom I find at all comparable with the Greeks in those qualities of vital and original ideas is one who may surprise you. He is Lucretius."

"Lucretius has something to say to the people of our time. *That* doesn't surprise me," I replied, "for I remember how Arnold Toynbee found the lines from a passage in Lucretius which argue that death destroys personality running in his head during the spring of 1918. They were written about one hundred and fifty years after Hannibal evacuated Italy, but the horror of that invasion was still so vivid in men's minds that Lucretius thought its mere memory made oblivion seem preferable to personal immortality. . . . And this brings up a question which I have been wanting to open with you. It isn't a very cheerful one, and I shall find it hard to phrase precisely, for it doesn't come from any single piece of evidence but, rather, from a thousand scattered impressions; what I read, what I see, what I hear, what I experience, and what I am left to infer. The effect is cumulative and the only way I know how to word it at last may sound banal, dreadful though it is. It is this: that we live amid a steady disintegration of what people are accustomed to call 'civilized life.' "

"I don't consider that banal," said he, "and I do consider it true. And I am afraid our old friend Adam Smith had something too much to do with it; not in the sense that one man's words can effect such vast consequences, but in the sense that he gave expression to a half-truth which was already lurking in men's minds, which, in fact, is always lurking there, and they took it as a whole truth and proceeded to act on it. I mean the idea of the predominance of the economic motive in man. Now I don't deny that the economic motive is there, but what plays the devil in human affairs is mistaking a half-truth for a whole truth. This elevated the material motive into good repute and allowed people to act on it with what they took to be good conscience. But no period of history has ever been great or ever can be that does not act on some sort of high, idealistic motives, and idealism in our time has been shoved aside, and we are paying the penalty for it."

"The very word 'idealism,' " I said, "has been a term of

derision since the first world war. Writing for readers of the daily press one grows very sensitive to what sort of ideas are and are not acceptable, and how the unacceptable ones must be rephrased to make them go down. And at about the same time it began to be noticed that there was a marked decline in the influence of Christian theology."

"Christian theology," said Whitehead, "took a fearfully wrong turning."

"Buddhist theology, though very elaborate, in fact too elaborate for me, does nevertheless strike me as being intellectually respectable," I remarked.

"The Hindus," added Whitehead, "had, among other things, grasped the resemblances between us and the animals and incorporated it into their religious thought, but you can hardly call it an equalitarian idea, for they considered that it was the job of all of us alike to get rid of our damned personalities." (He said this smilingly, but immediately turned serious again.) "As for the Christian theology, can you imagine anything more appallingly idiotic than the Christian idea of heaven? What kind of deity is it that would be capable of creating angels and men to sing his praises day and night to all eternity? It is, of course, the figure of an Oriental despot, with his inane and barbaric vanity. Such a conception is an insult to God. . . . I will tell you, though, that on its emotional and aesthetic side, Christianity plays an enormous part in the lives of people who are not over-intellectualized; women especially, and it gives them a sustainment which is often quite touching. One of the worst pieces of luck that has befallen Europeans was that when it came time to reform the Church, the new forms were set by Martin Luther, who threw away the aesthetic and emotional appeal, and left only the dry bones of theology."

German theology led to a discussion of German scholarship and its distinctive qualities as viewed beside the scholarship of France and England. Whitehead presently generalized the three impartially by remarking:

"German scholarship shares a defect which I find common to most scholarship. Scholars insist upon using words as though the meanings of those words existed in a vacuum. They will say, 'This man said *that* about *this*,' as though the words themselves were all there were to it, and quite ignoring the emotional content of those words in the historical environment in which they were first uttered. What was the total emotional connotation of those terms when they were originated, and how have the historical changes which have occurred since altered our understanding of them?"

" '*Er hat zu viel gelesen*,' was the verdict of a young German who came out from a lecture by one of the eminent savants at Berlin, with Bliss Perry when he was a young student there. Bliss heard Mommsen, whom he did admire, and von Treitschke, whom he admits he didn't see through at the time, and also many of the university bigwigs of that period, and he was left thinking that a good many of them had also 'read too much.' And men who read too much are likely to be contented with half-truths."

"Most propositions are that," said Whitehead. "Under one aspect it may be false; and under another, true. Whether it is true or false will depend upon its relevancy. In the aspect in which it is relevant we call it true, and in the aspect in which it is irrelevant, untrue. Actually it is neither, and it is both, depending upon the relevancy in which it is seen. A half-truth, you see. And it is taking these half-truths for whole truths that raises the mischief."

"Do you consider that the economists have been any worse offenders with half-truths than historians?"

"The more history I read," he replied, "the less I think of historians. Most of them strike me as men who presume to write authoritatively about events which they are not qualified to understand. Or else they accept the official documents of an epoch at their full value, omitting to reflect that its real significance lay in the emotional atmosphere which activated its people and the general ideas under whose sway they lived. I make two exceptions: Gibbon is one and the other is Thucydides. Gibbon had had some practical experience of managing men in that regiment of his, the Hampshire Volunteers; he had had experience in politics; he had known an interesting set of literary men in London; and then just at the right moment, he emigrated to Geneva where he came into contact with the point of view of travelled and cultivated people on the Continent. These, with his other qualifications, gave him an equipment for the writing of history which is unique among modern historians. As for the ancient one, Thucydides was a general who had been a part of the life and times which he depicts."

XXXIII

May 9, 1944

ONE of those oddities which keep happening in wartime occurred on my way to dine with the Whiteheads. Each spring on fine evenings the Harvard and Radcliffe choirs sing from the steps of Widener Hall, the university library, in what is generally known as the Sever Quadrangle. These massive stone steps mount to an imposing classical façade of red-brick academic Georgian with Corinthian columns. They are spacious enough for several hundred persons, and they face a somewhat similar portico of the Memorial Church across a greensward and elm grove, making a pleasant out-of-door concert hall. The church was built to commemorate the Harvard men who were killed in the first world war.

Half a dozen undergraduates, three of them in uniform, were trundling a small cabinet pianoforte on a wheeled carrier toward the steps; people were already assembling; evidently it was for a Yard concert. The boys did not know what the programme was going to be, but just then Professor Wallace Woodworth, the choirmaster, arrived and told me: they were to sing three movements from Brahms's *German Requiem*. We agreed that it was a piece of historic irony which might be taken in any one of several ways.

The May evening was golden of late sunlight behind the fresh green of the budding elms, a pink dogwood tree was in full flower over by the church, and the robins were already choiring.

At the Hotel Ambassador the Whiteheads were sitting beside their westward windows, which were wide open; for in four warm days spring had come at a bound. We dined beside another window opening westward, still in the late rays of the setting sun, and dined scrumptiously, albeit without a single rationed item on the table, unless it were a few snicks of butter or sugar. As the meal went on, Whitehead spoke of what the sudden access of wealth had done to Spain in the sixteenth century.

"That influx of gold from the West Indies and South America ruined Spain in about the span of two lifetimes," said he. "As soon as they had exhausted what the natives had accumulated, there it ended. Not that the Spanish people saw much of it, for Charles V used the gold to finance his European wars and political manoeuvres. No new industries were started and so the stream of bullion from the New World created no lasting wealth. Food and manufactured goods were largely imported, and it has been said that the only articles of export were 'soldiers and priests.' Now the true prosperity of a country is derived from its *internal* industrial activities. Of course, the fruits of these activities must be more or less equitably distributed. But if the wealth comes from outside and without any particular exertion from the most of your people, its effects are ruinous. A nation flourishes and survives by its internal activity. Even if your loans to other nations are never paid after this war—and I don't suppose they will be—you still have in this country your immense industrial equipment, your agrarian productivity, and your people with technical skill; and by these your recovery is sufficiently assured."

[276]

"The Spaniards had two other misfortunes at about the same time," I remarked. "There is a striking page in Gilbert Murray's *Tradition and Progress* in which he says that persecution, however disastrous its remoter consequences, may be a complete political success, instancing the treatment of the Protestants and the Jews in Spain, where 'the blood of martyrs' was certainly *not* 'the seed of the church.'"

"Toleration," said Mrs. Whitehead, "pays such immense returns. The Jews have done a great deal for England and, *as* Jews, I would say, are tending to disappear. You need your Jews in this country. They make an admirable ingredient in your population—are more acute and more subtle than our Anglo-American stock. Your Negro problem, on the other hand, is a real problem. When English people deplore their having been brought here, I want to ask them, 'Who began it?' Your Southern planters and Northern shipowners continued on a larger scale what the English started, and it is all very well for us to point out that we abolished it legally by the year 1833, but black slavery was never in *our* islands. It was a colonial problem."

"Bringing them in was so fearfully short-sighted in the first place," said Whitehead. "A little imagination should have warned anybody what was being incurred. The immediate motive of individual profit is of too limited a range to serve as foundation for a stable society—and so, for that matter, is the immediate advantage of any single nation, as I should think we should all have learned by now."

"Do you ever see Dr. Brüning?" asked Mrs. Whitehead.

"Only now and then, and not with much opportunity for personal conversation."

"He was here once, and he and I spoke together by ourselves," she replied. "One thing he said was that he could have succeeded as chancellor of Germany if Britain and America had supported him! What kind of government is it that needs to be sustained by two other governments?"

"Once, at Dr. Hans Zinsser's, where we were only five at table," I said, "and probably because Zinsser was of German descent, Dr. Brüning spoke very freely. What he told in detail of Hitler's rise to power sounded like melodrama; Brüning seemed to have known what was going on and what Hitler intended, yet he seemed to have been powerless to stop it."

"Brüning is a very devout man," observed Whitehead, "but a man may be devout without being good. He may be a man of conscience, but his conscience may be a damned *bad* conscience, for conscience presupposes that its promptings are socially beneficent."

Dinner ended, Mr. Whitehead and I were shooed into the living room, where we sat by the open window in the soft twilight until Mrs. Whitehead had cleared the table. He asked what I thought of the government's eviction of Sewell Avery from the offices of Montgomery Ward in Chicago.

"The most eloquent comment on it," I thought, "was the newspaper photograph of Avery being carried out, cat's-cradle fashion, by the two soldier boys. It was much worse than if the boys had been laughing; for they were gentlemen and trying hard to keep their faces straight. But I will tell you who *were* indignant about it—the small business people and every little property-holder hanging on for dear life to what property he has in the midst of a world war in which the young men, who have not yet lived, are dying."

"The idea," said Whitehead, "of supposing that in the midst of the greatest crisis in the history of mankind, people should not be disturbed in their accustomed procedures and routines! I would have liked to be there in order to kick Avery!"

"It was a carnival for the Roosevelt-haters," I observed.

"To hear them talk," said Whitehead, "you would think that Mr. Roosevelt had entered the Presidency in an era of unprecedented prosperity."

"I am patient with their dialectic," said I.

"It is not dialectic," said Whitehead, "it is ranting."

Before settling down for the evening we roamed around the living-room a little, looking at its various pieces of Spanish mahogany, now no longer obtainable, Mrs. Whitehead remarked.

"The desk," said Whitehead, "is a museum piece. One of those Jacobean chairs is a bad Victorian imitation. The other is genuine Jacobean."

One of the pieces had a family genealogy of four generations, having been transmitted from a ninety-year-old great-grandmother to a grandmother, who in turn lived to the age of ninety or more. Taking one of her dining-room chairs into Boston for repairs, Mrs. Whitehead had asked its value. "How many of these have you?" inquired the dealer. "Half a dozen," said she for reply, for some of them are in her children's house. "Two hundred and fifty dollars," says the dealer. "For the half-dozen?" she asked. "No. Apiece."

"So I am having them insured," she said in epilogue.

Midway in a discussion of how our world has been jolted loose from what it thought were its most impregnable ideas, not alone in theology but even in physics, Whitehead remarked, "I have been rereading Huxley's *Letters*, especially the second volume. He strikes me as one of those men who fall just under the first rank, immensely able but not great. Darwin, on the other hand, is truly great, but he is the dullest great man I can think of. He and Huxley had grasped the principle of evolution in material life, but it never occurred to them to ask how evolution in material life could result in a man like, let us say, Newton."

"There was one man who saw that omission very early, and said so. He was Samuel Butler."

"They didn't like him," said Whitehead.

"Like him? They tried to ignore him, but he was a hard man to ignore."

"Darwin's dismissal of the transmission of acquired characteristics is another lapse. Who knows where our bodies begin or end, or how characteristics may be transmitted otherwise than by heredity? There may be a thousand predispositions in a child due to the occupations of his immediate forebears. A certain type of activity may have been going on in the family for generations, and the child is predisposed to it. Is that 'environment' or is it heredity?"

"Harvey Cushing came of four generations of doctors, first in this state, then in Ohio," I remarked. "Clevelanders can't remember a time when there wasn't a Dr. Cushing, and he couldn't remember a time when Cushings weren't doctoring someone. How vastly that must have increased his initial momentum."

"My father," said Whitehead, "my grandfather, and my uncles all had to do with education or local administration, or both. And so have I."

"You are a changeling, though, all the same," Mrs. Whitehead remarked, "as different from the others as could be imagined. I have always attributed the Celtic fire in you to that Welsh grandmother of yours, Mary Williams."

"That supine reliance on heredity," continued Whitehead, "had a bad effect. People felt safe in neglecting environment. 'Heredity would take care of all that.' If you want a civilization to progress, there are two or three things you must do. The forces that are constantly playing in upon our minds and bodies are inconceivably innumerable—for instance, rays from some star millions of light-years away from us—forces as fantastic as that . . . and the forms of life which might be lived on other stars millions of light-years away and millions of years hence could be infinite and admit every possibility that the imagination could conceive. The thousand thoughts that drift through a man's mind day by day he should entertain and turn over and consider in every aspect, give them their share of consideration. We need to entertain every prospect of novelty, every chance that could result in new combinations. But at the same time we need to entertain those with sceptical examination, and subject them to the most impartial scrutiny, for the probability is that nine hundred and ninety-nine of them will come to nothing, either because worthless in themselves or because we shall not know how to elicit their value; but we had better entertain them all, however sceptically, for the *thousandth* idea may be the one that will change the world!"

"People in our time, having seen the incredible achieved so often," I said, "are prepared to admit that possibility in the world of scientific discovery, but not yet in the larger world of general ideas."

"I will give you an example," said he, "of how unpredictable these chances of novel origination are. Seated in this room with an apparatus, we can convey thought to someone seated in another room in Boston or farther away. But seventy years ago if you wanted to communicate quickly with Tokyo you had to telegraph. Today you can speak to somebody in Asia who has with him an apparatus no larger than that one in the other room. Marconi thought that such communication might be possible; at the start, of course, he couldn't be sure. But there were plenty of first-rate men of science who could tell him that it wouldn't work, and could tell him why; the vibrations, instead of continuing around the earth, would go up into the stratosphere and disperse. They did go up into the stratosphere, but instead of being dispersed they were reflected back down to the earth, and so we have wireless communication. No one foresaw that fact which made it possible; not even Marconi at the outset. Something unknown and unpredictable—a mere chance, if you care to call it that—determined the success of this still almost incredible means of human communication. Now some general idea, equally inconceivable to people now living, might change our manner of life on this planet even more than wireless has affected intercommunication."

"Europe, for all its ructions," said I, "has produced no lack of novel origination—at least since the Renaissance, and for centuries before the fall of Rome. But if enough young men are slaughtered in these wars, and civil societies are repeatedly disrupted, I wonder where the impetus for novel ideas will come from."

"Russia is a possibility," said he.

"But tinged with the Asiatic: don't forget that," said Mrs. Whitehead. "That makes it not quite the same thing."

"There is not much reason thus far to suppose that the impetus would come from South America," continued Whitehead. "I look for it to come from you, here in the United States, in North America. If you people cannot produce it, I think the world will be in a bad way. You may need another century to coalesce your races; and I believe you will gain by the admixture of the brilliant southern European strains. Left to itself the old Anglo-American stock is a little too stolid."

"This fusing of races," I said, "is only just beginning. As yet, it is likely to take the form of gifted individuals rising spectacularly. The races are mixing but we don't yet know what the result will be. It might be brilliant—or it might be stupid."

"I have never ceased to entertain the idea," said he, "that the human race might rise to a certain point and then decline and never retrieve itself. Plenty of other forms of life have done that. Evolution may go down as well as up. In Asia we have seen how life can stagnate for centuries. A part of that stagnation seems to come from religious mysticism. 'Never mind about this world,' or 'Our misfortunes are our karmas incurred in previous incarnations, and must be expiated' or 'The overruling purposes of the universe are inscrutable, and who are we that we should question them?' "

"The West, in contrast," said I, "has seldom hesitated 'to take arms against a sea of troubles.' "

"Static religions are the death of thought," said Whitehead.

"Would that be because they presume to answer all questions before they have been asked?"

"Any dogmatic system of thought does that. When a priesthood becomes dominant in a society, freedom of inquiry is discouraged; and if their dominance continues long enough, the level of general intelligence is depressed."

XXXIV

August 29, 1944

SUMMER ending, the Cambridge elms already beginning to look like September with brown leaves fallen on the green-swards. It was seven-forty when I rang the bell of the White-heads' apartment. They were both looking uncommonly well. "But then," as I told them, "why shouldn't you? Back from a month on your island in Maine, and then this deluge of favour-able war news? You must wonder, as we all do, whether we are living in the same world as that of 1940–1942."

"It is true, these events are staggering," said Whitehead.

"Are they really unprecedented," I asked, "or are they only on a larger scale physically?"

"Nothing like it that I know of has happened in a thousand years, and when it did it took a hundred years to happen, while this takes only a matter of months. Formerly the magnitude of such events could be seen only afterwards, and then mainly by historians and scholars, but these can be seen happening by everybody, from day to day, almost from hour to hour."

"I come to you almost blind from reading newspapers or hanging over the office teletype, and this since June 6th. As you read these events, what, in essence, do you think it is that is happening?"

"Two things. First, sheer self-preservation. We have been forced to defend ourselves against not now one, but two types of German military men (acting, of course, as agents for people in the background); one, the regular German army officers of the old aristocratic class; and two, these new, low-class adven-turers. They both thought, 'Wouldn't it be great to enslave the whole of Europe!' And they threatened us with a slavery of a new and horrible kind. Most previous conquerors have been willing to leave regional cultures fairly intact! . . ."

"The Romans preferred to," said I. "Conquered territories were easier to govern that way."

"But these Germans," said he, "set to work extirpating all that. I'm not sure they meant to 'rule the world'; at least not yet, but if they had won they would have made plenty of trouble for you acting through South America. The other thing that is happening, as I see it, is this: you cannot wage a war of such magnitude as this without inaugurating a new epoch. We have been fortunate in Churchill. He is an admirable leader to arouse the patriotism of his people in a desperate war; but he doesn't think sociologically in terms of a new epoch. I doubt if he would be so admirable in the making of the peace."

"Churchill thinks in terms of the eighteenth century," said Mrs. Whitehead positively. "He has two sides to his nature; on one side he is a British statesman of the type one knows, and, in many aspects, admires. But I knew his mother—a lighter-headed young thing . . . and on that side he is a back-slapping Rotarian, singing jovial songs with 'the boys.'"

"You are more fortunate in your man," continued Whitehead. "Mr. Roosevelt does, I believe, think largely in terms of a new epoch. It was shown before this war began in his domestic policies, which so infuriated some of our wealthy friends. Let us hope he lives to have a large hand in the shaping of the peace. And in the epoch to come, again, I look to Russia."

"When I think of the 'bad press' Russia has had in America for twenty-five years, to see ourselves now locked in fraternal embrace . . ."

"You Americans, it seems to me, are rather narrow-minded in your views about the excellence and general applicability of your own form of government," Whitehead spoke slowly, weighing his thoughts. "How is it that the Russians have been able to do what they have? For the previous century, or century and a half, before their Revolution, whenever they came into the affairs of western Europe it was usually to support the wrong side, as they did Metternich at the Congress of Vienna. There were, it is true, charming and gifted people at the top of their society of whom one knew, and they did well in the arts—literature (those novels of Tolstoy, Dostoevsky, and Turgenev, that are so much better than ours of the same period), and drama, music, and painting. . . ."

"Don't omit the dance. . . ."

"Also," said he, "their defeat of Napoleon—as such great events usually are—was an advance notice of what was to come. But it is not until our own century that the world has seen the true greatness of which Russia is capable."

"Where do you date it? November 1917?"

"Rather, from the departure of Trotsky and the arrival of Stalin in power."

"Lenin," observed Mrs. Whitehead, "being a revolted aristocrat, had it in for his class, as such rebel sons usually do. But Stalin is a man of the people and much more representative."

"Stalin's being a Georgian, I think, does have a good deal to do with it," agreed Whitehead. "He has had this concept that Russia, with its enormous diversifications and extent, could be coalesced into one great people. And how this vast array of talents has been elicited from the masses of the Russian people in such a short time is worth looking into. Take their generals in this war; they are mostly a young set. Presumably someone had to pick them, and I don't suppose Stalin chose them by chance. It is a main function of society to release the widest possible spread of talents, and this appears to have been being done in Russia. When great departures come in the lives of peoples they are generally the result of two or more causes coming together; but although one man cannot initiate such great changes, once these changes are in motion, one man may be able to give them their direction, this way or that. Napoleon rode into power on the ideas of the French Revolution, but he never, at heart, was interested in those ideas. One reason was that he was too good a general; the application of military science interested him more; the revolutionary ideas stoked, as it were, his war-machine."

"Would you agree that Napoleon's star rose as long as he subserved the great ideas of the French Revolution and began to decline when he supplanted them with his own imperial ego?"

"Yes. And we English were on the wrong side all along. Our ruling classes and landed aristocracy were frightened by the Terror and the beheading of the king."

"As if the English hadn't beheaded a king . . ."

"Yes," said Mrs. Whitehead, "but that was 'different.' "

"Haven't I heard that there was some religious revulsion in it, too; that the English nonconformists regarded the deism of the French *philosophes* and revolutionary leaders as sheer atheism?"

"That would have placed our people solidly behind our aristocracy," said Mrs. Whitehead, "where, as a matter of fact, they were."

"And yet, to think of our American War of Independence having had, from start to finish, a sizable block of favourable votes in your British House of Commons."

"I do," said Mrs. Whitehead, "but I wish I could convince some of my American friends that that was the fact."

"Is it only when people have gone through some fearful personal or social ordeal that they can sufficiently universalize their minds to identify the movements for human liberation on whichever side of a national frontier they may be?"

"It doesn't always follow," said Whitehead. "Take the type of Frenchman so often produced by complete opposition to the Church; that type strikes me as unfortunate. The Reformation was one of the most colossal failures in history; it threw overboard what makes the Church tolerable and even gracious; namely, its aesthetic appeal; but kept its barbarous theology."

"What oppresses me," said Mrs. Whitehead gravely, "is where we are to find, since Christianity is losing its hold, a place where humanity can collectively express its good will. I don't deny the fearful suffering that Christian theology has inflicted on the more sensitive and imaginative spirits. That has been shocking enough, God knows! But just as the family is the only place one can turn to when he has behaved disgracefully (and we are all capable of so behaving at some time in our lives, even unintentionally) so there needs to be a place where people can come together, not to do specifically this or that, but to remind themselves and one another of their benevolent intentions, their general good will. If I thought the church, or any form of organized Christianity, were still doing this, or could still do it, I wouldn't be saying what I am. The need still exists; how can it be filled?"

The objection that multitudes of church-goers might say that the churches are still filling just that need was not raised because, so often, what one solitary voice is saying today the multitude may be saying tomorrow. Instead, the question was raised whether aesthetic experience might not be a form of religious worship: "Are not aesthetics a form of ethics?"

"No," replied Whitehead, "the two move in different realms."

"Wait a moment; let me try to rephrase that. . . . Isn't there a high moral content in the work of great artists?"

"What do you mean by 'moral content'?"

"I mean the effect on the spectator or the listener of artists who have lived and worked at a consistently high level. Surely, it isn't stretching things to say that we are getting a higher voltage of the spirit when hearing good performances of music created by men of genius than when listening to the Reverend Doctor or the Reverend Father. . . . And I encounter a good many others who think the same way. How can the effect of such works be other than religious?"

"While you were speaking," said Whitehead, laughing at

me, "I was of two minds. One said, 'Yes, that sounds all right,' and the other said, 'What the devil does he mean?' No," he continued, "the only question in aesthetics is: is the work of art good or bad? If you and I were enjoying together, say, a fine sunset, I wouldn't nudge you and ask, 'I say, what do you propose to do about this sunset?' We enjoy aesthetic experiences purely for their own sakes. That is all we have any right to expect of them."

"Well, perhaps what you have been hearing from me is the hang-over from two sets of dissenting grandparents: one, New England Puritans, the other Philadelphia Quakers."

"The artist," said Whitehead, "has, and must have, a continuous flow of fresh aesthetic experiences. These he translates into an art-form, and it is through these works that his experience passes into the lives of others." He let it go at that, but he knew, and I knew, that what he had said meant more than met the ear.

"So morals have nothing to do with good poetry?"

"Was Byron 'moral'?" he inquired, smilingly.

Of a sudden he had me on his side:

"This is one thing which ails so many of our American nineteenth-century poets. They are entirely too 'correct'—in their printed sentiments at least. Reading them now, one finds himself thinking: 'You didn't really believe that. It's not possible that you didn't know better. Only you didn't dare say so!' A sample in prose of that timidity is the feeble 'moral' which Hawthorne ventures at the end of *The Scarlet Letter*: 'Be true! Show freely to the world, if not your worst, yet some trait whereby the worst can be inferred!' Even as a boy, reading that, I knew it was evasive. 'If you can't be true, be as true as you can!' "

"The one of your poets who escapes all that," said Mrs. Whitehead, "is Whitman. And American poetry has never elsewhere reached such heights as in his elegy for President Lincoln."

From here the discussion moved to the impact of scientific technology on our modern world:

"These new techniques," said Whitehead, "have created a situation absolutely unprecedented. At the beginning of this evening you asked me if I thought these world events—the military action and the consequent social changes—are really more significant than similar crises in the past, or merely on a larger scale physically."

"Yes: are these events of today 'greater' or only 'bigger'?"

"They are probably no bigger and no greater than the collapse of Athens at the end of the Peloponnesian War seemed, or was, to the Greeks; and probably no greater or no bigger than the fall of Rome was to the Romans of the fifth century A.D.; but I will tell you what *is* new. In those earlier crises in the history of mankind, and in others like them, it took a hundred years to bring about changes which we have been watching in the past five years; even in the past five months. That *is* new, and the spectacle is terrific. For one thing, the apparatus for communication works with a rapidity which is almost instantaneous. Already we are all so accustomed to this that to mention the fact seems trite. Yet the fact itself is far from being trite. Again, the acceleration of new techniques is such that since 1900 the rate of technological innovation is double that between 1800 and 1900. I was born in the year 1861. And I would almost venture to say that the techniques of living have changed faster and more between 1861 and 1944 than they did, going backward, between 1861 and . . ."—he paused, smiling —"I was going to say—between 1861 and 61 B.C.!

"Furthermore," he continued, "the effects of these new techniques are interactive. Their alterations in our ways of daily living affect our moral ideas, and the alterations in our ways of thinking in turn react upon the uses to which we put our new techniques and, in turn, produce fresh novelties. As I have often told you, I can hardly think of a concept which was accepted as fundamental truth when I was a young man in the 1880's, that has not been profoundly modified if not rendered obsolete by the changes of which we have been speaking. Thus our moral ideas are affected by these floods of change and the fluidity of ideas reacts upon the uses to which the new techniques are put."

"A while ago," said Mrs. Whitehead, "when we were speaking about the impulse of worship, I was asking myself, 'Where —finally—does it come from?' What is this moral sense that we have? A child has it, a mere baby, and feels guilty, poor lamb, when he thinks he has violated his little vision of the good."

"As you speak, I can see Eric's tiny boots sticking out from under the bed," said I.

"We never knew what he thought he had done that was wrong," said she. "Our first intimation of anything amiss was that only his heels were visible. I never pumped him. He was very glad to be taken by one foot and hauled out on his little tummy, but we never found out."

"He was the most fascinating human being I have ever known," said Whitehead absently. "His colonel came to see us afterwards, and told us a good deal that we hadn't known. He said, among other things, that while there was a good deal of bawdy talk at table, it was always moderated when Eric was there, not because Eric was a prig, for he wasn't, but out of deference to some quality in him. He was full of fun and if there was a 'rag' he would be one of the ringleaders."

"They couldn't believe," said Mrs. Whitehead, "that he spent his evenings on leave at home. 'I say, Whitehead, where do you go?' Directly he arrived home the telephone would start ringing. 'May I speak to Eric?' One evening it rang five times. I said, 'What ails them? Can't they let you alone for a single evening?' He explained: 'They are charming fellows. What they do doesn't seem to harm them in the least; it glides off them like water off a duck's back; but if I did the same, I couldn't look you in the face.' What sort of homes they had been reared in I don't know; perhaps their mothers were of the order of women who are too pure to discuss sex with their sons."

"That restraint on rough tongues in the presence of a well-bred boy is a mysterious process. I have seen it work but can't say I ever understood exactly what was going on. The Signet Society in Harvard when I was an undergraduate was a group of brilliant young men, and the first place I ever heard young men talk well; but there were two or three upperclassmen who were quite disagreeable. With the first Junior Seven came in a Philadelphia boy with, I judge, a personality somewhat like Eric's. Almost at once it was noticed that when he was at table the three disagreeables moderated their pitch. It wasn't that he ever said anything or perhaps even thought anything. But what *might* he think? And one wouldn't want to be thought badly of by Spencer Ervin."

"This awareness of worth in human beings," said Whitehead, "develops very early. Most attempts to formulate it in words fail."

"When I meet it, this quiet worth, where there is the most of it, in common life, I can see that it is a value above all other values, that it outranks all other ranks, and yet its dignity is totally unselfconscious. This was my first discovery when I went to work in a city. Boston in those years was a good deal wickeder than it is now. It was really grim, and there were places in it that were downright sinister. And yet . . . one kept encountering this silent, innate worth in the most unlikely places: on the docks, in police courts, in slum tenements; there was no name for it, yet there it was, and one always knew it when encountered. Truly, I may say to you that this is the only thing of any importance that I know; and, as you see, I cannot communicate it; all I can tell you is that I have 'seen something.' But there are no words for it."

"Words," said Whitehead, "do not express our deepest intuitions. In the very act of being verbalized they escape us. The trouble is that we are in the habit of thinking of words as fixed things with specific meanings. Actually the meanings of language are in violent fluctuation and a large part of what we try to express in words lies outside the range of language."

"Music often seems to come nearer expressing our deepest feelings."

"Another form of profound expression is sculpture," said he. "I am thinking more especially of ancient sculpture, for that, I think, was the principal art of the ancient world. They had their literatures, too, very great ones, and music, though we know little about that. . . ."

"Christianity," said Mrs. Whitehead, "—if we accept the historical figure of Christ, complicated and garbled though the historical records are—tried to express some of this idea of human worth."

"It did get some useful principles formulated," said Whitehead, "but in general it was too simple-minded and too ignorant."

"How shocked I was at myself, when I first began to realize that!"

"When was it?" asked Mrs. Whitehead.

"After the first war. The realization had been growing for several years before I knew what it was."

"Did it take specific form?"

"It took dozens of them. One that I remember best was, 'Christianity did not invent human worth.' "

"As this war goes on," said Whitehead, "and so many young men die before they have had time to live, I keep asking myself what it is that can inspire such heroism and devotion. If our side had failed in this war, life on our earth would not have been worth much, and multitudes have finally realized that fact. Manifestly most of these young men in uniform are not animated by complex political concepts, and only a small proportion, I suggest, consciously think of themselves as Christians. Their ideas are multiform, and, taking them by their millions, often

[292]

conflicting. Yet there is one which they have in common, and, while it isn't verbalized by them, and while we have admitted that there are no words for it, it is, as nearly as we can come to a definition, the idea of human worth. They are dying for the worth of the world."

XXXV

November 14, 1944

WHEN I arrived, Mr. Whitehead was asleep in his study. It was eight o'clock of a mild autumn evening, with moist air and the residential streets smelling agreeably of fallen wet leaves:

All in a death-dumb, autumn-dripping gloom.

Coming almost directly from the office my brain was full of the horrors of the Germans' massacre of the Greek village of Distomo, which had just been verified in detail and published in the final edition. The philosopher found Mrs. Whitehead and me threshing out the question of German cruelty half an hour later when he came out of his study. One remark he made was that in other cases anywhere remotely comparable, "cruelty has been practised for some purpose, but the Germans practise it for its own sake, and even when it is senseless, no advantage to be gained, and, as they retreat, merely making things worse for themselves."

"I have some good news for you" (it seemed to me a good idea to shift the subject), "and more edifying; our friend Livingstone has been made vice-chancellor of Oxford; 'admitted,' I believe, is the correct verb."

"Has he? I am pleased."

"He says he will read '(but with adequate humility, I hope) Plato's remarks about the return of the philosophers to the cave. However, Plato's philosophers had more power than vice-chancellors, and no doubt had the advantage of being better philosophers.' Will this office grind up much of his time and strength in administrative tasks?"

"Not excessively, I think. There is a committee of which he will be chairman, but nine-tenths of the administrative work is done by the heads of the colleges."

"I have been told the vice-chancellorship isn't considered any dizzying altitude, but that it is a demerit if you don't get it."

"Not as serious as that," said Mrs. Whitehead smiling, "only a hush-hush" (laying finger to her lips) "on the part of one's friends."

"The office," said he, "is passed around in rotation among the heads of the colleges, and each one has a turn at it unless he is considered incompetent. How old is Livingstone?"

"About sixty-one, I think."

"Isn't he older than that? I would have said seventy."

"Nonsense!" exclaimed his wife. "They were just young people when we first knew them."

"Let's look him up in *Who's Who*." He went into his library and returned with the volume. Holding it down to the lamp with a big, heavy-lensed reading glass, he scanned the page, and announced: "Sixty-four . . . and I say, what a lot he has done! vice-chancellor of the University of Belfast from 1924 to 1933, then president of Corpus Christi, Oxford, and a great deal of public work. I first came to know him well in 1920 when we were both on the prime minister's committee to look into the study of the classics, and respected him immensely."

"Add to that," said I, "all his books. They begin with *The Greek Genius* in 1911. That's a remarkable book to have been written by a man of thirty-one."

"I don't dispute the quality of the book," said Whitehead, "but the age at which it was written doesn't strike me as remarkable. It is not unusual for men to begin producing their best work at the age of thirty or thereabouts."

"You score off me: Beethoven, Goethe, Michelangelo."

"The basic ideas of a man's life-work may be well in his mind by the time he is thirty. He may give them widely different forms later, and more extended development; but their main outlines can be already present."

"Wouldn't you consider Livingstone's one of the solid contemporary English careers?"

"Yes. Since Murray is less active, I suppose Livingstone is his successor. What a useful book *Who's Who* is," he continued, turning over the thick, red-covered, closely printed volume in his hands. "If I were to be cast on that desert island and allowed to take only one book, I would certainly take *Who's Who*," he looked up at us laughing.

"It would last a good while," I conceded, "but the entertainment to be had from it presupposes your equipment."

"What is Lady Livingstone like?" asked Mrs. Whitehead. "I remember her only as a young thing, rather shy, when her second baby was in a pram."

"Quiet and effective. To know her is to admire. I could enlarge on this theme to some extent. Also, she is exactly the wife for the head of an Oxford college."

Midway in a discussion of Livingstone's books, Whitehead remarked:

"I am struck by the fact that mankind has not advanced morally, to speak of, for the past two thousand years."

"You could make it longer than that."

"Say, three thousand, then."

"I would have said about twenty-five or twenty-six hundred."

"Well, my own figures would come to about that."

"The period I was thinking of was the fifth century B.C. in Hellas, and the preceding sixth century in which its forces were gathering. If you say fifth-century Athens, then yes, it's not only a matter of modern man not having made an advance, but also a question of whether we have kept up to their mark." I cited certain undisputed historical facts as reasons for thinking so.

He weighed them awhile, then said:

"I consider it not at all impossible (though I hope improbable) that man might reach the apex of his intellectual powers and go into a deterioration lasting thousands of years. In fact, I have often thought that this war might be determining his future one way or the other. The momentum, the impetus of independent thought is so easy to lose. Men might sink into mere routine repetition of habitual acts and accustomed social processes at a fairly low level, almost brainless, as certain insects can run a stable society though they have no brains. . . . And, too, what a mess mankind has made of its religions!"

"Those who know their histories are apt to find themselves hesitating to use the very word religion."

"Have you considered how many of the great religious founders take their rise about in the fifth century B.C.?"

"I hadn't. Where does Buddha come?"

"About then, I think. Let's be sure." Again he went into his study and came back this time with a volume of the *Britannica*. Sure enough, fifth century.

"How about Moses?" I asked. Neither of us was sure—with good reason, as the event proved.

"Let's look him up, too."

"I don't want to make you a lot of work. Let me."

"No. I want to see for myself." He went for another volume of the *Britannica*.

"'Moses'; now where are his dates?" Holding the big volume to the lamp and scanning it with the reading glass, he could find none. I looked along with him. No dates.

"Why, this is queer!" said he. "They don't even give you any idea of where he comes within two centuries. 'Moses!'—in a vacuum."

"Suppose we try 'Exodus.'"

We tried it. Page after page, column after column, subheading after sub-heading, we peered together at the print, up and down, down and up. No dates. The co-authors whose initials were signed at the end of the article were certainly cagey. Perhaps they had heard, as I had, doubt cast on the idea that such a historical character as Moses ever existed, and that "the great character in fiction is Jehovah."

"I say, those men *must* be first-rate scholars," murmured Whitehead, "to give us so little help. Let's look up their initials in the front index and see who these asses are."

It was a bad knock-down for both of us.

"Cook!" said I. "A member of your own sainted Cambridge University, and co-editor of my sainted *Cambridge Ancient History!*"

He replaced the volume on its shelf.

"When I read history," said he, "I want to know where I am. The date should be at the top of each page."

"Trevelyan, at least, will do that for you in his one-volume *History of England.*"

"When I was going through old Froude, as a young man," continued Whitehead, "I would read along page after page, almost chapter after chapter, and never a date."

"With a really swagger historian," said I, "perhaps dates are considered *infra dignitatem*. Lots of times in the *Cambridge Ancient History* you can find the event quite explicitly on one page, then have to read pages before and pages after to corner the exact year when it happened."

"They can't be bothered!" said Whitehead. "Dates interrupt the beautiful, even flow of the literary style."

"Tell me," I asked, "did you ever have much luck with Buddhism?"

"I can't say that I have. It all seems to lead in the end to an unfruitful passive meditation. Perhaps that enervating climate had something to do with it. In such a situation it is easiest to sit still and do nothing. But it leads to social stagnation, as the world has seen."

"It is said not to have made much headway in this country except with bored wives; but in the 1920's, when I was studying it—and very respectfully, I assure you—I thought the psychology often hit pretty close to the facts of life. But I hadn't spent the previous twenty years in coughing up one theology to swallow another whole."

"Never swallow anything whole," said Whitehead emphatically. "We live perforce by half-truths and get along fairly well as long as we do not mistake them for whole-truths, but when we do so mistake them, they raise the devil with us."

"That experience of yours as a young man, of seeing the Newtonian physics, which were considered fixed as eternity, blow up under you, must have made a powerful impression."

"It taught me," said he, "to beware of certitude. We supposed that, except for a few dark spots which might take a few years to clear up, everything was known about physics, and then, by 1900, it was found that while the Newtonian physics were still a useful and convenient way of looking at things, they were, in any absolute sense, gone. Now, as I have told you, this would have astonished Aristotle but it would not have surprised Plato. If you will let your mind run over his *Dialogues* —excepting the *Laws,* which, though they contain admirable matter, show him in his old age when his ideas have begun to harden—you will remember that when the Dialogue, whichever one it is, is ended, nothing is finally settled. Everybody has had his say, the subject has been examined from many sides, some of the aspects are more persuasive than others, but it is erroneous to identify Plato entirely with any single one of them. He is passing us around through various points of view, knowing that each of them has, more or less, some truth in it, but no single one the whole truth. The final effect of this on a receptive and flexible mind is about right; we are left with a fair working knowledge which we must then learn to apply for ourselves. Nothing is entirely true, but there is some truth in each aspect. That, if we understood ourselves better, is about the way we do deal with experience, unless we begin to dogmatize—when we immediately get into trouble. We do fairly well with half-truths so long as we remember that they *are* half-truths."

"And now, since we are speaking of certitude, what can you say in defence of the zealot?"

"He is a useful member of society."

"You surprise me. Time was when I thought he was our only hope. Today I look on him with suspicion!"

"The zealot gets things done. He cuts through established routine. A certain amount of zealotry is necessary to get habituated mortals out of their accustomed ruts. It is so easy, you know, to keep on doing and thinking the same things just because for generations those are the things that have been thought and done. And it is also very dangerous, because, left to itself, humanity has a tendency to keep grinding around in the same grooves. The zealot is one form of the element of novelty in life, and though his ideas may not be original (and, in fact, seldom are) his energy and persistence are one form that is taken by the power of origination."

"He has given me a sociological defence of zealotry," said I to Mrs. Whitehead. "Can you give me a personal justification of the zealot?"

"Yes. He makes the comfortable classes uncomfortable."

"That is what our abolitionists did. Some of them were intensely disagreeable—had congenital grouches which they indulged under the pretext of anti-slavery agitation; some were people who loved mercy and justice; and some were of the stuff of heroes."

"People come to accept the most shocking wrongs inflicted on others," resumed Mrs. Whitehead, "because it is customary, or not inconvenient to themselves, or through insensitiveness, or lack of imagination. The element of excess in the zealot is demanded by the lack of feeling in those he finds it necessary to rouse."

I said that sympathetic imagination was a rarer quality than those who have it are prone to suppose, and Whitehead added, smiling, "So is the power of origination. . . . You may recall a sentence of mine which Livingstone quotes in his book on education. . . ."

"I do recall it. 'Moral education is impossible without the habitual vision of greatness.' He adopts that as one of his main themes."

"Last Sunday morning"—Whitehead smiled with relish—"a man was calling on us who is a fellow of Livingstone's college; he had read the book and said, 'I have been trying to think where that sentence comes from. It sounded familiar. Where did you find it?'"

XXXVI

January 19, 1945

AT New Year Whitehead had been awarded the Order of Merit by King George VI. This was founded by Edward VII at his coronation and the number of British members is fixed at twenty-four. I had written about it in the *Globe* ("Philosopher and King") concluding:

> *One of Plato's remedies for the ills of this world was that philosophers should be kings. This was Plato's little joke, for philosophers are kings already. Kings rule only in the material world; but philosophers create that out of which worlds are created. This king has honoured himself in honouring a philosopher.*

"You patted me on the back," was Whitehead's greeting as he came out of his study. "It occurs to me that Livingstone might have had a hand in my receiving this."

"There are plenty of other people in England who would have seen to it besides Livingstone." (In Oxford, at Easter, 1947, Sir David Ross, then provost of Oriel and sometime vice-chancellor, told me that he had proposed Whitehead for the order. It is quite possible that they both had.)

"I don't know," Whitehead continued. "Livingstone is now quite important. The vice-chancellorship of Oxford sounds like second place, but it is really first. The chancellor is like the king, the vice-chancellor is prime minister."

"He writes to me interestingly about his administrative problems; that, like all other administrative work, it consists in being pushed by events, finding immediate answers to immediate questions, and the difficulty is, behind their urgency, to remain aware of anything ultimate, to avoid mortgaging the future. He says it makes him realize how much people live in the immediate present and how little any view of ultimate aims enters their minds."

"Those are unusual thoughts for an administrator, and that is why administrative work should be done by such men as Livingstone."

"By the way," said I, "your New Year's honour, I understand, won you a great success in the Basement." (The "Basement" is the lobby of the hotel, slightly below the surface-level of the street.)

"Oh, rather," says Mrs. Whitehead. "The manager told me, 'It was read to me before daylight this morning by the night-watchman, who sent word to Mr. Whitehead grandly, "Tell him he deserved every bit of it!"' And when I went down to the news-stand at ten o'clock, here was the news-stand woman reading it aloud to an admiring circle of our fellow-tenants. Knowing that I can't see to read, she offered to read it aloud to me. I explained that I had to rush away, so she sold me her last copy. Then that afternoon when Alfred went out to walk, the newsboy spoke to him about it, and said, 'and besides that, it was better written!' The reason the newsboy knew was that he is Jewish."

"They have been my best audience for thirty years. Hebraism and I kissed and made up long ago," said I. "We may disagree amicably, but I know my friends when I see them."

"How strange it was," said Whitehead, "that it should have

been Hebraic thought which went northward among the European peoples instead of Hellenic."

"We were barbarians," said she. "It represented something better than we had."

"Christianity was the form in which the intellectuality of Alexandria went north into Europe. Most of what we don't like in its content and its results," said Whitehead, "comes from its oriental tinge; its asceticism, its despotic quality, its rigidity of dogma. But without Alexandria we might never have received Hellenic thought at all. Alexandria systematized it; in being systematized it lost much of its force, but it wanted a certain amount of systematization to preserve it, for in its pure form it is fluid and evanescent. Alexandria gave us the clues by which centuries later we were able to recover its true content. But systematization is entirely alien, I don't say to Aristotle, but certainly to Plato. In the *Laws*, the work of his old age, it is true, there are elements of dogmatism—certain types of people, he says, are not to be tolerated—but in the work of his prime he is careful, as he says in one of his letters, that he does not give us a 'system' of Platonic philosophy. He says there is none, yet in the nineteenth century how the German classical scholars laboured to construct a Platonic system of philosophy! 'Now what, *exactly*, did Plato mean?' He was at pains *never* to mean anything exactly. He gave every side of a question its due. I have often done the same, advancing some aspect which I thought deserved attention, and then in some later work, presenting its opposite. In consequence I am accused of inconsistency and self-contradiction."

"Perhaps I can suggest a reason why. Your idea that all truths are necessarily half-truths took me months, perhaps I should say years, to grasp. Yes, I heard your words the first time, remembered what they were, wrote them down, and thought about them; but it is only gradually that a realization of what the idea means grows clear and becomes active in one's unconscious thinking. Ibsen, as I now realize, must have had the same idea. In the period of his social dramas, say from *Pillars of Society* on to the end, he would write one play, as he did *Ghosts*, to present one side of a case, and another, as he did *The Wild Duck*, to present the other. I believe the late plays move to a large extent in such pairs. . . . But why should it have been Hebraic thought that travelled northward through Europe and not Hellenic?"

"Hellenic thought has a way of becoming whatever the peoples who receive it are themselves. In Alexandria it became Alexandrian, in Rome it became Roman."

"But in neither was it truly Hellenic," I said.

"No. But they transmitted enough of it to us so that we could find its true form for ourselves. Alexandria provided the intellectual framework for Christian theology, and the man who, I suppose, did more than anybody else to distort and subvert Christ's teaching was Paul. I wonder what the other disciples thought of him—if they thought anything. Probably they didn't understand what he was up to, and it may well be doubted whether he did himself. It would be impossible to imagine anything more un-Christlike than Christian theology. Christ probably couldn't have understood it."

"Could Greek thought of the Great Age, do you suppose, ever have come into being without that matchless instrument of thought, the Greek language?"

"The same innate genius which begot one," said Whitehead, "begot the other."

"Its precision, its flexibility, its power of expressing exact shades of meaning, its sheer beauty of sound and splendour of resource, and, through all, its simplicity," said I, "are a never-ending amazement."

"How fortunate it would have been," said he, "had Greek become the language of Europe instead of Latin."

"We might have been spared a lot of confusion for one thing, for a Greek sentence generally means exactly what it says, and nothing else. Since the drill in the ancient classical languages has been dropped out of our school curricula, the results are glaring in the work of contemporary writers. We used to learn our English grammar in Latin and Greek. If an English construction was grammatical in Greek or Latin, it was generally good English. But many of these people writing English today seem to be semi-illiterates."

"I was never taught English grammar at all," said Whitehead. "My father, who had been a schoolmaster before he became a clergyman, taught me at home until I was fourteen. He did not send me away to school until then because as a child I had been frail. He taught me my Greek grammar out of a Latin grammar. It was written entirely in Latin and I learned and recited its rules in Latin. Greek grammar, as such, I never studied at all; yet I read Greek as easily as English."

"One result of this abandonment of the classics is that English novels are now 'taught' in our secondary schools. I am properly respectful towards the men who teach them for they are able and devoted schoolmasters, but the idea of being 'taught' English!"

"When I was a schoolboy," said Whitehead, "we read novels, but we read them for fun."

"So did my generation. It would never have occurred to us to 'study' them. Tell me, where did your novel-reading begin?"

"With *Pickwick*, as a child of six, seated on a hassock beside a fire at the feet of my grandmother's maid, Jane Wychelow. . . . My grandmother was a wealthy woman. She made the mistake of having thirteen children, and by the time even a large fortune is divided among thirteen it is no longer large, and when it came to the grandchildren, not much came to me. But as a child I spent a good deal of time at my grandmother's house in London, and it was Jane Wychelow, reading to me by the hour, who first gave me my taste for literature, and it was *Pickwick* which gave me my first insight into the English social system."

"You don't consider it overdrawn then—caricature?"

"Bless you, no! Dickens's people were all around us; they were Londoners, or South of England. Pickwick, you notice, never goes very far north—as far as Norwich, say. . . . I am standing now at a window of my grandmother's house . . ." he mused.

"Eighty-one Piccadilly?" supplied Mrs. Whitehead, wistfully.

". . . looking out over the Green Park," he continued, "and there is Queen Victoria going by——"

"You would have seen her? . . ."

"Bless you, yes; and not once or twice but every day or so."

"Imagine your having seen the old queen as often as the grocer's delivery wagon!"

"She wasn't 'old' then; she was in the prime of life, and not very popular. It was only after the 1870's that she began to be popular, and she ended by becoming such an institution that when she died, we couldn't believe it."

"Even the poor went into mourning," said Mrs. Whitehead. "If they couldn't afford to buy black clothes, they dyed their ordinary clothes black. They were in mourning for the Victorian Age—though they didn't know that then," she added sombrely.

"We had grave apprehensions about Edward VII," continued Whitehead, "and he was far from popular when he came to the throne, but by the end of his reign he was well liked. The two Georges since (I think) have paid their way."

"Though George VI seems to me a somewhat colourless figure," said she, "after his father. George V had a temper."

"It's amazing that the monarchy has lasted until 1945," said I.

"Oh, no, it isn't," said Whitehead. "The English never abolish anything. They put it in cold storage. That has its advantages. If they should want it again, there it is!"

"If you will permit me to say so, sir, that also goes for their Established Church."

[305]

"As I have said to you before," remarked Whitehead, "the Reformation seems to me one of the calamities of history. If given more time, I think the Church would have reformed from within. Erasmus had about the right ideas and he was offered a cardinal's hat before his death, though he refused it. But the revolt of the Protestants hardened the Church's resistance; and the Protestants threw out precisely that part of the Church which makes it gracious and tolerable; namely, its aesthetic and emotional appeal. If I were to choose among present-day Christians, I would prefer the Unitarians, but I wish they had more influence. They are, I realize, close to the Congregationalists, and I think it would be well if they were closer, for it would not surprise me if in another hundred years the United States were predominantly Catholic."

"The one aesthetic and emotional appeal which the Protestants didn't throw overboard," I remarked, "was music."

"Religion," said Whitehead, "cannot exist without music. It is too abstract."

"That's so! Even the New England Puritans, who did away with church organs and instruments, kept their psalmody!"

"Music comes before religion," said he, "as emotion comes before thought, and sound before sense. What is the first thing you hear when you go into a church? The organ playing. What is the last thing you hear as you come out? The organ. And in the Catholic service, the mass itself is sung. Music comes aeons before religion. You can't tell me that the nightingale is singing to his mate out of anything but the joy of life, for the love of singing. These things lie deeper than thought, as sound strikes deeper in us than sight. When we were savages, I venture to suppose, we were much more impressed by the sound of thunder than by the flash of lightning."

"We can protect ourselves from sight by closing our eyes," remarked Mrs. Whitehead, "but we cannot close our ears. From sound we are defenceless. As a young woman when I went to the theatre, the love-making on the stage would some-times offend me by its exhibitionism. I had only to shut my eyes."

"You once said to me that you thought mankind had paid an overdue share of attention to the impressions that come to us by the eye."

"Our education does," he replied, "rely largely on what is written and printed."

"But sound evaporates; writing, print is fairly permanent. Pericles delivers the Funeral Oration, but we have it because Thucydides wrote it down."

"The oration is Thucydides, probably; not Pericles, you know," Mrs. Whitehead corrected me smilingly.

"If so, it is none the worse for that!"

"Perhaps better," says she.

"What has saved writing," assented Whitehead, "is the survival value of its relatively permanent form. But sound speaks to the emotions, the emotion then becomes thought, and the thought action."

"The emotion may become action without ever going through the stage of thought: remember that," corrected Mrs. Whitehead.

"I do," said he. "The relationship between sound and action may be much more direct than between sight and action. That which we see suggests, in general, thought; that which we hear, emotion. Music speaks directly to the emotions; it may, I admit, suggest thoughts, too. . . ."

"But if it suggests them too explicitly," said I, "it is likely to be not very good music."

"When the children were little," said Mrs. Whitehead, "I started them on Mozart. It was thought snobbish of me, but they never heard any trash at home, and when they did hear it, later, they knew it was trash and never cared for it."

"Music," said I, "is amoral. It is like any other great force of nature—in itself, neither good nor bad. All depends on how it is used. It energizes what is already in us; if bad, bad; if good, good."

"I don't agree that music is amoral," said she. "Wagner's music is often distinctly sensual. I don't consider it 'pure' music either aesthetically or morally. Mind you, I like it, at times; but I know what it is doing all the same."

"Music," said Whitehead, "can be both moral and immoral. Take Wagner, if you like. You Americans love his music, and I can't see that it has done you a bit of harm; but I think it has done immeasurable harm to the Germans. To them it suggests dreams of power which lead to violence."

"Wagner, I admit, can still be a controversial figure, but Beethoven must be exempted. Where is there a purer religion than the music of his last quartets? And it is pure sound, too."

"I am inclined to agree with you," said Whitehead, "and I think one of mankind's earliest emotions was in response to a solemn sound."

XXXVII

May 25, 1945

LUNCHEON of the Saturday Club. It was radiant spring weather, and since the interdict on taxicabs had been rescinded, Whitehead came in one. Bliss Perry brought as guest Professor Carl Weber of Colby College, who made that unique collection of memorabilia of Thomas Hardy. He told me, "I wanted to study Hardy and no collection existed, so I had to make one. Just now I am working at Cambridge and often, for wanted materials, I wish I were back at Colby."

About fifteen members were at table. Whitehead and I were at the lower end by ourselves. "You must be careful what you say to me from now on," said I. "I'm your boss, having been made one of the Visiting Committee for the Department of Philosophy."

"Oh, but so am I!" says he.

"In that case, we start over again."

By way of being careful what he said, he was next remarking, *sotto voce*, at my ear:

"Imagine a Being capable of creating a world for the express purpose of its creatures praising him!"

"Isn't it strange that although Christianity is occasionally criticized by capable men, the prevailing attitude is that, however indifferent people may be in practice, Christianity is immune from criticism. If anyone ventures to view it from the outside, it is regarded as a foolish eccentricity."

"The educated people who have been brought up as Protestants and then embrace Catholicism—as a few did in the 1920's and '30's," said he, "—strike me as people who have read history without understanding it, or else as people who do not know history. No one who had even meditated on the meaning of historic events, could knowingly so retrogress. Stagnation of thought is one of the pitfalls of mankind. It is easier to grasp from the history of mathematics than from theology. *Mathematics is the study of possibilities*. Beyond the immediate practical applications of the multiplication table, say at 12 × 12, mathematics in fifth-century Athens was useless. It was a form of speculation. Plato was immensely excited about the subject. His mind was full of mathematics; he used it as an instrument of thought, and it suggested to him all sorts of hitherto unguessed possibilities. If you had talked to Aristotle about him at that time, no doubt Aristotle would have remarked to you privately, 'Poor old Plato! All bogged down in those useless mathematical ideas.'" (He smiled drolly as he said this.) "Now, as a matter of fact, in Plato's time those mathematical ideas *were* useless, and they remained useless for roughly sixteen or seventeen centuries. Then, beginning at about the twelfth century A.D. those mathematical ideas which had so excited Plato, made possible the modern world."

"Was there any specific reason that we know of for their

coming to fruition as they did between the Renaissance and, say, the seventeenth century in France and England?"

"No. Everything necessary for modern science and technology existed in the time of Archimedes. People think I am making an idiotic joke when I say it, but I am quite serious when I say to you as I have said before, apparently all that was lacking was that in Sicily or Magna Graecia people did not sit by their fires and watch the lids of their kettles lift from the steam of boiling water."

"Then we are here back at the *diffusion* of a given experience. As you have remarked to me, an experience needs to be widely diffused in order to elicit the response from the widest possible spread of talents—as you didn't get concert pianists from a western cattle ranch in the nineteenth century, no matter how brilliant the potential talent may have been. There wasn't any piano."

Until the chairman at the head of the table raps for order, conversation is usually in pairs, so Whitehead asked me what news had been coming into my office that morning. I told him, then remarked:

"Can you think of a single Western nation which has had access to the civilizing ideas of the past twenty-five centuries since ancient Greece which could have been made to do what the Germans are now shown to have been doing?"

"There is nothing new in their specific deeds," said he. "To be knocked down, robbed, and murdered, perhaps tortured, has always been going on somewhere to some extent. What is new with the Germans is the scale. It has never before been done on anything like such a scale as this."

"What would you give for the chances of their behaving themselves after this?"

"They knocked over the Roman Empire," said he. "They knocked over the system of the Middle Ages; and they have knocked over the civilization of modern Europe—and I mean the one which originated about five hundred years ago, say at the Renaissance. They will probably go on trying to knock things over, because they like to knock things over."

Here the chairman, Mark Howe, rapped the table and tossed the subject of Japan into discussion. Langdon Warner, who has lived and travelled widely in China and Japan, and Cameron Forbes, who has been ambassador to Japan as well as governor-general of the Philippines, carried most of the discussion, urged on by leading questions: What, in the event of victory, should be done with the Chinese treaty ports, Manchuria, Korea, island airplane bases? What sort of government for the Japanese home islands? . . . Cam thought the treaty ports should be returned to Chinese sovereignty but perhaps bases to Britain to save imperial face, all but Hong Kong, which he considered too centrally vital for anything less than inter-nationalization. Whitehead saw no reason why Britain should have back the treaty ports. "Singapore, however," said he, "is important to us on account of Australia and New Zealand."

"I am uncertain about the Chinese," continued Whitehead. "Their cultural development shows no continuity of process. From about 500 B.C. to 1200 A.D. there seemed to be no development to speak of; and in modern times, they appear to be trying to make themselves as much like Americans as possible. But suppose they do succeed in making themselves like twentieth-century Americans; when they have done so, have they the capacity to go on developing in their own way from there, or will they merely remain for centuries to come like twentieth-century Americans?"

Of the Chinese Communists, Cameron Forbes said, "They are so different from the Communists of Soviet Russia, the historic origins which condition them go back so far and are so peculiar to China, that when you use the word 'communist' of them, you are hardly talking about the same thing as what is understood by communism in Russia."

"What you say interests me," said Whitehead, "for people appear to think that when they have used the word 'communism,' they have designated something exactly, and know what they are talking about. Now, as a matter of fact, not only should there be, as you have suggested, half a dozen varying ideas and definitions of communism in people's minds when the subject comes up for discussion; there ought to be nearer six hundred varying definitions."

The party rose at about half past three. Whitehead and I hailed a taxi at Brimstone Corner, rolled up Park Street and down Beacon to Charles past the rich May greenery of the Common. "I never heard Cam speak with such admirable good sense," said he. "Generally, when he begins, one gets ready to disagree or make allowances or maintain a discreet silence. But to my astonishment, I found myself substantially in agreement with everything he said."

We rolled across the Longfellow Bridge and into Cambridge, which also is looking fresh and comely in its new May-green dress. There were stalks of pale-blue larkspur in the vases of Mrs. Whitehead's living-room and brilliant afternoon sunshine streamed in at the west windows. She was given some of the table talk at second hand, by request, and it went on into a discussion of the American social system.

"I tell you what," said Whitehead positively, "I believe the American social system to be, on the whole, the best that has ever existed. It has grave defects; the English system has points of superiority, but yours remains the best that has been done so far. The paradox is that you are not really a 'political' people. About one-third of your citizens I would say are genuinely first-rate; but they are not in politics. Of the remaining two-thirds, about half, I should say, are second-rate but still good. The other half" (he hesitated, then went on), "are criminal."

"Including many of our politicians," I supplied.

"Yes," said he.

It was decided to change the subject.

"I am invited to the party on June sixth," said I, "and

hastened to accept before they should have had time to take it back."

"One is supposed to go to Buckingham Palace to receive it, or, if in this country, from the hands of the ambassador," said Mrs. Whitehead, "but as Lord Halifax has plenty else to do, it is to be given by the British consul."

Whitehead was of the opinion that too much fuss might be made about it.

"Not from the point of view of the university," I remarked. "Whenever before has an American university had as its emeritus professor of philosophy a man with the Order of Merit?"

"That is nothing," said Whitehead.

"I know it is nothing. But this university has made some bad blunders in recent years. One was allowing Harvey Cushing to go away to Yale. Another was George Pierce Baker . . . ditto. There have been still others." I told them Harvey Cushing's account of that affair as he recited it to me one Sunday afternoon in the summer of 1932 when we were alone in his old house on Walnut Street in Brookline.

"This custom of retiring a man perforce in his sixties," said Whitehead, "is idiotic."

"With surgeons it is said to be a necessity," his wife corrected him. "I understand they can no longer be sure of a steady hand."

"Cushing didn't complain of the retirement age of sixty-three. He had set it himself when he organized the Peter Bent Brigham Hospital. In fact, he didn't complain of anything. He only said that devious financiers, whom he had trusted, had wiped out a large part of his estate, including his patrimony from old Dr. Cushing of Cleveland, which he had never touched, but salted down for his old age. As you remember, his health was gone, and, all this being well known, he was offered at Harvard a professorship without salary."

Whitehead looked grim.

"How old were you," I shifted gears, "when you first felt a sense of conscious mastery of your subject?"

"I have never felt it at all," said he.

"Then I have asked my question clumsily. Perhaps what I was trying to ask was, when did you first begin to feel an adequacy to your work?"

"I have never felt adequate to it."

"Good heavens!" said his wife. "Don't I know? Not a year went by bringing back September and the resumption of his teaching, that he didn't have a bad case of the jitters."

"You are a competent witness."

"I have only observed him for fifty-one years."

Whitehead, who had been listening absently, now said, "I will tell you what, about this custom of enforced retirement; it is idiotic, because, although a man may not think of anything new after he is sixty, he often finds new ways to use what he already knows."

XXXVIII

May 29, 1945

THERE was a party for the Whiteheads given by Mr. and Mrs. William James, at 95 Irving Street, in the big, comfortable house which Professor James had built in the 1890's, and where he lived until his death in 1910. I remembered the study from having gone there as an undergraduate to consult him about a thesis subject.

The guests had been asked to come "any time after half past eight." It was a mild May evening, Cambridge was quiet, and the fresh greenery of the elms and ivies in the College Yard was a temptation to loiter. When I arrived, the Whiteheads and several other guests were already in the study. There was a group around the hearth where a wood fire was burning, and others kept arriving until the room must have held thirty or forty persons. The guests were seated but the groups kept changing, and I noticed with what skill and tact the combinations were managed.

At intervals I was able to renew my acquaintanceship with this room. It was still walled with books, but William James, the second son, who joined me presently for a chat by ourselves over in a corner beside his father's study table, said: "They are not all the books, nor all his books, and they have been rearranged, largely by sizes and sets. His was a scholar's library, in which books of every size and shape stood side by side arranged according to subjects."

"That seems more as I remembered it; a good many paper-backed volumes, and pamphlets. . . . I notice up there on the next-to-the-top shelf a complete set of the Edinburgh Edition, Constable & Company, of George Meredith."

"That was Uncle Henry's. It was a present from Meredith."

On the fireplace mantelshelf was an excellent photograph, about four inches by eight, framed under glass, of the two brothers, William and Henry. The centre table was gone, and so was the green-shaded kerosene study lamp of other years, but here was the big black-walnut study table, long enough for a tall man to stretch out on as bivouac, and carried on two pedestals of black-walnut desk drawers. It looked, indeed, as though it might have antedated Professor James's tenancy, having perhaps belonged to his father. His son said:

"Father used to work on the other side of it, in that corner."

It was a sore temptation to forget the party and browse along those shelves taking notes of titles and authors, as I have once or twice been able to do in Whitehead's library. Beside the hearth Professor Ralph Barton Perry, the biographer of William James, was in conversation with Whitehead.

It was necessary for me to leave early. Out in the hall, when my coat and hat had been picked up, I ventured the remark to my host, who had come out with me:

"What are we going to do about an oil portrait of White-head?"

"Charles Hopkinson has made two sketches in oils," said he; "one not so good; the other, *very* good. Then, as so often happens with us painters, he took it along to his studio to 'finish' and some people think he spoilt it."

"I have seen the two sketches in his studio. One, I thought, was pretty close to it. I spoke to Charles about it a few days ago, and he said, with admirable modesty, 'I doubt if I am up to painting Whitehead.' . . . But are we going to let Whitehead get away from us without a good portrait? You owe it to yourself to have painted a portrait of Whitehead."

"When I was young," he replied, smiling, "I would ask anybody to sit for me. Now when I am trying to learn a language, I hesitate to ask a sitter until I shall have learned to speak that language."

As the front door of 95 Irving Street closed after me and I went out again into the May evening, I had a glimpse of that spacious dooryard to the south of the house, overlooked by the windows of the study. There, on a September afternoon in 1903, I had seen William James for the first time. My entrance examinations were safely passed, and I was not yet an under-graduate but in two days more I would be. It was two years since I had begun to read what William James had written, and, as a seventeen-year-old lad in a small town of the Midwest, two essays of his in especial had put heart and courage into me. I was grateful to him and loved him *in absentia*. Being in Cambridge at last, it had suddenly struck me that, after having gone to Concord and seen where Emerson and Hawthorne had lived, I could walk around and see where William James lived. A college directory gave the street and number. This time, the hunting was considerably better than a house. There in his dooryard seated in a lawn chair conversing with some callers was William James. Not a doubt of it! I had seen photographs of him. The tones of his voice, a genial tenor or high baritone, though not his words, carried out to the sidewalk. This was, I suppose, the first time I had ever seen an eminent man in the flesh. It is quite an eye-opener: had you not been told, you might not have guessed. He could easily have been supposed to be not much different from anybody else; and this was true, and at the same time, was not true. At any rate, there sat William James in a lawn chair chatting with his friends like an affable archangel, and if I had had to choose between being given a glimpse of an archangel or William James, I certainly would have chosen William James. I still think that choice valid.

XXXIX

June 6, 1945

WEDNESDAY afternoon at four o'clock in the Faculty Room at University Hall the Order of Merit—Badge and Grant of Dignity—was presented to Alfred North Whitehead, D.Sc., LL.D., S.D., F.R.S., F.B.A., and Professor of Philosophy Emeritus in Harvard University.

This was at three removes. Had he been in England he would have been expected to go to Buckingham Palace; were the British ambassador less preoccupied, it would have been presented by him either in Washington or Cambridge; things being as they are, the presentation was by the British consul-general at Boston. Considering the dimensions of the world Whitehead lives in, and those of the British Empire, the notion of bestowing dignity or merit upon him seemed like my Swampscott dory towing the S.S. *Queen Elizabeth*, and in fact Whitehead himself had dismissed the idea of its being of any intrinsic importance. I remembered too that George Meredith, who received the Order of Merit in 1905, said that what the letters *O.M.* meant was that he was an old man.

The scene, however, was picturesque. We had produced our

equivalent to a June day in England, a south-west wind with alternate sunshine and showers, and white-backed grey-breasted clouds tumbling about a pure blue sky. By four o'clock the afternoon sun was pouring in at the high-arched windows on the west side of the hall, while the faculty chairs, about two hundred, I should say, had been arranged to face the equally high eastern windows which look out into the green foliage of the Sever-Widener-Memorial Church Quadrangle.

The room has an aspect of reticent dignity. Its height is two stories, the second and third of University Hall, and its architect was Charles Bulfinch. The walls are tinted a pale green which, in certain lights, looks light blue, and between the arched windows white fluted Ionic pilasters rise from floor to cornice. From the ceiling hang four crystal chandeliers.

The marble busts on plinths around the dais which runs along the wall on the long dimensions of the hall were distracting my attention from most of the immediate company. There is an excellent one of Benjamin Franklin, by Houdon I think; another of President Eliot and another of my old friend and teacher Dean Briggs, startlingly real, almost to the twinkle in his eyes and to the least wrinkle in his lean Yankee jowls. The walls on all four sides are hung with portraits of Harvard presidents and eminent scholars from the past three centuries. Here was my old Greek grammarian, W. W. Goodwin, his crimson doctor's hood over his shoulder, his complexion fresh and rosy, his hair pure white, and his smile bland and unworldly. With certain notable exceptions, the men on the walls were more interesting than the people in the chairs.

On each chair was laid a programme bound in a heavy greenish-grey paper. "The Proceedings" were begun by President Conant, who said, among other things, that Whitehead, after a long and distinguished career in England, came to Harvard to give his first course of lectures in philosophy, and "the first lecture in a course on philosophy which you had ever attended was the one given by yourself."

The consul narrated the institution of the Order of Merit. Looking down the list of its present members, eighteen in number, I noticed the names of Gilbert Murray, G. M. Trevelyan, J. W. Mackail, Vaughan Williams, John Masefield, and Augustus John. It had often occurred to me that a good many eminent men in England would feel silly accepting feudal titles, and that perhaps this Order of Merit was tardily devised as a method of the government (including the monarchy) to climb aboard the bandwagon of continuing British genius.

A photographer flashed two bulbs while the consul was hanging the badge by a ribbon of the order around the philosopher's neck. As a decoration it is quite striking.

The participants in the ceremony, including Dean Buck of the faculty, who assisted as a benign presence, had been seated at a large round table, which looked as though it might have been the one around which William James, Josiah Royce, and George Herbert Palmer had their portraits painted sitting together.

Over on the north wall is a noble portrait of William James. He is standing beside his breast-high writing desk in his study at 95 Irving Street. Behind him are bookshelves and rows of brown-backed volumes. His writing desk is of brown walnut, he wears a brown suit, his hair and beard look brownish, touched with grey, the light in the study is an atmosphere of mellow autumnal brown, and his face is ruddy as if from a summer in the open at Chocorua, New Hampshire. He is made to look a bit more severe than his usual genial self. The canvas was well lighted by the late afternoon sunshine which poured in through those western windows. After the ceremonies, as I was admiring it, Professor Ralph Barton Perry, first his pupil, then his colleague, and finally his biographer, came over and spoke.

"When was it painted?" I asked.

"About 1908, I think," said he.

"How satisfactory is that portrait to you?"

"Very! Miss Ellen Emmet painted with bold strokes."

"Nineteen-eight was only two years before his death. He must have been frail" (in fact, we both knew that he was) "but here he looks robust and vigorous."

"He always looked more robust than he was," said Professor Perry, "perhaps because his mind was so vigorous."

I have noticed the same thing about Whitehead; he speaks, because he thinks, with the vigour of a young man.

After the presentation I had asked him if he had a copy of his response. Our interchanges have been so almost entirely oral that I had only two scraps of paper written in his hand. He said he would send me the MS. Next day it arrived. The text is as follows:

President Conant: It is impossible for me to express adequately the obligations of my wife and myself to the University over which you preside. Both as an institution and as a group of individuals, Harvard has made it possible for me to express ideas which had been growing in my thoughts for a lifetime. I wish to emphasize my admiration and personal affection for so many Harvard friends, some of whom are present today. During my life I have had the great happiness of teaching in two countries which have contributed so greatly to learning and to the dignity of mankind.

XL

June 19, 1945

It had been a day of thunderstorms, two by the sea—one at Marblehead, another at Nahant—and a third on the editorial floors of the *Globe*, where one party was indignant at the publication in the paper of Ciano's diary, as Fascist whitewash, the other laughing at its exposure in all directions and giving the public credit for knowing a hawk from a handsaw.

The second view was shared by the Whiteheads. They were

in Cambridge passingly for a few days between their return from the Pickmans' at Bedford and a month in Maine, whither they go next Friday. All the windows of their apartment were wide open to the humid night air, a light breeze drawing through; huge white peonies nodded in the vases; all the rugs were up and the window hangings down, giving the rooms a cool, bare, refreshing look. With the June flowers scenting the air, these familiar rooms had taken on an unfamiliar aspect, looking summery.

We had been speaking of how the high polish of the now bare hardwood floor reflected the mahogany and white peonies, when Whitehead came in from his study.

"Why, our rugs are up, aren't they?" said he. "I hadn't noticed it."

"Yes," said she, laughing at him, "and me hustling around to get them off to the cleaners." She rose and went to a tall, mahogany cabinet, saying, "We have something to show you." It was in a dark-leather case and lay on velvet of an off-ivory shade. It was the badge of the Order of Merit. The Maltese cross is a rich amber-coloured enamel on gold, with a gold crown mounted above it, and a circle of pearls around the centre of royal-blue enamel on which the inscription, *For Merit*, is laid in gold. Around it is a wreath of laurel.

"They don't do it by halves, do they?" I remarked.

"Fortunately for us," she said, "it cost us nothing. Every other decoration, those given by the government, must be paid for by the person who receives it; but not this, which is a gift of the Crown."

"The Crown paid something, I should say. And I should also remark how neatly the university ran that ceremony; no long speeches, no fatigue, no fuss or feathers, and just about the right number of people. Tell me: was that a typical faculty audience of two hundred persons?"

"It was typical," said he smiling, "of those who were there. They were members of the philosophical department–"

[321]

M

"'Cock and hen,' of course," said she.

"–and the Junior and Senior Fellows–"

"Those I was able to identify, as I knew some of them–"

"–and, to my great satisfaction," he continued, "the secretaries of both departments, men and women who carry so much of the administration load."

"We had nothing to do with the invitations," explained she. "The only ones we invited were our John and Mary, who are, of course, a part of the family. *That* gave us a good deal of satisfaction. It wasn't certain until the last minute whether Alfred would be able to attend. He lay down all day, and finally got up to try it. The moment he arrived at University Hall, he felt all right. . . . Your invitation, by the way, came through your official connection with the department of philosophy."

"I have some good news for you": (it was now my turn to produce) "he didn't say I wasn't to tell, but I have told no one so far. Livingstone is coming over to lecture at Toronto next September."

"We would love to see him," said Whitehead. "Is there any prospect of his coming here?"

"I'm not sure. He says he spends his hours turning his mind from one university problem to another, and that he will lecture in Toronto if he can get the lectures written."

"When you write him," said Whitehead, "will you say that if we don't see him we shall be greatly disappointed?"

In some detail we discussed ways and means.

"His two booklets on education have been republished in this country in one volume by Macmillan's, and called just that—*On Education*. The salesmen at the Old Corner Book Store tell me it is going very well."

"It deserves to," said Whitehead. "I have read them in the English edition, and thought highly of them."

"When was your *Aims of Education* published?"

"Let me see. I've forgotten." He went into his library,

returned with the volume and read from the preface the dates of its various chapters. Most of them came between 1912 and 1922. "My writings on philosophy," he continued, "were all after I came to this country; but the ideas had been germinating in me for the better part of a lifetime. Some of them I had had when I was at school before ever I went up to the university. Education I had heard discussed continually since I was a little lad: my father and two uncles were in it. And at Cambridge I was, as you know, a member of The Apostles."

"This was somewhat unusual, wasn't it?" said she. "Weren't you the only mathematician in the group?"

". . . Perhaps because I was the only mathematician interested in general ideas," he replied.

It then transpired—"transpired" in the correct use of that verb—that Whitehead had only taken his examinations for the fellowship at Trinity as a chance shot (you are given three tries) and with so little expectation of being accepted that afterwards he went away for the summer without leaving his address.

"Until I first read *Aims of Education*, in 1933," I said, "I doubt if I had ever met such compactness of thought in English sentences. Is writing easy for you?"

"Yes," he said, "if it's something I want to write." His wife looked sceptical. "What would *you* say?" he asked of her.

"You are full of ideas," she reminded him, "and first you write them all down; everything is in it. But after that comes the rearranging and pruning—"

"With your help. . . ."

"Well, you read it aloud and I listen. . . . He has a wretched tendency," she imparted for my benefit, "of getting going on some particular word—'thereby,' or 'whereas'—and on every other page that damned word will turn up. . . ."

"Does he do that too? Tautologies are a species of self-hypnosis."

"I don't see how you can write as often as you do," she added, to me.

"Neither do I. And the answer is, I don't. Twice a week nowadays, or thrice at a pinch; but with absences of months to refuel. What do you do to protect yourself from exhaustion?" I asked Whitehead.

"Lectured twice a day for years, since I was twenty-four years old," he replied, smiling blandly at my discomfiture. "It is true, the summer vacation ran from late June to early October, and we also had four weeks at Christmas and five at Easter. The schedule was really not heavy."

"But it is also true," she reminded him, "that you never stopped working. If we travelled on the Continent, there was not a blank envelope-back in your pocket that wasn't written all over on your knee in railway trains or hotels as ideas occurred to you; and if we stayed in England somewhere in the country, you were always just the same, pursuing your private philosophical Boojum."

"You evidently," I addressed him, "don't think a man uses himself up and works himself out by continual expression— within limits of his time and vitality." (I was thinking of more than one academic scholar who appears to have talked out as lectures what might otherwise have been a good book; also of the exhaustion which I see around me among journalists who cannot or will not pause long enough.)

"No," Whitehead replied. "I think one gains by such expression. He brings vague ideas into precision by putting them into speech or writing; and by expression he develops his ideas and finds his way to new ones."

"Perhaps what I was trying to ask was, Do you *enjoy* writing?"

"Yes. I like being in that world."

"The compactness of thought in your style—do you suppose it comes from your mathematical training? You learned one technique of expression, and then moved on to another. It is as if, having had one severe intellectual discipline, you moved easily into the art of writing and speaking."

"William James had something of the same sort," said his

wife. "A hard intellectual discipline in medicine first; then he moved on into philosophy, psychology, and, one might almost say, *belles lettres*."

"At Trinity," said Whitehead, "and later, in a wide experience of educational problems at London University, I had the advantage of general discussions. It was precisely the kind of education that Plato approves. Mathematics must be studied; philosophy should be discussed."

This shot landed heavily. He saw it land and gave me breathing space to take it in.

"You must allow," he went on presently, "for the imprecision of language. It is a point I cannot make too emphatic. Again and again I return to it. The notion that thought can be perfectly or even adequately expressed in verbal symbols is idiotic. And that supposition has done philosophy immeasurable harm. Take the simplest statement of a fact: that we three are sitting in this room. Nearly everything of importance is left out. 'This room' presupposes a building, Cambridge, the university, the world around us of which we are a part, stellar systems of which our world is a part, the infinite past from which we have come, and the endless future which is streaming through us and out ahead of us. It presupposes our separate individualities, each quite different, and all that we know, we are, or have ever done. That verbalization of our sitting here means next to nothing; yet, in much more serious subjects and on a far more ambitious scale, we are constantly accepting statements of historic fact, and philosophical speculations which are much more lacking in accuracy or in any relationship with exact truth. When such over-simplified ideas are addressed to persons who cannot supply the omitted presuppositions, they mean nothing, are not comprehended, are not even taken in. . . ."

Two wine glasses, his and mine, stood on a little table at his left hand. He touched them, saying, " 'One and one make two.' One and one what? One glass, or one glass partly filled with wine? Or one and one where? On a table, in this room, or in this universe? But two glasses are not and cannot possibly be made exactly equal. Nor can they be filled with equal amounts of wine. Then do we mean 'one plus one' after all the necessary deductions and additions have been made? But the glasses are also raging with molecular activity, and, if we were not in the habit of measuring time by the ridiculously inadequate yardsticks of our consciousness in this human life span, we should remember that those glasses are disintegrating before our very eyes. I refuse to be taken in by such monstrous inexactitude in the use of words."

This was quite a headful for one while. Circling around it a little, he asked, "Do you suppose the Greeks were the first people who ever wanted something reduced to exactitude in language? They wanted a correct version of Homer. When was that?"

"Probably somewhere in the sixth century B.C. It's supposed to have been done at the command of Peisistratus."

"About when would you say the great Hebrew literature begins?"

I spoke of the familiar JEPD, adding, "The Old Testament and the Homeric poems are both 'traditional books,' taking centuries to grow. In their editing, the one by the ancient Hebrews, the other by the ancient Greeks, how characteristic the differences of method and spirit are of the two peoples: one produced a manual of morals; the other, a work of art."

"How unique the Hebrew genius is," said he. "It was profoundly moral. The Hebrews were one of the most remarkable peoples that ever lived. And yet," he ruminated, "I don't think I would have cared to live among them. The Greeks were more reasonable."

"All the same," said I, "the Hebrews produced one of the greatest books in history. It has outsold the *Iliad*!"

"If you accept the divine authorship attributed to the Bible," said Whitehead, his eyes twinkling, "it seems a little odd that a person like Solomon, with his million wives and thousand concubines, should have been chosen to write parts of it."

"If he did, it must have been as a young man when he had only about ten wives, and was just getting started in life," I suggested.

"Before his heavy family responsibilities had begun," added Mrs. Whitehead demurely.

"David," I remarked, "is a much more 'sympathetic character.' His palace memoirs are certainly more candid than that class of literature generally is. Legions of gentile boys are still being named David—long after Hector has gone out of fashion. David is quite a beautiful name. As for Solomon, aren't his million-and-one wives merely a tall tale? After all, when telling a whopper, why not tell a good one?"

"Is there any reason to suppose," asked Whitehead, "that the surrounding nations took much notice of the ancient Hebrews—that is, before the period of the Roman conquests?"

I pleaded ignorance, but the impression was that there had been comparatively little.

"What I would like to know," he continued, "is to what extent, if at all, the Semites and the Hellenes re-expressed ideas which were generally current in that part of the ancient world—ideas that flowed down to them from older peoples and the surrounding nations. Of course we know that some of that did happen; some of the Eastern notions were known to Plato; and the older prophets anticipated, mostly, the ideas of Jesus."

"When I am asked, as I often am, how to account for the explosion of genius in Greece from the sixth century to the third B.C. I hardly know where to begin."

"The Eastern Mediterranean, you must remember," replied Whitehead, "was a remarkable place, and had been for a long time. Besides the Hellenes and Semites you have the Minoan-Mycenaean culture, the Phoenicians, and the three big empires of Babylonia, Assyria and Egypt."

This glance at the monotonous regularity with which empires collapse caused him to remark on how much faster our world of today is changing than it ever changed before.

"In fact," Mrs. Whitehead remarked in parenthesis, "if we can arrange it, Alfred and I have agreed to come back once in every fifty years and see what has happened."

"We only want to stay two months at any given time," said he.

"Like Tom Sawyer, you want to 'die temporarily.'"

"No. Three months," said she. "We would need that much time to assimilate what we can."

"Whether you date this acceleration of change from a hundred and fifty years ago, or from fifty years ago," Whitehead pursued the main theme, "the alteration in our society exceeds anything in history. The long-term views of human nature have not been changed; those have to do with how we think, feel, and act. What is new in our situation is"—he paused, smiling, then continued—"what I may call 'the dodges.'"

"Precisely what do you mean by 'the dodges'?"

"The names given to various devices of statecraft to make them go down more easily, the methods of meeting various sociological exigencies, the nomenclature of social change . . . that sort of thing."

"I will give you an example," interposed Mrs. Whitehead energetically. "When your government finds itself obliged to pursue imperialistic policies, you call it 'the good neighbour'; but you will keep the Pacific islands just the same—and so you should. They have cost you something. But when Britain does the same sort of thing, you call it 'spheres of influence.'"

"Do you believe," I appealed to Whitehead, "that the United States is imperialistic?"

"Certainly," said he calmly.

Having ascertained their opinions, I did not pursue the subject. Instead I returned to the definition of "dodges."

" 'The dodges,' then," said I, "are how people go around corners on two wheels without hitting the hydrant."

"They don't always miss the hydrant," said Whitehead.

" 'The dodges' are fairly familiar to me," I remarked. "They occupy by far the major portion of newspaper space. But about the long-term views of human nature—how we think and feel, why we behave as we do . . ."

"Those are fairly familiar to you also," said Whitehead. "They were written down by the Greeks. The singular thing about Greek literature is that it doesn't age. It is just as vital today as it was when it was written."

"It is more," said I. "We study it to understand things about ourselves which our own writers are not able to say as clearly."

"The mortality of literatures is a singular study," continued Whitehead. "Suppose Greek literature had perished completely, as it might easily have done; we would never have missed what we had never known and yet how immeasurably poorer all of our lives would have been! It was the university at Alexandria, I suppose, which saved it, preserved the papyri and diffused their influence and their contents widely enough for survival. Sometimes I ask myself what constitutes the survival value of a literature. The literature of the eighteenth century, for example, has already lost much, perhaps most, of its interest excepting in so far as one reads it in order to understand how people lived and thought during that period. And the rapidity and violence of social change in our own times is certain to condemn much other literature—including some of our esteemed contemporaries—to the discard. It is the *social* literatures, I think, that tumble overboard when the vessel has to be lightened to ride out a gale."

"I'm not quite sure what you mean by the social literatures."

"Literatures which presuppose the continuance of an existing social system—namely, the social system on which they are based."

M*

"That makes it clearer. Already, one can think of numerous highly respected nineteenth-century works of literature—actually first-rate in some instances—which social change in our epoch has pitched over the dam."

"The late sixteenth and early seventeenth-century writings are more durable," said he.

"You have also, I think, defined the durability of Greek literature. While it is based on a then-existing social system, that social system is subjected to such constant critical scrutiny from the sixth century to the fourth, its existence is so often in jeopardy, and its forms are so diverse and can change so rapidly, that most of the great Greek authors seldom, it seems to me, fall into the way of taking it for granted as a necessarily permanent fixture; and some of the greatest of them—Plato, Thucydides, and Aristophanes—toward the end of the fifth century have a pretty clear notion that their social system is threatened with dissolution."

"If you want another example of one of the 'dodges,' " said Whitehead, "I will give you the treatment of the big industrial corporations. We began by treating them as 'persons.' For England in the eighteenth century in its dealings with India that concept served well enough—though I wouldn't guarantee that the Indians found it equally satisfactory. But by the time you reach the end of the nineteenth century, that conception is obviously untenable. The corporations, for better or for worse, have reached into all corners of our lives, and to pretend that a corporation is a 'person' is nonsense. A person has feelings, emotions, desires, aspirations; a corporation is an impersonal entity. It is idle to suppose that they will not be brought more and more under public control."

Ten had long since boomed from the clock tower of Memorial Hall, which they see from their windows; and rain was falling.

By previous agreement, Mrs. Whitehead drew up a chair to the big six-drawered mahogany escritoire and began rummaging for the promised photograph of Alfred. This developed into a major operation: drawer after drawer was pulled out, contents turned over, or heavy manuscript packets dropped on the floor. Her manner of doing it, all in complete absorption, was interesting and a dash picturesque; totally unselfconscious and yet so watchable for its own sake that the idea, which has so often crossed my mind before, crossed it again: "That act would be effective on the stage: she is looking for something in an escritoire, the contents are rummaged out interestingly, some of them plumped on the floor, others examined in her lap: this woman could probably have been a fine actress. I get it by flashes." She was handsomely gowned, and earlier in the evening, while we were turning over his badge of the Order of Merit, had laid it against the texture of her dress to show how the colours blended; but hang it around her own neck? Not she!

I said, "Oh, give up the search. That's too hard work. Wait till some other time."

"If you wait," said she, "you'll never get it."

"That's true. I've already waited nine years."

Finally she produced what she was looking for—a photograph of Alfred in his study when they lived out in Canton. He is seated in his leather-upholstered chair with his writing-board laid across its arms and his hands folded on a heap of manuscript sheets. Behind him are rows of books on shelves and beside him on a low table one of those familiar cups in which we have so often had chocolate.

"I like this better than the Harvard Tercentenary photograph," said I, "because in that one he is looking down and one doesn't see the eyes."

"Let me show you the first picture that was ever taken of me," said he, and going into another room brought back an old album. Paging through it, "I can't find it," he said finally. "But here is the headmaster of Sherborne when I was there as a boy, one of the greatest schoolmasters I have ever known; and here is my grandfather."

"He looks the typical Victorian Englishman. Does he fall entirely in the nineteenth century?"

"Nearly. He was born in 1794 and lived well into his eighties. This photograph was taken when he was about eighty years old."

"If that face isn't nineteenth-century England . . . !"

"He ruled the town," said his grandson, in a tone of humorous reminiscence, "and as a mob orator he was without peer."

"How big was the town?"

"Twenty thousand."

"We call that a city. I was reared in a 'town' of three thousand."

"We call that a village."

"Here it is," said Mrs. Whitehead, suddenly producing from the penetralia of her escritoire a small photograph in an oval fillet of ormolu mounted on a faded but still-deep crimson velvet. It was framed and backed in embossed leather and equipped with a brass ring from which to hang it on the wall. He showed it me.

"That is my first picture," he said.

On the lap of a smiling matron who bends over him fondly is a year-old baby in a white muslin dress, with plump features, fair hair not yet long enough to cut, a strongly modelled head, firm features, and rather a determined expression. Had I been shown the picture and asked to guess, I think it would have been easy to guess that this baby was British.

They said they were off to Maine on Friday.

"What is your address?"

"Battleship Island, Little Sebago Lake, West Gray," said Mrs. Whitehead. "The island is about a quarter of an acre. It has the great advantage," she glanced sidewise at Alfred, "that one cannot go on too long walks."

XLI

In August, 1945

IN August the war of 1939–1945 was crashing to its close. Two of those detonations were the atomic bombs dropped, the first on Hiroshima on August 6, the second on Nagasaki on August 9. Preoccupation with public events had become so intense as to reduce one's personal affairs to the estate of a waking dream. The evening after the first atomic bomb was dropped, I was with the Whiteheads. Professor Henry Maurice Sheffer, of the department of philosophy in Harvard, was there. My expectation had been that Whitehead would discuss the possible social consequences of atomic fission; instead, after having politely noticed the subject, he dismissed it. A year or two later he did discuss it, but at that moment he was one of the few who knew enough to know what it was that could not yet be known.

Charles Hopkinson was painting his portrait. The two sketches had been trial trips. Now there were seven sittings of two hours each, from 11 A.M. to 1 P.M., about as long as Whitehead could sustain the sessions, which were lightened as far as practicable by conversation among the four of us. Most of this had to go unrecorded because of the pressure of public events, but fragments of it remain. Being asked, "Which are more important, facts or ideas?" Whitehead reflected a while, then said:

"Ideas *about* facts."

During a discussion of William James's *Varieties of Religious Experience*, he said:

"The difficulty of communication in words is but little realized. If I had to write something about your personality, of course I could—but how much would remain that couldn't be put into words. So, when the rare balance of knowledge and perception appears, as in William James—one who could communicate so much more than most—it is perhaps an advantage that his system of philosophy remained incomplete. To fill it out would necessarily have made it smaller. In Plato's *Dialogues* there is a richness of thought, suggestion, and implication which reaches far. Later, when he came to be more explicit concerning some of those implications, we have a shrinkage.

"Something similar can happen in scholarship. There is, of course, great importance in scholarship—exact knowledge, rationalization—but a great many scholars are engaged in reducing men of genius to the commonplace.

"Consider John Dewey. In carrying on the philosophy of William James, I think he enormously narrowed it. With James the consciousness of the ever-present complexity and possibility in human experience is always implicit in his writing. Dewey is without it. William James's awareness of the wide scope and the interrelations of all questions made him one of the great philosophic minds in history. Furthermore, that awareness is so sensitive and so vibrant that even if he did not survive as a philosopher, he would survive as a man of letters. But his philosophic thought does have the quality of permanence. When I was passing examinations for my mathematical degree, the physical and mechanical aspects of the world were considered to be all known and settled, with the exception of a few out-of-the-way problems which were being worked on by capable persons and which would no doubt be solved before long. Then it all blew up. The character of William James's mind was such that he could stand the shock of that explosion, which was the death of many others."

Those conversations during the sittings for the portrait were sometimes gay as well as grave, for, yes, by now we did know that the slaughter was nearing an end, temporarily at least. The Whiteheads entertained us with stories of their young married life at Ramsgate and in Cambridge. One was of Lady Jebb and her irascible Sir Richard.

"She was playing chess in their library, with young Arthur James Balfour," recited Mrs. Whitehead. "Sir Richard kept going in and out of the room and it put them off their game.

Finally Lady Jebb rose and locked the door after him. He came back, tried it, rattled the knob, and then began kicking it. Whereupon Lady Jebb called out, 'Kick away, Dickie. It's your ain paint and your ain dure!'"

Whitehead was equally informative:

"My father's church at Ramsgate," said he, "was an ancient Norman building roofed by a barrel vault. It was more impressive as architecture than it was helpful with acoustics. If you sat in the rear of the church you could hardly distinguish one word in ten, but when my father preached, that didn't matter, his voice was so powerful and sonorous it rolled reverberating the length of that barrel vault freighted with such moral earnestness. He was an Old Testament man; the New didn't mean so much to him, but he had the fervour of the old prophets, and when you heard him, that depth of feeling penetrated in his tones. You didn't need to know the words; his tones were enough. What was so intensely moving was the sincerity of a solemn sound. Wasn't that so, Evelyn?"

"Entirely!" she agreed. "And 'the converse is also true.' When we were engaged you insisted on taking me to vespers at St. Mary's in Cambridge. I dressed in my best bib and tucker for I well knew that I would be under public inspection; in addition to which, quite as I had apprehended, we were led up almost prematurely to the altar and seated far forward, where there was no difficulty in hearing. And what do you suppose happened?" she appealed to me.

"Either something quite distressing or very amusing. It wouldn't have been anything halfway."

"It was both," said she decisively. "A young vicar preached. Toward the end of his sermon he said—that was once when the words didn't help the sound—he said, 'Finally, my brethren, for well-conducted people life presents no problems.'"

"He didn't!"

"He did. Alfred and I had exemplary control over our facial muscles, but when we were outside and beyond earshot, I said to him, 'Catholicism may have its defects, but at least in a Catholic church you would never hear anything like that,' and Alfred replied, 'My dear, even in a Protestant church one doesn't very often hear anything as good as that.' "

When he lived in London, being obliged to ride about on buses, Whitehead said he had made a practice of taking along with him one or another historic personage, seated at his side, usually on top of the bus. They held animated conversations, he explaining what was meant by what they could see from the bus-top and then listening to his companion's comments. Who were they? Well, he often took along Sir Isaac Newton, Aristotle, or Archimedes, but never Plato. But why not Plato? He never could be brought to say, perhaps didn't himself quite know, but Plato was never taken along.

This led to some chaffing about Europeans who come over here on a whirlwind tour, then go home and write a book explaining all about us.

"Oh, but," said Whitehead, "that's the only way to do it. Having lived here more than twenty years, I wouldn't dream of writing such a thing now, but if I had written my impressions of America after I had been here my first three months, *that* would have been the book of books!"

One forenoon we were speaking of revolutions, in especial, those of France and Russia.

"The real destructiveness of revolutions," said Whitehead, "is not their overthrow of a ruling class or the execution of a monarch. England got on quite well enough without Charles I and France could well spare Louis XVI. The Hohenzollerns were no great loss to Germany nor the Hapsburgs to Austria, let alone the Romanoffs to Russia. Even when it comes to the overthrow of ruling classes the social dislocation may not be serious. During the French Revolution, even under the Terror, life in Paris within a few streets of the Place de la Concorde and the guillotine flowed on much as usual. But the real destructiveness of revolutions comes in the displacement of the people who carry on the minor social services, those who do the day labour of carrying forward the normal processes of civilized life, and I do not mean the so-called learned professions, law, medicine, the clergy, but rather the teachers, the small civil servants, the skilled artisans, people who know how to do the unspectacular but necessary tasks. They are the cambium layer under the bark of the tree, and if that is girdled, the tree dies."

*   *   *

To bring Charles Hopkinson, then in his seventies, to those sittings had taken some manoeuvring. In summer he lives at "Sharksmouth," his place on the North Shore at Manchester, and the train ride to Boston followed by the subway journey to Cambridge would have brought him to his painting in an advanced state of August wilt. Fortunately the Marblehead Rationing Board saw the light and was gracious enough to grant the extra petrol necessary to carry him from the Salem railroad station to Cambridge and back. This went on until mid-August; then the surrender of Japan released supplies of petrol in their former flood. Besides, it had long been understood that petrol rationing had been primarily for the economizing not of petrol but of rubber for tyres.

The portrait was finished about September 1st. In a thunderstorm the painter and I drove over to the Boston Museum of Fine Arts to show it to Mr. Constable, the curator of paintings. Constable and Hopkinson went into an abstruse discussion of its merits. It was later exhibited in the rooms of the Society of Fellows at Eliot House.

As the month went on, Whitehead questioned our good faith about keeping our every next appointment for a sitting:

"I say, shall we expect you next Thursday forenoon punctually at eleven on the dot while the bell of Memorial Hall is striking the hour?"

"But why not?"

"The war may end any day, in which case you will be dancing in the streets, or standing on your heads."

On August 14th Japan surrendered and rejoicing was frenetic, though some of those who had seen the armistice in 1918 were not so sanguine. The war did end September 2nd with a formal surrender. Since then, peace has been defined as a pause between wars for enemy identification.

Yet that month of August, with those quiet forenoons of painting and conversation in the Whiteheads' living-room, sun shining on the treetops beneath their windows, the still, sultry air fragrant from white phlox in vases of gleaming black enamel, and the deep-voiced bell of Memorial Hall punctuating Whitehead's discourse first with the strokes of twelve, then with the stroke of one, and all this preceded by the drive from Salem to Cambridge through a countryside smiling with summer where the purple loosestrife blossomed in marsh meadows along the way, still remains an idyl of peace in a world of war.

XLII

September 11, 1945

So the war had ended, but people were still benumbed and not yet fully able to realize it. Summer was moving toward the threshold of autumn in a procession of days glowing with sun-gold and sea-blue. Since the slaughter had stopped it was once more possible to feel that the world was beautiful, and on the shores of Nahant Bay it is never more radiant than at summer's end.

In the midst of this, Sir Richard Livingstone had arrived from England by plane ("high priority" for a civilian) and had gone to spend two days at the Institute for Advanced Study in Princeton. His destination was Toronto, where he was to deliver four lectures at the university. For another two days of rest and quiet beside the sea he came to Swampscott; we then drove on Thursday forenoon into Cambridge for luncheon with the Whiteheads. As there was a strenuous fortnight awaiting him at Toronto before his return to England by plane, he had made no other engagements.

His younger son, Captain Rupert Livingstone, had been killed in this second war, as had Whitehead's in the first. This bond was present wordlessly.

The four of us sat in Whitehead's book-walled study. It was flooded by golden sunshine through a south window which stood wide open to the warm, still air, and in the trees outside the cicadas were shrilling. Scot and Englishman, the two are a contrast in type, Whitehead, the fair, florid Briton of Kent and East Anglia; Livingstone, tall, slender, sandy-haired and sandy-complexioned, though just now unwontedly reddened by exposure to the blazing sunlight and sea-glare of New England's September on the North Shore.

Their renewals of acquaintance were quickly disposed of; a brief pause, then Livingstone asked:

"What do you think has been the effect of science on our world?"

"Before I answer, what do you think?"

"Hasn't science abolished slavery?"

"If you had said that about the year 1900, yes. But the acceleration of change in the past, let me say, fifty years has altered the whole situation. I'm not speaking of the atomic bomb for the present, since it is only the latest in a series, and too recent to be appraised anyhow."

"When the atomic bomb was announced," said Livingstone, "the scientists, it seemed to me, were somewhat frivolous in their view of it, but the people were alarmed."

"I mean," resumed Whitehead, "that the conditions of our lives have been basically more altered in the past fifty years than they were in the previous two thousand—I might say three thousand. My answer to your first question would be, I think that we are on the threshold of an age of liberation, a better life for the masses, a new burst of liberated creative energy, a new form of society; or mankind may all but exterminate itself and desolate this planet."

"Suppose," said Livingstone, "some of the greatest Greeks were to come back and see us as we are now . . . Thucydides, Plato, Pericles, Aristotle?"

"Aristotle would be inexpressibly shocked at the way his generalizations have gone overboard. Mind you, I don't say his ideas—species, genera, and all that sort of thing—haven't proved vastly useful. Aristotle discovered all the half-truths which were necessary to the creation of science."

"Aristotle's *Ethics*, on the other hand," rejoined Livingstone, "seem to me to stand up better."

Whitehead looked dissent. "I grant you, they are admirably definite," said he. "Plato's ideas on that subject tend, in comparison, to be vague. But I prefer the vagueness."

"The Greeks didn't like vagueness," remarked Livingstone. "In that sense Plato may almost be said to be atypical. They liked outline to be distinct and subject matter to be clearly organized within definite form."

"I prefer Plato," Whitehead resumed. "He seems to me to have been the one man in the ancient world who would not have been surprised at what has happened, because his thought constantly took into account the unpredictable, the limitless possibilities of things. There is always more chance of hitting on something valuable when you aren't too sure what you want to hit upon."

He turned again to Livingstone, and continued, "There's something I want to ask you: am I right in thinking that German scholarship is quite wrong in trying to identify Plato with some explicit conclusion in his *Dialogues*, with some single speaker and a final point of view? It seems to me that was just what he was trying to avoid. Take his letters: assuming that he wrote them, and even if he didn't, they would state a prevailing frame of mind in ancient times about his work: namely, that there *is* no Platonic system of philosophy. What he did was explore various aspects of a problem and then leave us with them. . . . He seems to me to have had, more than anyone else, a supreme sense of the limitless possibilities of the universe."

"About German scholarship, I'm not at the moment prepared to say," replied Livingstone, "but all through Aristotle one can see his resistance to the influence of Plato, and all through him the influence of Plato's thought is inescapable."

"Let me speak personally for a moment," said Whitehead. "I had a good classical education, and when I went up to Cambridge early in the 1880's my mathematical training was continued under good teachers. Now nearly everything was supposed to be known about physics that could be known— except a few spots, such as electro-magnetic phenomena, which remained (or so it was thought) to be co-ordinated with the Newtonian principles. But, for the rest, physics was supposed to be nearly a closed subject. Those investigations to co-ordinate went on through the next dozen years. By the middle of the 1890's there were a few tremors, a slight shiver as of all not being quite secure, but no one sensed what was coming. By 1900 the Newtonian physics were demolished, done for! Still speaking personally, it had a profound effect on me: I have been fooled once, and I'll be damned if I'll be fooled again! Einstein is supposed to have made an epochal discovery. I am respectful and interested, but also sceptical. There is no more reason to suppose that Einstein's relativity is anything final, than Newton's *Principia*. The danger is dogmatic thought; it plays the devil with religion, and science is not immune from it. I am, as you see, a thorough-going evolutionist. Millions of years ago our earth began to cool off and forms of life began in their simplest aspects. *Where did they come from?* They must have been inherent in the total scheme of things; must have existed in potentiality in the most minute particles, first of this fiery, and later of this watery and earthy planet. Does it not strike you how absurd it is to start from the five and one-half or six feet of our own bodies as our scale of physical measurement?"

"Overdoing the idea," said Livingstone, quoting it in Greek, "that 'man is the measure of all things.'"

"Our notions of physical dimension," assented Whitehead, "are absurdly arbitrary. It doesn't strike me as at all impossible that the smallest pebble might contain within it a universe as complex as the one we know, and that the universe or universes which we have recently begun to apprehend may be as minute in the scale of what lies beyond as that in the pebble to the one we know; or that the vastness might be as much greater in the opposite direction—the direction of what we consider the infinitely small. . . . Development, I believe, goes by jumps. Fifty thousand years ago, let us say, there would have been a lucky jump; embodied in one man, or in one family, or in a few families, and, after an interval, another great advance following from that."

It was suggested that we may be living in the midst of one of those "jumps"—if it doesn't extinguish us.

Whitehead considered this, then said, "Why talk about 'the laws of nature' when what we mean is the characteristic behaviour of phenomena within certain limits at a given stage of development in a given epoch—so far as these can be ascertained?"

As the laughter subsided, he said to Livingstone, "But come, let's drop all this; I want to talk about your admirable books on education, especially adult education. How idiotic it is to dismiss children from school at sixteen, or even at eighteen, and consider them capable of coping with the complexities of life. . . ."

"My idea, as you know," said Livingstone, "is that education must continue throughout life for everybody, at the varying levels of ability and aptitude, and that that is the only way a modern democracy is workable or can continue to exist."

"What we want," said Whitehead, "is to elicit as nearly as possible all the latent capacities of human talent. No way of doing this adequately has ever been devised. A certain class of talents will be elicited under certain forms of social organization favourable to their development, but in a very limited range and in very limited conditions of space and time. We never seem to have found a way to elicit the complete spread of man's potential capabilities."

Mrs. Whitehead returned to the study. Luncheon was not quite ready, so seating herself on the cushioned leg-rest of her husband's arm-chair facing the two Englishmen, she plunged into a discussion of our two countries:

"The thing one mustn't do," she was addressing herself to Livingstone, "and it is so fatally easy, is to compare. They are not comparable; each is itself. We have lived here twenty-one years, and it is the differences which keep coming out. When we first came here after the other war, the hope that I saw in the faces was 'choky'—all these young things looking forward to life eagerly . . ."

"Having just arrived by airplane in Baltimore last Sunday afternoon," said Livingstone smiling, "I am in a perfect position to write a book about America."

"The longer one lives here, the less competent one feels to write it," said she. "But don't be put off by externals: to us, many of them are misleading. . . ."

"I'll tell you one of them," said Whitehead, "if Lucien will forgive me; the newspapers."

"I could damn them more specifically. But go on."

"To glance at their front pages," he continued, "you might suppose that a principal occupation was murdering one another."

"Remember, Altie," she cautioned him, "that when we used to go from England to the Continent, the crime on the Continent seemed tremendous, and *was* tremendous."

"I do remember, and the impression given by the front pages of the newspapers is quite fallacious. It isn't news when you ask a stranger, anybody in the whole scale of American life, the direction to some place, and he goes out of his way two streets to set you right, yet it is this that is absolutely typical among these people who seem to me to possess more native kindness than any people who ever lived on the face of the earth."

"Were you required to sign papers for admission to this country?" she asked of Livingstone.

"I don't recall anything unusual or formidable."

"Oh, but that is so; you wouldn't. It was when we were coming over here to stay—this is what I mean by not being put off by externals—Alfred and I were required to sign sworn statements that we had never spent longer than ten months in jail!"

"No, I don't remember signing anything like that," says Livingstone.

"But Gilbert Murray does," I offered a correction. "When he came over here in 1926, like you merely to deliver a series of lectures, he said, foreigners had to sign a paper answering the questions: Are you an anarchist? Are you a polygamist?"

"My God!" said Mrs. Whitehead.

Regaining her equanimity, she continued: "For nine years, after we came here to stay, we used to have students in, one evening a week. First and last, the number of boys and girls who went through our rooms would have run into the hundreds. They came from all sorts of homes, including the farms and what you would call something next door to a slum, and yet I tell you that the gentleness of their manners, their good taste, and really good breeding was virtually invariable. That was in the brave days of the Volstead Act, when people, and especially older people, were filling up before ever they started out to dine. And yet in all that time only one drunk came, and he, if you please, a scion of Boston blue-blood! At the other extreme was a boy who turned up from New York, the East Side. About half-way through the evening he stretched himself, sighed, and said, 'Isn't the world wonderful?' . . . 'What do you mean?' I asked him. 'Why,' said he, 'a few weeks ago I was rolling barrels in the streets of New York, and now here I am amidst luxury and all these books.' (Well, of course, our apartments down by the river were never anything special.) What he meant was that this was his first time in such surroundings—but not his last! He became one of Alfred's most brilliant pupils, and has done very well."

"The social constituency of English universities," remarked Livingstone, "has changed greatly." He cited instances: "The net incomes of the parents of our last year's scholars in Corpus were £400, £688, £361, £318, £1,065." (These figures have, of course, been made precise since that conversation.) "Two did not claim the extra emolument and therefore were well off; but there were two weekly wage-earners, £3 10s. 0d. per week, and £8 per week."

"It seems to me," said Whitehead, "that the English universities, Oxford and Cambridge perhaps in especial, are returning more nearly to their function in the Middle Ages, of training the gifted boys from the poorer classes. In the eighteenth century they trained young aristocrats at most, or the sons of country squires at least, with few scholars from the poorer classes, and in the nineteenth century, they drew largely from the more prosperous parts of the middle and professional classes—people like us, for example, for whom the world seemed to have been made fairly safe and enjoyable; but now they are beginning to get the children of the working class."

"From what you have been telling me," said Livingstone, "and from what I have observed here on previous visits and even a little on this one too, it seems to me that democracy in England is vertical, that is, an equalitarian feeling that runs from top to bottom of society, cutting through classes—and that in America, where classes are less defined, democracy is more horizontal." He indicated the two dimensions by gestures of his two hands.

"Let us give you an example of how horizontal it is here," Whitehead said. "Taxicab chauffeurs here in Cambridge and

Boston are good conversationalists; they have something really interesting to say. Quite recently we had one driving us home from Boston; he slowed down, and drove by side streets (explaining to us that he wasn't lengthening the distance, but only the time), conversing animatedly with us, and we with him, and when he let us out at our door, he said, 'This is the most enjoyable conversation I have had for a long time.'"

Luncheon was announced. We went out to the table. Conversation turned to English novelists.

"Women, it seems to me, write better novels than men," said Whitehead. "Men are too apt to go off in search of abstract ideas and try to fit life to them; women are more likely to give us the intimacies which make life and character vivid to us. How does it seem to you?" he appealed to Livingstone.

"As you spoke, I was thinking of Mrs. Gaskell, and I would agree."

"One exception I would make," Whitehead continued, "not a genius of the first rank, but an admirable talent for precisely what he did; present the average life and thought of his time through a fairly representative class, the clergy. I mean Anthony Trollope."

"You ought to know," exclaimed his wife. "Heavens, you were steeped in it and so was I, from my early twenties on. . . . And don't forget that it all but spoilt every member of your family in your generation except you. I grant you that Trollope does it well; only perhaps a trifle too well."

"At least, pettie, he got it right," said Whitehead, beaming across the table at her. "We agree about that! Reading him, I can hear my father and his clerical friends talking. Even the jokes sound natural. We lived near Canterbury and saw a good deal of the cathedral clergy."

"But women novelists don't draw men well," conceded Mrs. Whitehead. "When it comes to their favourite figures of men, something usually goes wrong."

The question arose whether men novelists drew women any

better, with comparisons between George Meredith and George
Eliot.

"Thackeray," said Whitehead, "has immense art, but he is
too narrowly confined to a class; he carries you all over England
and the Continent, but in the end they are always about much
the same kind of people."

"He was writing of a class, too," added she, "to which he
didn't belong, and saw from the outside with a mixture of
fascination and repugnance, never able to make up his mind."

"One nineteenth-century English novel that I think *will*
last," said Livingstone, "is *Pickwick*." (In his *Greek Genius* he
parallels the jollity of Christmas at Dingley Dell with the
picture of country life in Attica in the *Peace* of Aristophanes
[verses 1127–1171].) "*Pickwick*," he continued, "is not only
literature; it is also history. That is what the English are
really like."

"A moment ago," said Whitehead, "I was saying that I
thought women wrote the best novels." (He paused and gave
us a mischievous twinkle.) "I would almost say that Dickens
was one of the best women novelists!"

"How about Galsworthy?"

Livingstone thought his people weren't very real.

"Galsworthy, like Thackeray," said Mrs. Whitehead, "was
another 'outsider.'"

"As with novels, so with letters," Whitehead carried it
forward. "Women write better letters than men. They put in
what we want to know, how people felt about things, how they
lived, what they ate and wore, what they worried about—all
those immediacies which make the life of an epoch live again.
History should be written more from letters. Who cares about
the Battle of Crécy, dates, places, and all that we are crammed
with in the name of history? What had they to do with it?
History is from day to day; and it is not events, it is sociology;
it is the progress of thought."

"The trouble with formal history, it seems to me," said

Livingstone, "is that it gives us the conclusions, the end results, without showing us how these results were arrived at."

"Precisely," assented Whitehead; "the clashes are only the last step in the process; what we need to know is the progress of ideas and ferments which produced the clashes."

"Another historical source which should be more used, though the French have made more use of it than the English, and effective use, too, is memoirs," said Mrs. Whitehead. "English literature is not very rich in memoirs and those we have are likely to be bleak and dreary. French memoirs, on the contrary, are vivacious and full of reality. It's true they often record scandalous escapades, but with such spirit that, while one does not condone, one is not depressed. The equivalents in English memoirs I find repellent, and the people unamiable."

They began casting about for those who could be said to have written history well in the nineteenth century in England:

"Not Macaulay," said Mrs. Whitehead, "with that much-touted 'style' . . . rhetorical periods, 'tum-te-tum-te-tum,' the sort of House of Commons speech that was effective in that epoch, and all quite superficial."

"Don't forget," says Livingstone, "that Macaulay managed to make the reading of history popular, no small achievement."

"So did Strachey," said she, "but that didn't make what he wrote *good* history."

"I don't like it," said Livingstone, "any better than you do, but it is often very good writing."

"That I grant you; and what he says is often very funny, but it is not funny when others try to say it like him."

We rose. Coffee was served in the living-room. Whiteheads and Livingstone, Cambridge and Oxford, began playing a kind of tennis game as between their two universities, comparing their whimsicalities, their contrasts, their merits and defects.

"I arrived there," said Mrs. Whitehead, "in the Year of the Thirty Brides, and I assure you, it was not an easy place for brides."

[348]

"There had just been a change in the university statutes," explained Whitehead, "permitting dons to marry. Before that, in order to marry, one had to take holy orders, and as most of them no longer believed in the Articles to which they were obliged to subscribe, they found ways of satisfying their consciences by all sorts of far-fetched interpretations of those theological concepts which, I should say, did the Broad Church no particular good. The result was, as Evelyn says, that thirty or forty brides arrived in Cambridge all at once, some of them, like her, quite young; others by no means young."

"But I learned fast," said Mrs. Whitehead. "Having been born and reared in France, I had read a good deal in French, but, being transplanted abruptly to England, hadn't read what one is expected to have read in English. One of the dons, seated next me at a dinner party, began questioning me about my English reading. Naturally, I didn't come off very well. 'I see that you read nothing!' said he, and ceased to attend to me for the rest of the evening. . . . And his lack of interest in me lasted some years. No, it was not an easy place for brides."

"Nor always for bridegrooms," added Whitehead. "You remember the Verralls and Jim Stephen?" he asked her.

She suddenly choked with laughter.

"But be sure and explain to Sir Richard," she cautioned him, "that that was before Stephen went 'off'."

"He was down visiting us at Cambridge," pursued Whitehead, "when we lived next the Verralls; our gardens adjoined—"

"Only a one-brick thickness of wall between them," Mrs. Whitehead put in.

"Now Verrall talked in a high, squeaky voice" (he mimicked it), "and Jim Stephen was a deadly mimic. He began mocking Verrall in an imaginary scene of Verrall proposing to his wife. Poor Evelyn was horrified and made frantic gestures to him to stop. 'They can hear; just over the wall,' said she in whispers. 'What of it?' says Stephen. 'Do them good!'"

As between the two universities, Livingstone questioned whether there was much to choose in man's inhumanity to man.

"At Cambridge," said Whitehead, "what civilization we got, came from outside. But at Oxford, you civilize your people inside the university."

"Oxford is more sociological," admitted Livingstone. "At Cambridge you train mathematicians and scientists."

"What saved me for civilization," said Whitehead, "were two things. One was The Apostles. It was a discussion club of twelve members, undergraduates."

"And what was the other?" asked Livingstone.

"Being taken out of Cambridge and plunged into the University of London for fifteen years."

"What do you think that did for you?" Livingstone inquired in a gently chaffing tone.

"Stirred me about among all sorts of people; and, added to that, was my experience in the university senate."

"The sociological cast of Oxford," observed Livingstone, "is generally accredited to the classical Greats. I say the classical Greats, because even the men who take modern Greats and do well in them admit that they aren't as effective, aren't as powerful."

"Just what do you conceive to be the effect on a man of the classical Greats?" inquired Whitehead.

"In Newman's *Nature of University Education* there is a definition of a gentleman," replied Livingstone. "It covers about three pages,[1] and comes nearer to defining what you inquire than anything else I know. It's all the more forceful since Newman doesn't approve of the type he is describing and leaves you in no doubt about it, for, as an example, he cites the Emperor Julian, 'the apostate from Christian Truth, the foe of Christian education,' " and he quoted, " 'a gentleman's religion is of a liberal and generous character; it is based upon

[1] On the scope and Nature of University Education, John Henry Newman. Everyman's Library; pages 186–188.

honour; vice is evil, because it is unworthy, despicable, and odious.' "

"Poor Newman," exclaimed Mrs. Whitehead, "that sensitive, defenceless, skinless creature! *Ecorce*. Who could blame him?"

"I saw him once," said Whitehead.

"To speak with him?" asked Livingstone.

"Yes."

"Can you remember what he said?"

"It is too long ago." Whitehead looked preoccupied for a moment, then exclaimed suddenly, "There's a question I would like to ask of a Jesuit priest. . . ."

"Then ask it in your study," proposed Mrs. Whitehead, rising. The conversation was temporarily adjourned.

"There was a question you wanted to put to a Jesuit priest," prompted Livingstone, when we were again in the study.

"Yes. It is this: 'Is there laughter in Heaven?' The humourlessness of the Bible is amazing."

"I tried rereading the Old Testament a while ago," replied Livingstone. "Much of it is superb in every way; but bits are . . . Well, you remember Oscar Wilde's 'When I think of all the harm that book has done, I despair of writing anything to equal it.' "

"Had the Hebrews no sense of humour?" asked Whitehead.

"When something is very serious, don't we lose a bit of it by laughing about it? Doesn't laughter diminish it in value?"

"Suppose we consider the arts," proposed Whitehead. "Do we find humour there?"

Livingstone thought it might be hard to find in the greatest art, say religious painting of the Italian Renaissance. "I doubt," said he, "whether it goes with the greatest thought or art."

"There's plenty of laughter in the comedies of Aristophanes," I said, "and his works are both art and religion."

"Yes," said Livingstone, "but I always think Aristophanes is at his best in the parts where he isn't joking."

"Still, on the main issue, I challenge you: Laughter is a divine attribute. And the absence of laughter from the Hebraic religions is a serious matter to us of the Northern European races, for laughter plays a large part in our lives, and we are forced to do our laughing almost entirely outside of our religion."

"How could it be done inside religion?" asked Livingstone.

"It has been done. There is a liberal arts college in New England which had better be nameless, since things were going badly in it during the 1920's and 1930's."

"You are quite right about that," said Whitehead, to my consternation. "I was invited there to lecture in 1930, and I could see that for myself."

"Then you must be clairvoyant, for we mean the same college. The boys were out of hand; were required to attend daily chapel and church on Sundays, but if they didn't like the visiting preacher (and they mostly didn't) they would cough him down and no way could be found to stop them. But there was one preacher who came there repeatedly, whom the boys heard gladly. He was a man of intellect and of great moral earnestness, and he also had a lively sense of humour. Between his passages of earnestness he could keep the boys rocking with laughter. They adored him. . . . As for laughter in Greek religion, we needn't stop with Aristophanes. It begins as far back as Homer, the first book of the *Iliad* ends with gods laughing on Olympus."

"There is a fragment of a lost satyr play," Livingstone conceded, "in which Prometheus has stolen fire from heaven, and the satyrs think it so beautiful that they try to kiss it and get their beards singed."

"The Hebrews," resumed Whitehead, "had a most intense ethical perception, though within a very limited range. It is 'the beauty of holiness.' In that, no one else approaches them, but the range is narrow."

(Sometime afterwards we did come up with sundry examples

in Holy Writ of what, by stretching the definition, might be interpreted as humour. One was the prophet Elijah taunting the priests of Baal with the impotency of their god, though he also ordered them to be slaughtered by their late sectaries [I Kings 18 : 40]; another was the prophet Elisha conjuring bears to tear two and forty children who had taunted him with his bald head [II Kings 2 : 24]; a third was Haman hanged on the gallows fifty cubits high which he had had built for Mordecai [Esther 7:10]; and a fourth was Saint Paul's incident with the silversmiths of Ephesus, which is first-rate satire [Acts 19 : 24]. But it had to be admitted that none of these was the kind of hilarity which has audiences rolling in the aisles.)

"The Greeks," said Livingstone, in reply to Whitehead's last remark, "had everything which the Hebrews lacked."

"Touching this problem on its modern side," Whitehead continued, "the Unitarians, I think, come the nearest to having found a way to adapt the Christian ideas to the world we live in now—and with the Unitarians I group those other religious people who are so nearly like them, the Congregationalists. And by the way, a few days ago I even had a letter from an Episcopalian bishop commending me for my philosophy. I couldn't but think he was a good deal more like an eighteenth-century English bishop in respect to his breadth of religious thought than a twentieth-century one. . . . See here," he said abruptly, turning to Livingstone, "at the risk of being rude, I am going to ask you a personal question: you needn't answer it if you don't want to: how did you vote in the last election?"

"For Labour."

"Good! So would I have had I been there."

"It happened that our local candidate was a very good one."

"I would have voted for the Labour candidate, even if he had been a poor one, unless he had been *too* great an ass."

"Did you expect the result that came?" asked Mrs. Whitehead.

N

"No," said Livingstone. "The most that anyone seems to have expected was a sharp diminution of the Conservative seats."

"What went wrong with Churchill's campaign?" she asked.

"He is thought to have got into the hands of Beaverbrook."

"We've known Churchill and followed his career since the Boer War," she continued. "He seems to be one-half hero and the other half bounder. In a fight he is superb, but the moment the fighting stops, the bounder comes uppermost."

"It's greatly to the credit of the British electorate, I think," said Livingstone, "that there was no raking up of dead bodies and dead issues. Baldwin and Chamberlain were left out of the controversy. The only time I know of when one of them was brought in was during a discussion in the House of Commons about sending our iron railings off to war. 'Leave Baldwin his railings,' said a member. 'He'll need them to protect him from the people!' The remark was drowned in boos, and it was made by a Conservative member."

"There is no diminution of Churchill's popularity," resumed Mrs. Whitehead. "He is still 'good old Winnie!' and gets the more cheers when he appears in public, more than the Labour premier. The people admire him and honour him, but they won't vote for him. To me it seems an extraordinary manifestation of political good-sense on the part of the British electorate."

"Yes," said Livingstone, who, being a Platonist, is well acquainted with the valid criticisms of "the democratic man."

"It makes one believe in democracy."

"What do you think are the chances of your getting a military man for President after this war?" Whitehead appealed to me.

"We have had two melancholy experiences in that kind which are pretty vividly remembered," said I.

"But General MacArthur is making a play for it," said Mrs. Whitehead.

"That may be. As a military man he is admirable, but he also has a sense of theatre and that, in American public life, doesn't wear too well."

"Eisenhower," said Whitehead, "is a really great figure. How about him?"

No one cared to predict.

"One great change in the American frame of mind which you must take into account," Mrs. Whitehead addressed Livingstone, "is that they now know that the world is not safe, even for them. We, for our part, never were safe, and we have mostly known it, unless it were for a brief period towards the end of the nineteenth century. What a comfortable—and vanished—world that was!—The world of Queen Victoria. What a figure of legend she is now!"

"Is Queen Victoria ever known to have made a joke?" asked Whitehead, suddenly reverting to our discussion of humour.

"'We are not amused,'" quoted Livingstone. "At least, she had a negative sense of humour; she knew what she thought was *not* funny."

"But she once said, 'Mr. Gladstone addresses me as if I were a public meeting.'"

"Yes," said Mrs. Whitehead, "but did she know that remark was funny?"

"Wasn't it disgraceful," said Whitehead, "the way 'Dizzy' sucked up to her. Disraeli's eminence is a striking instance of political detachment. They didn't like him, but they knew he had ability and accepted him as a political representative."

The clock in the tower of Memorial Hall struck a booming "Three"! There was an afternoon train for Toronto which Sir Richard must be aboard. We stood, to take our leave.

"Shall you," asked Whitehead genially, "feel let down when no one any longer walks before you carrying a poker?" The allusion was to the degree ceremony at Oxford, when the academic procession enters the Sheldonian Theatre, the vice-chancellor preceded by his staves as the symbols of authority.

N2

"My children," replied Livingstone, "amuse themselves by asking why I don't turn around and walk in the opposite direction. At the same time our registrar, who has had long experience in it, says that the custom of standing when the vice-chancellor enters the Hebdomadal Council does have a good effect on getting to the business seriously. Ritual has a place in life. The deference may not be for a personality, or even for the institution; but it can be for the ideas embodied in the ceremony."

XLIII

November 11, 1947

ARMISTICE DAY. Evening with the Whiteheads, an autumn storm raging outside, with a gale of almost hurricane force and torrential rain.

At first they both seemed a little limp. This was scarcely to be wondered at, for their daughter-in-law, Mrs. North Whitehead, had died after a lingering and dreadful illness; and Mrs. Whitehead herself had had to go to Phillips House, Massachusetts General Hospital, for what threatened to be an emergency operation. She referred to it coolly as "knife work." Privately, before he came out of his study where he was having a nap, she said that it had been rougher on him than on her.

"He can meet these things when they happen, but he no longer has his endurance, and they take it out of him after they are over. Here I am, as usual—well, not *quite* as usual—but with him"—she paused and regarded me with a comic glance —"you might suppose I had been cremated and dispersed!"

The living-room was full of flowers, chrysanthemums, yellow, bronze, lavender, artistically arranged with fronds of green. I spoke of them. "Yes," said she, "I am being spoilt, and how I love it! You would think I was a film actress from the way flowers arrive."

Rising, she went to her big mahogany escritoire and took out a sheaf of letters.

"There is something I wish you to know," said she, "though nothing must be said about it at present." She kept opening letters and scanning them, speaking along as she did so.

"As you know, our income from England was cut down during the war. Financially for us it was quite a tight pinch. But I managed. What I want you to know is that three times during the war, the bank manager where we have our accounts received anonymous certified cheques to be deposited to our account. Each time the sum was the same, three hundred dollars. I asked if he knew who. He said he didn't but could communicate through the other bank. We couldn't accept anonymous gifts, of course, but I asked if it was possibly in payment of some forgotten debt or obligation. The answer came back, 'It might be considered so.' No. We're too old for that. Our hearty gratitude was conveyed but we couldn't accept. . . . I can't find the letter I'm looking for. Do you put things away and lose them?"

"Do I? Last spring I brought home as gifts some things from Oxford, which I put away carefully. It is now November and I haven't found them yet."

"You make me feel better. . . . I would have preferred you to read the letter; but can tell you. The college has had an anonymous gift of money for a scholarship, to be known as the Alfred North Whitehead Scholarship, the income of which is twelve hundred dollars a year, to be paid to Alfred during the remainder of his life and to me if I survive him; after that to the student holder of the scholarship. What impresses us both most is the generosity of it; also the tact and delicacy. It is paid to the college. That makes it quite different. We have no say in the matter. And what pleases Alfred most is that it leaves a permanent connection of his name with the college in a living form."

She added, "The endowment sum is thirty thousand dollars at four per cent."

No conjectures were offered as to who the donor might be, but there were two or three strong probabilities.

"Well, that is it." Rising, she put the papers back in the escritoire and, resuming her arm-chair, lighted a cigarette. The telephone rang. "Oh, damn!" says she, and answered it. Her surprise was a joyful one, for it was somebody she dearly loves. That conversation being ended, she knocked at the study door, went in softly, and spoke in a quiet voice: "Lucien is here. Now don't bound up: wait a few moments before you rise."

Presently he came out of the study, not quite fully awake. But after bathing his face in cold water, he came back feeling fit.

They were most entertaining. It seems that his publishers' envoys had been to call. This meant that a representative of the English firm had been brought by one from the American branch.

"The immediate occasion," said he, "is that they are planning an omnibus edition of my work."

"Will it include *Process and Reality*?"

"Some of it. . . ."

"We would have preferred," said she, "to have all or nothing of each work, instead of all the works with cuts by editors, and were quite let down when we found that the editors had taken it upon themselves to cut the works, in some cases whole chapters."

"Why, the colossal . . . what shall I call it?"

"And what do you suppose Alfred said?"

"Well, what did he say to anything like that?"

"'No doubt they've improved it' . . .!"

"I always said he is too good for this world. But it's wonderful news that *Process and Reality* is to be republished in any form. I can't get a single-volume edition. The Old Corner Book Store has been advertising for one for me these two months. I remember your telling me that it is the book you most wanted to write."

[358]

"In the preface to it," said he, "I wrote something which ought to have been repeated in the opening sentence of the first chapter, and repeated at frequent intervals all through the book: namely, how impressed I am with the inadequacy of any human being's attempt to express such philosophical ideas at all; how utterly beyond our scope are these universal processes. All one can do, in venturing on such subjects, is to *offer suggestions*."

"Is it true that a single-volume edition of *The Aims of Education* has been reissued in England?"

"Yes," said she, "they sent us a copy."

"That is more good news, for at least half a dozen of my friends, headmasters and such, have been trying to obtain it."

"Look here," said he, "I'll give you this one."

He went to his study, brought it back, and laid it in my lap. The plates (it was an English firm) were obviously the original ones, but the dark-blue binding was different and in better taste than the crimson cover of the 1928 edition. Later in the evening he autographed it.

"We had a pleasant time with the publishers' representatives," said Mrs. Whitehead, "but there was one ghastly moment. What do you suppose the publishers wanted to do? *Print a photograph of Alfred on the cover of* Life *magazine!*"

"Good God!"

"Imagine Alfred's face being hawked about the streets," said she, grimacing.

"How did you get out of it?"

"I told them, most gently, that he had made it a lifelong rule not to give interviews and not to be photographed for the press —except at the Harvard Tercentenary, of course, when all the old boys were photographed."

"Imagine Alfred joining the publicity hounds!"

"The publishers' men were very kind about it," she resumed. "They agreed to drop it."

"When is the 'omnibus' to appear?"

"We don't know. They gave us no idea."

"My own guess is," said Whitehead, looking at me with a mischievous twinkle, "—mind you, I don't know, and perhaps I shouldn't say this; but my own guess is that they mean to postpone publication of this until shortly after I have quitted this earthly sphere."

"If that's the case," said his wife, "I question their judgment. If they want a 'Whitehead boom,' it is on now. Have you seen the new volume of excerpts?"

"Yes. So far, three copies have been sent me."

"What do you think of it?"

"It strikes me as very well done."

"*The Wit and Wisdom of Whitehead*," said she, "—what a title! I grant you the wit, and some of the wisdom, but—"

"The title is not exactly new. It was used for those excerpts from George Eliot during her lifetime, and again for George Meredith during his. No doubt the alliteration of the three *W*'s was an irresistible temptation. But looking it over I thought the selections were made with care and skill; a good many of them I recognized, but others I didn't, and the result is that I shall do what I expect the excerpts will cause a good many others to do—go back to the books themselves."

Dinner was quite sumptuous. The beating of wind and rain against the windows reminded them of "Bleak House" at Broadstairs, where they first met, for Alfred's Aunt Susan had lived in it; but long after Dickens's sojourn there. And bleak it was, for the building was high, narrow, and exposed, and although built of flint-stone, on nights like this it shook in the gales off the North Sea. They said there had been numerous shipwrecks on that headland.

From Bleak House they moved in imagination to the vicarage at Ramsgate.

"It was of brick," said Mrs. Whitehead. "There were fine trees, spacious grounds, and a lovely garden—under which, you are to understand, was a sizable cave."

"Rock-walled?"

"No. In the chalk."

"An entrance to a cavern yawning in your garden?"

"No," said Whitehead. "It was entered through the coach-house."

"It sounds a bit like sword-and-cape melodrama. Was the vicarage interior interesting?"

"Yes. Not impressive, you understand," said Mrs. Whitehead, "but interesting. There was a wide hall, though the staircase was not good. It was something new that had been added by a predecessor of Father's. But the old stairway was lovely; that had been moved back into the servants' wing. Of course the tone of the interior had to be ecclesiastical. The dining-room was properly dark. Dining-rooms were expected to be gloomy. The darkness set off the family silver, of which there was any quantity."

"What was that amusing tale you were telling Livingstone here at luncheon about Archbishop Tait and his son? So much went on in those four hours that I couldn't remember it all."

"That's Alfred's story," said she, laughingly. "He was there. I wasn't. Though I know it almost as well as if I had been."

"Tait was a very great man," said Whitehead. "He should have been Prime Minister of Great Britain; but Providence made a mistake; he went into the church instead and became Archbishop of Canterbury. Living so close by, he became a great friend of my father's and was often at our house. Sometimes he drove over after morning service from Canterbury for Sunday dinner at the vicarage. On this particular day he brought with him Bishop Gore of Oxford, a man who had found religion. Now, being eighteen years old by that time, I was well aware that Archbishop Tait had quite a name for peopling posts of good emoluments with his relatives, and when I heard Bishop Gore ask Mrs. Tait, by way of making table conversation, 'And what profession does your son seem inclined to enter?' I realized they were on thin ice. There was a pause. Gore leaned forward solicitously over the table, and I listened intently for the reply. 'We have considered a great many possibilities,' said Lady Tait, 'but it seems, after all, to come back to one thing—we think dear Gordon will take holy orders.' Another pause. Then Gore said, as if to himself, 'Quite!' "

When we rose they asked if the epidemic of war-scares in the newspapers had begun to subside. All I could say was that we hadn't had a war with Russia for thirty-six hours.

"If either this country or they start a war with these new instruments," said Whitehead, "civilization is done for. It won't wipe out the human race, but it will set civilization back thousands of years."

"Do you see any bulwark against such a disaster?"

"Only the appearance of half a dozen eminent men."

"Can you descry half a dozen such on the horizon?"

"They don't appear on the horizon; they appear in our midst and cannot at once be identified."

"Shall I confess? I go about my accustomed occupations, among my friends, amid my favourite scenery, all with a sense of unreality, a sense that all this may be blown to atoms within the next few years."

"So do I," said Mrs. Whitehead.

"This much I will say," said Whitehead. "When you consider the past history of Russia, who the Russians are, what they endured under the czars, and the vast extent of their territory and population, it seems to me that it has to be admitted that their present government is the best obtainable by them, and enough better than any they have ever had before. And this notion that in any part of the earth, no matter how barbarous its previous history or how backward its people, all you need do is give everybody the vote is idiotic."

He added that although modern weapons, especially since the atom bomb, had rendered all previous forms of warfare as obsolete as fists and cudgels, "this has not been grasped by the

military people, for all their talk about it, or by hardly anybody else. Take this room; it looks solid, stable, and used to be
thought so. As a matter of fact it is a raging welter of activity,
nothing permanent about it at all; merely different rates of
change, decay, disintegration, ranging from weeks to thousands
of years, which in the time span is nothing. Almost no one has
grasped the fact that our world has so changed since 1900 as
to make any future utterly unpredictable, and any attempt to
apply the standards of the past to the present very risky. The
nineteenth century was dead by the 1880's; the 1870's was its
last lush decade; 1914 was only the mace-blow, which con-
firmed the fact of its previous demise. But we are now in an
epoch where change is far more drastic than that which slew
the nineteenth century."

I asked, somewhat circuitously, if he had ever had a sense of
being seized by a force not of himself, while writing.

"In all I have written," said he, "I have been trying to
express common sense."

Discussing the "half-truths," he continued:

"People make the mistake of talking about 'natural laws.'
There *are* no natural laws. There are only temporary habits
of nature. . . .

". . . What is more, we are too stuck-up in our notions of
size, measuring everything in proportion to our bodies. From
what science has discovered about the infinitely small and the
infinitely vast, the size of our bodies is almost totally irrelevant.
In this little mahogany stand"—he touched it with his hand—
"may be civilizations as complex and diversified in scale as our
own; and up there, the heavens, with all their vastness, may be
only a minute strand of tissue in the body of a being in the scale
of which all our universes are as a trifle. Man has only just
begun to understand, not this vastness, for we cannot grasp it,
but that such vastness exists, and that it throws out all his
previous calculations. Dead knowledge is the danger. It is the
peculiar danger of scholarship, of universities; and it is

N2*

considered quite respectable. If you 'know' a great deal, that is supposed to suffice. Now what is wanted is 'activity in the presence of knowledge.' Novel viewpoints; knowledge applied to experience."

I asked him whether he thought he had learned more from books or from people. He said: "I have learned, I suppose, far more from people than from books."

As we discussed this, Mrs. Whitehead exclaimed:

"You two men talk like sated gluttons! If you had struggled all your lives under the handicap of not having had a formal scholastic training, you would speak of books more respectfully. The paralysing thing is the uncertainty, the never feeling quite sure of your ground. What the formal training with books does for you is enable you to organize what you know."

She had us, we knew it, and meekly retired from the fray. Whitehead resumed our theme in a different development:

"I am impressed by the inadequacy of language to express our conscious thought, and by the inadequacy of our conscious thought to express our subconscious. The curse of philosophy has been the supposition that language is an exact medium. Philosophers verbalize and then suppose the idea is stated for all time. Even if it were stated, it would need to be restated for every century, perhaps every generation. Plato is the only one who knew better and did not fall into this trap. When ordinary methods failed him, he gave us a myth, which does not challenge exactitude but excites reverie. Mathematics is more nearly precise, and comes nearer to the truth. In a thousand years it may be as commonly used a language as is speech today. Most of what we think and say with our conscious minds and speech is shallow and superficial. Only at rare moments does that deeper and vaster world come through into the conscious thought or expression; they are the memorable moments of our lives, when we feel—when we know—we are being used as instruments of a greater force than ourselves for purposes higher and wider than our own. Men of genius have the moments more often, but nearly everyone has had a few moments of such illumination. The poets are important here, because they express these vast intuitions in words, often better than most philosophers, and in words, however inadequate, that do nevertheless somehow stir in the reader or listener some corresponding sense of the infinitude of thought or feeling or experience which is being talked about. I mean of course only the very greatest poets."

"Should poets know a good deal?"

"Some poets should have known more (especially today); others would have been better poets had they known less. Shakespeare wrote better poetry for not knowing too much; Milton, I think, knew too much finally for the good of his poetry."

"You remember our old friend Walter Raleigh," said Mrs. Whitchcad.

"Yes. You always said that he should have been a poet, not a university don."

"I stick to it. He did have just such glimpses of infinitude. There was a quatrain of his, it was published years ago, and I can remember where—in the *Westminster Gazette*—that has stuck in my memory ineradicably." She quoted it:

> *Stand on the trestles of the world*
> *And view the humours of the fair*
> *Where knives and fiery balls are hurled*
> *And God leads round his starry Bear . . .*

★   ★   ★

It was growing late, and later than I thought. The autumn gale was still pelting and pouring outside. As the evening went on, it had kept occurring to me that my first visit to them at Canton more than a dozen years ago had been on an April 6th, anniversary of our entrance into the first world war, and that this was Armistice Day, another such anniversary. The idea annoyed me a little, for of late each time I had seen him it had been to wonder if it might be the last. The notion was dismissed, for earlier in the evening though he had looked frail and tired, he was now speaking with the vigour of a young man, of the creative force in the universe.

"It was a mistake, as the Hebrews tried, to conceive of God as creating the world from the outside, at one go. An all-foreseeing Creator, who could have made the world as we find it now—what could we think of such a being? Foreseeing everything and yet putting into it all sorts of imperfections to redeem which it was necessary to send his only son into the world to suffer torture and hideous death; outrageous ideas. The Hellenic religion was a better approach; the Greeks conceived of creation as going on everywhere all the time *within* the universe; and I also think they were happier in their conception of supernatural beings impersonating those various forces, some good, others bad; for both sorts of forces *are* present, whether we assign personality to them or not. There is a general tendency in the universe to produce worth-while things, and moments come when we can work with it and it can work through us. But that tendency in the universe to produce worth-while things is by no means omnipotent. Other forces work against it.

"God is *in* the world, or nowhere, creating continually in us and around us. This creative principle is everywhere, in animate and so-called inanimate matter, in the ether, water, earth, human hearts. But this creation is a continuing process, and 'the process is itself the actuality,' since no sooner do you arrive than you start on a fresh journey. In so far as man partakes of this creative process does he partake of the divine, of God, and that participation is his immortality, reducing the question of whether his individuality survives death of the body to the estate of an irrelevancy. His true destiny as co-creator in the universe is his dignity and his grandeur."

EPILOGUE

Mrs. Whitehead speaks:

"On Christmas Eve I was putting up the holly and mistletoe around our living-rooms. Alfred was in a state of complete happiness, even of elation, holiday high spirits. You would have thought from his praise of our rooms that we had spent our previous years living in kennels. I said so. I said, 'This place isn't anything.' He said, 'I know it, but what does it matter?' What *did* it matter? He had long since ceased to live in it, perhaps never had lived in it at all. On Christmas Day we had our usual family gathering. The next day he wasn't so well, and on that day it came. I saw it happen. He raised his left hand and let it drop, to tell me that he knew, for it was already half paralysed. And I knew the end was not far off."

He lingered four days, but without regaining consciousness, and died December 30, 1947, in his 87th year.

Such was the end, Echecrates, of our friend; concerning whom I may truly say, that of all the men of his time whom I have known, he was the wisest and justest and best.

President Conant: It is impossible for me to express adequately the obligations of my wife and myself to the University over which ~~passide~~ you preside.

Both as an institution and as a group of individuals, Harvard has made it possible for me to express ideas which had been growing in my thoughts for a life-time.

I wish ~~more especially~~ to emphasize my admiration and personal affection for so many Harvard friends, some of whom are present today.

During my life, I have had the great happiness of ~~pursuing~~ *teaching in* two countries which have contributed so greatly to learning and to the dignity of mankind.

Manuscript page in Alfred North Whitehead's handwriting

On the occasion of Whitehead's receiving the Order of Merit from the British Crown at University Hall, Cambridge, Massachusetts, June 6, 1945.

Books by

ALFRED NORTH WHITEHEAD
(1861–1947)

A Treatise on Universal Algebra (1898)

Principia Mathematica (with Bertrand Russell; 3 vols., 1910–1913)

Axioms of Projective Geometry (1906)

Axioms of Descriptive Geometry (1907)

An Introduction to Mathematics (1910)

The Organization of Thought (1916)

An Enquiry Concerning the Principles of Natural Knowledge (1919)

The Concept of Nature (1920)

The Principle of Relativity with Applications to Physical Science (1922)

* Science and the Modern World (1925)
* Religion in the Making (1926)
* Symbolism: Its Meaning and Effect (1927)
* The Aims of Education (1928)
* Process and Reality: An Essay in Cosmology (1929)
* The Function of Reason (1929)
* Adventures of Ideas (1933)
* Nature and Life (1934)
* Modes of Thought (1938)
* Essays in Science and Philosophy (1947)

* *Written in the United States.*

INDEX

Index

Applied mathematics equipped scientists with a complex medium, 66

Aptitude, superior forms of, in humble people, 248

Arabic numerals easier to manage, 66

Archimedes, 211; we might have had the Industrial Age in the time of, 226; everything necessary for modern science and technology existed in the time of, 310

Architecture, 253

Argument, spontaneous conversation should follow where (it) leads, 13, 165

Aristocracies welcome talent, 88

Aristocracy, in America, (it) had a black eye, 62; that shirks its leadership is done for, 63; almost for the first time in history, with a religious tinge, 130

Aristophanes, 28, 352

Aristotle, 142, 165, 213, 226, 309; *Politics*, 129; invented science but destroyed philosophy, 165; *Ethics*, 340

Art, easy for a good period of, to die, 23; greatest, speaks to the common people, 23; theory on relation of technique to, 96; flourishes when there is a sense of adventure, 169; great, is dealing with simple subjects freshly, 178; is the imposing of a pattern on experience, 225

Art-forms, life cycles of, 97

Artisans seeking intellectual enlightenment, 7

Artist, or amanuensis, 30; and America, 177; place of, in our national development, 178; must have a continuous flow of fresh aesthetic experiences, 288

Artists, great, exhaust an epoch, 23; not to be blamed for what is done with their works, 72; germinating power of, in American civilization, 168

Arts, sterility among Bostonians in, 40

Ascham, Roger, 70

Athens, 166

Atlantic Monthly, 204, 205, 230

Atomic bombs, 333

Audience of ten persons, a man writes for, 64

Augustus Caesar, 119, 120, 199; President Roosevelt compared with, 34; saved Rome from the Romans, 158

Aurelius, Marcus, 37; *Meditations*, 167

Austen, Jane, 28

Average comfort and literacy, diffusion of, major achievements in human history, 53

BACKWARD REGIONS, revolutionize life in, 144

Battle was on higher ground (to Whitehead), 17

Bayreuth, festival in, 71

Beauty, unschooled people (have) more true feeling for, 60

Beethoven, Ludwig van, 64, 227, 267; *Diabelli Variations*, 11

Belgian Women, The, 35

Best, damnable heresy that people don't want the, 257

Bible, 130–1, 179–80, should have closed with Funeral Speech of Pericles, 17; humourless, 28, 107, 195, 351, 353; "not one of my students had ever read," 102; has been a best seller, 107; excels in suggestion of infinitude, 130; allusions to, and classical tradition on the wane, 154; *Iliad* compared with, 196

Biography, satirical, 23

"Bitch Goddess," 111

"Bleak House," 5, 360

Book, kind of, about which one must do something, 167

Boss, what service does (he) perform 83

Boston, 110; ought to have done better, 245–6; wickedness in, in early twentieth century, 291

Bostonian, a correct Puritan, 34

Bostonians, sterility in the arts among, 40

Bottle-washing job (London University), 7

Bourgeois virtues, 259

Brahms, *Fourth Symphony*, 10; *German Requiem*, 276

Break-up, our own time a period of, 23

"Bright boys, the," 97

British seamanship, excellence of, 51

Brothers, have as many (of them) as you like, but no cousins, 222

Brüning, Dr. Heinrich, 277–8

Brutality, always an element of, in religion, 157

Buchan, John, *Cromwell*, 41

Buchman sect 31

Buckingham Palace, 103

Index

Index

Old Testament man, 1
Order of Merit awarded to Whitehead, 300, 317–20, 321
Oriental despot, figure of, an insult to God, 273
Origination, power of, 159; man's capacity for, 169
Oxford University, 22, 47; a high level of mediocrity at, 43; returning more nearly to its function in the Middle Ages, 345; is sociological, 350

PASSIVE ACCEPTANCE of polite learning, 60
Past, sense in England of, 204
Past centuries, living voices of, 3
"Pastlessness" in America, 203
Paul, Saint, 131; no evidence that (he) ever saw Jesus, 57; (his) idea of God is the idea of the devil, 186; the man who distorted and subverted Christ's teaching was, 303
Pavlov, Ivan, 76–7
People, far more learned from, than from books, 364
Perfection just precedes a change, 52
Periclean Age, Whitehead a figure of, 18
Pericles, 37, 119; the Bible should have closed with the Funeral Speech of, 17
Perry, Bliss, 196, 144, 274
Perry, Ralph Barton, 49, 50, 53
Persecute, better to pacify than to, 264
Persecuting temper, the, 86–7
Persecution, more harm than heresy, 138; may be a complete political success, 277
Personal destinies, where (they) are decided, 189
Phillips, William, 236
Philosopher, what it means to be a, 17; what (he) should do, 128 30; conditioned by what is or is not known in the time when he lives, 225
Philosophers are kings already, 300
Philosophic adventure, death of, 5
Philosophies, need for (them) to be rethought, 129
Philosophy, "my (Whitehead's) writings on, were all after I came to this country," 323; should be discussed—mathematics must be studied, 325
Physical personality, overtones from, 184
Pinero, Sir Arthur Wing, *The Second Mrs. Tanqueray*, 39

Plato, 71, 132, 159–60, 165–6, 179, 182, 213–14, 226; *Republic*, 11; an unparalleled genius, 129; speaking of "the receptacle," 159; union of (his) God, with a God of the universe, 214; *Theaetetus*, 213; *Dialogues*, 263, 298, 340; not much "system" in, 302; mathematics of, 309; was one man in the ancient world who would not have been surprised at what has happened, 340; vagueness of, 340
Platonic method of instruction, 4
Pliny the Younger, 264 n.
Plumber in a Vermont village, 203
Poetry, science hostile to, 24; lends itself to brilliant work by young persons, 74; in, is a fragrance of experience, 191; morals have nothing to do with good, 288; knowledge and, 365
Poet's rewards, question of a, 121
Polite learning, passive acceptance of, 60
Political myth is to safeguard the lot of the common man, 265
Political opposition, how the English manage, 139
Posterity, bequeathing to, a changed form of society, 145; what (it) really wants to know, 181
Power States, 36
Precipitates, a series of, 47
Precocity, specimens of, 73
Priesthood, when (it) becomes dominant in a society, freedom of inquiry is discouraged, 282–3
Print, damaging effect of, 166
Prism, his thinking is a, 14
Process and Reality (Whitehead), 8, 358
Process is itself the actuality, 210
Professional crusaders, 106
Prohibition, 204
Prose fiction, why nineteenth-century England should have been favourable to writers of, 118
Protestant sectarianism, branches of, 32
Protestant sects, mistake (they) make, 154
Protestantism in America, 58
Protestants, people brought up as, who then embrace Catholicism, 309
Provincial in time, men can be, 48
Prying into minds, craze for, 31
Published works, never liked to be quizzed about, 16

QUIRKS, people with, 148

[381]

Index

RACES, fusing of, 282
Racial mixtures, best civilizations come from, 158
Radiation, phenomena of, 4
Railway came at exactly right moment in America, 144
Raleigh, Walter, 365
Rand, Edward Kennard, 55
Ranting and wandering from the point, 27
Reading, speed of, 167
"Receptacle," Plato speaking of, 159
Reformation one of most colossal failures in history, 286, 306
Regimentation an utterance of the undermen, 77
Religion, of one God, if that, 111; problem in, to link finitude to infinitude, 131; always element of brutality in, 157; resisted new ideas and suffered, 212; as means of keeping order, 252; cannot exist without music, 306
Religious experience, lacks something which is found in artistic expression, 58; emotions aroused but not satisfied by, 59
Religious founders, how many, take their rise about in the fifth century B.C., 296
Religious persons fond of a joke, 59
Religious services, two most impressive, 156
Renaissance, 23; Low Countries transmitters of, 47; backward-looking traditionalism came in at, 55
Reputations made by machine publicity, 39
Research, abuse of, 124
Research scholars, students qualified to become, are few, 109
Retirement, custom of enforced, idiotic, because after he is sixty, a man often finds new ways to use what he already knows, 314
Revolutions, real destructiveness of, in displacement of people who carry on the minor services, 336-7
Rigid dogma destroys truth, 165
Rigid system, anxieties lest (one) be imposed on mankind, 251
Rolland, Romain, *Jean-Christophe*, 130
Roman Catholic Church generally found resisting change, 125
Roman Empire, 271; the bottleneck through which culture of ancient world passed into Northern Europe was, 200
Roman numerals were clumsy, 66
Roman period of the Civil Wars, 150
Romans, 114, 120; not yet bored with their civilization, 120
Rome, Augustus saved (it) from Romans, 158
Roosevelt, Franklin D., 284; compared with Augustus Caesar, 34; state of funk over, 41
Roosevelt-haters, a carnival for, 278
Routine repetition, men might sink into mere, 296
Royal manners in the eighteenth century, 35
Royce, Josiah, 8
Russell, Bertrand, 179
Russia, 77, 362; aims of contemporary, 268-9; accomplishments of, 285
Russian novelists, 268, 285; comparison with English, 224

SAINT FRANCIS OF ASSISI, 173
Salon in the eighteenth-century French meaning, 9
Salvation Army, upper-class, 31
Santayana, George, 8, 261-2; *Persons and Places*, 260; irony of, 261; philosophy of, 262
Satire is the soured milk of human kindness, 28
Satirical biography, 23
Saturday Club, 229, 230, 308
Sceptics and scientists the leading dogmatists, 5
Schiller, Johann, 122
Scholar in twentieth century, 70
Scholars, hounding of, one of symptoms of social decay, 76; timidity of, 124
Scholarship can ask itself three questions, 73
Science, hostile to poetry, 24; why has (it) kept advancing with such strides since 1900, 65; effect on our world of, 339; abolished slavery, 339
Science and humanism balance in Whitehead, 4
Science and the Modern World (Whitehead), 8, 267; how (it) was written, 4, 146
Scientific revolution in the past fifty years, 212
Scientists, and sceptics the leading dogmatists, 5; many, are little more than technicians, 67; are naïve, 171

[382]

Index